Study Guide with *ActivPhysics 1*

Volume 1

Alan Van Heuvelen
The Ohio State University

Jeffrey J. Braun
University of Evansville, Indiana

Christopher Wozny
Waycross College, Georgia

Physics with Modern Physics for Scientists and Engineers

Wolfson • Pasachoff

ADDISON-WESLEY

An Imprint of Addison Wesley Longman, Inc.

Menlo Park, California • Reading, Massachusetts
New York • Harlow, England • Don Mills, Ontario • Sydney
Mexico City • Madrid • Amsterdam

ACKNOWLEDGMENTS

Publisher: Robin Heyden
Sponsoring Editor: Sami Iwata
Project Coordinators: Bridget Biscotti Bradley, Catherine Flack
Accuracy Checkers: Gordon Aubrecht and Mike Ziegler, The Ohio State University
Senior Production Editor: Larry Olsen
Copyeditor: Mary Roybal
Cover Designer: Yvo Riezebos Design
Director of Marketing: Stacy Treco
Channel Marketing Manager: Gay Meixel
Cover Photo: Copyright © Image Bank

ISBN 0-321-05148-3

3 4 5 6 7 8 9 10-CRS-03 02 01 00 99

 **ADDISON-WESLEY**

2725 Sand Hill Road
Menlo Park, California 94025

Studying Physics

Physics is a complex subject encompassing a great variety of phenomena. It will challenge many of your long-held, common-sense beliefs about how the world works. It will introduce you to phenomena on scales too tiny to see with the unaided eye and so vast that they are difficult to comprehend. Underlying the subject of physics are a rather small number of fundamental laws. Success in physics comes from learning the underlying principles and applying them to a wide variety of situations. The crucial steps toward achieving success are:

- Developing an intuitive feel for the concepts.
- Developing problem-solving skills to apply the concepts and make quantitative predictions.

Each of you will eventually discover the study techniques that work best for you, but successful physics students tend to have one thing in common: They are *active* participants in the learning process. An hour spent in an active study procedure is far more beneficial than an hour spent in a passive process. Effective studying, however, can include activities from *both* columns in the following table:

Passive process	Active process
1. Listening to a lecture.	1. Taking notes during a lecture.
2. Underlining (or highlighting) while reading the text	2. Writing review notes and summarizing a chapter in your notes.
3. Having someone tell you how to solve a problem or just reading through the solution to a problem.	3. Working through a homework or *ActivPhysics* problem.
4. Watching the instructor solve a problem on the board.	4. Explaining a problem to another student
5. Checking the correctness of your answer against the solution	5. Determining whether your answer is physically reasonable.

This *Study Guide* will be a powerful ally as you work through your physics course, whatever your learning style or needs. We have combined:

- An overview of the material from your textbook—equation summaries, key definitions, and hints on avoiding common pitfalls; and
- Interactive simulations on the *ActivPhysics* CD-ROM to provide visualization of physical processes and allow you to change variables, test assumptions, make predictions, and develop intuition that only such hands-on activity makes possible.

We have also provided support in the form of guides to *ActivPhysics* that show you the topics in your course where *ActivPhysics* will be most useful. These guides will help you use the simulations and worksheets in ways that complement your personal learning style and increase your understanding of the material.

How To Use This *Study Guide*

Study Guide with ActivPhysics is encyclopedic in scope. It is designed to provide you with a range of options for each topic in your course. It is intended to be a reference for you so that you can choose and use those parts that best address your needs. These needs are likely to change as you work through your physics course. The *Study Guide* is divided into three parts:

Part I Study Guide matches your textbook chapter by chapter to provide a useful overview and summary of material. The Summary of Equations sections include the significant equations in each chapter of your textbook. These sections include a short discussion that covers new variables and conditions for use. The Definitions section lists all the terms you should understand after studying a topic. The Avoiding Pitfalls section gives hints and suggestions for avoiding common mistakes. Each chapter of Part I concludes with suggestions about where *ActivPhysics* simulations can help you most.

Part II Guide to *ActivPhysics* This part of the *Study Guide with ActivPhysics* will guide you to use *ActivPhysics* in a way that will complement your personal learning style, whether methodical or intuitive. Each part of your course will provide different challenges, and *ActivPhysics* is designed to help you meet those challenges. Read the Introduction and Game Plan sections to give you an overview before you spend time with the *ActivPhysics* simulations. The icons in the margins of your textbook indicate key topics that *ActivPhysics* can reinforce, and those icons plus this Guide will provide a map for using *ActivPhysics*.

Part III *ActivPhysics* Use the *ActivPhysics* CD-ROM and worksheets to help you visualize a physical process and analyze problems. You can use the questions as you would a homework problem. By changing simulation variables, making predictions, and drawing diagrams, you will develop intuition and imagery that will help you to understand the material presented in your class and to solve problems. *ActivPhysics* will support you each step of the way with an Advisor section that provides hints and solutions.

Study Tips for Learning Physics

1. *Budget enough time.* A useful rule of thumb is to spend between two and three hours outside of class for each hour spent in class. While some other courses may not require this much time and effort outside of class, physics simply cannot be learned by listening to a lecture or reading the text. You must become an active practitioner of the science.

2. *Go to class.* This may seem obvious to you, but there is indeed a strong correlation between students who do not go to class and students who do poorly in the course. A few professors are superb lecturers, with a well-organized plan, spellbinding oration, and dramatic demonstrations. A few professors are unsure of themselves, possess little eloquence, and seem rather disorganized. Most fall somewhere in the middle. But you should realize that every professor chooses as the topic for the day's lecture the ideas and concepts he or she feels are the most important or that most need explanation. By coming to class *every* day, you see for yourself the topics that most need your attention when you return to your room to study.

3. *Read the chapter before coming to class.* You will undoubtedly receive a syllabus that tells you the sequence of topics and, perhaps, the date on which the instructor expects to deal with that chapter or section. By reading over the chapter *before* going to the lecture, you accomplish two objectives: (1) You will have heard the terms and concepts before and you will find it easier to see where the lecture is headed. (2) You will know which parts of the chapter seem fairly straightforward and which parts seem rather difficult or confusing to you. You can then pay particular attention to those sections that have given you trouble and can ask questions immediately. (If you haven't read the chapter, it is too easy to tell yourself, "Well, this will make sense when I get around to reading this section."

4. *Take notes.* You don't have to be a stenographer and record every word of a lecture. Rather, be sure you write down the topics the instructor is emphasizing. When he or she intrpdices new material or presents an alternative approach to a topic, then you should get very busy. If, however, you know that the example being worked on the board is straight out of the book, then it is not necessary to copy down every word and symbol from the board. (By the way, if you have not already read the chapter, how would you know if the lecture is straight from the book or is presenting new and priceless information?)

5. *Don't recopy notes.* When you get back to your study area, don't waste your valuable time recopying or typing out your class notes. There are much more beneficial things to do, such as the following.

6. *Re-read the chapter.* That afternoon or evening, re-read the chapter and work through the sample problems. You should be able to cover up the solution and solve the problems yourself. If not, re-read the solution and try again. It is important to actually *write out* your solutions.

7. *Work the assigned problems.* Now you are ready to attempt the homework problems. Give each problem your best effort before turning to the back of the book or to your friends. Once you have finished the problem, or reached a dead end, then seek help. Help may come from a number of places.

   a. Occasionally, a look at the answer in the back of the book will trigger something in your mind, and you will be able to get started again.

   b. Use the *ActivPhysics* simulations to help you visualize a physical process or concept, and use the questions as you would a homework problem. The Advisor section will give hints, and many of the application exercises include the full solution in an Advisor section. You will quickly discover that the best way to truly understand the problem is to try to solve it without the assistance of the Advisor, but the Advisor is there to provide support should you need it. *ActivPhysics* simulations and questions are written in a way that promotes and encourages student interaction and discussion, and you can learn a lot by working with other students.

   c. Working with a group of students can sometimes be a blessing and sometimes be a curse. The crucial element for success in study groups is for each person to spend time alone working on the problems *before* meeting with the others.

   d. Also, your instructor will be glad to help you with your difficulties, *if he or she sees you have been working diligently on your own before coming in for help.* Even in large universities where other pressures tend to make the professor less accessible, study centers exist, teaching assistants abound, and many other resources have been set up to help you.

Physics is a subject that has challenged some of the greatest scientific minds through the centuries, but it also, in many ways, is the simplest and most fundamental of the sciences. Whether this is the first of many physics courses or this is the only course you will take, success requires an effort on your part. Arnold Sommerfeld was one of the greatest physics teachers of all time, and his advice to Werner Heisenberg (then a student of his) still applies today: "Just do the exercises diligently, then you will know what you have understood, and what you have not."

PART I

Study Guide

JEFFREY BRAUN

Connections to *ActivPhysics* by Christopher Wozny

This chapter gives you a brief overview of the science of *physics*. The greatest portion of this course will deal with classical physics-the description of the behavior and structure of the physical universe that we encounter in our everyday lives. Modern physics—physics developed primarily during the twentieth century—deals with the world of the very fast and the very small. We shall find that relativistic effects (for the very fast) and quantum effects (for the very small) play a crucial role in the behavior of the world at these extremes.

As part of this introductory chapter, we trace the development of the metric system, review some basic rules of handling units and significant figures in calculations, and demonstrate the power of making "order-of-magnitude" estimates.

DEFINITIONS

You should know the definition of each of these terms. (The number in parentheses is the text chapter and section in which the term is introduced.)

(1-Intr) *Physics* is the science that deals with the laws that govern the structure and behavior of matter and energy on a fundamental level.

(1-1) *Mechanics* is the subfield of physics that deals with the motion of bodies and includes concepts such as velocity and acceleration, force, energy, and momentum.

(1-1) *Wave motion* (in mechanics) refers to a particular type of motion in which the oscillations of one particle can set up oscillations in its neighbors, resulting in a traveling disturbance called a wave.

(1-1) *Thermodynamics* is the subfield of physics that deals with heat, temperature, and thermal energy, and the relationships between heat and work.

(1-1) *Electromagnetism* deals with electric charge, electric and magnetic fields, and electromagnetic energy.

(1-1) *Optics* is the subfield of physics that deals with the propagation of light and the formation of images.

(1-1) *The special theory of relativity*, developed in 1905 by Albert Einstein, compares measurements of physical quantities taken in two reference frames moving with constant velocity. This theory revises our understanding of the nature of space and time and has become the foundation of our understanding of the behavior of matter at extremely high speeds.

(1-1) The behavior of matter at the atomic and nuclear level is profoundly different than the behavior of the macroscopic world of our direct senses. *Quantum mechanics* is most strikingly characterized by the wave nature of subatomic particles and by the quantization of many physical quantities.

(1-3) A particular subset of units chosen from the metric system, the *SI system* of units is based on seven fundamental units (including the meter, the kilogram, and the second) and is the preferred system of units in scientific literature throughout the world today.

(1-3) *kilo-, centi-, milli- :* (I have included these three prefixes because they are used so frequently that their meanings should be memorized. The other prefixes will be introduced as needed, but you can always look them up.)

kilo- 10^3 = 1000

centi- 10^{-2} = 0.01

milli- 10^{-3} = 0.001

(1-4) To improve the ease of interpreting extremely large or small numbers (and to eliminate ambiguities about the number of significant figures), *scientific notation* writes numbers as a decimal number between 1 and ten, multiplied by a power of ten. For example, $1500 = 1.5 + 10^3$, and $0.00075 = 7.5 \times 10^{-4}$.

(1-4) The number of *significant figures* in a quantity is found by counting from the left all the digits in the quantity, starting with the first *nonzero* digit. Trailing zeros in a quantity with a decimal point are always significant; trailing zeros in a whole number (with no decimal point) may or may not be significant.

AVOIDING PITFALLS

1. **Metric prefixes:** First, there's no need to memorize all 20 prefixes in the metric system. You probably already know the three you will use during most of this course: kilo-, centi-, and milli-. Two errors to watch for: "milli" means one-thousandth, *not* one-millionth. Also, be sure to distinguish between the prefix *m* (10^{-3}) and the prefix *M* (10^6).

2. **Units conversions:** If you write out the conversion fractions and honestly check that the units are canceling as you expect, then you won't

make the mistake of dividing by 1000 meters instead of multiplying by 1000 meters (or vice versa). Also, when using the square (or cube) of a conversion factor, don't forget to square (or cube) the *numbers* inside the parentheses as well as the units! For example, when converting area units,

$$(100 \text{ cm/m})^2 = 100^2 \text{ cm}^2/\text{m}^2 = 10^4 \text{ cm}^2/\text{m}^2.$$

3. **Exponents:** Although scientific calculators make arithmetic involving power-of-10 numbers simple, it is still important to know the rules of combining exponents when dealing with algebraic quantities:

   - Adding or subtracting: *The exponent (or power of 10) of each term must be the same.*

   - Multiplication: *The exponents of the factors add.*

   - Division: *The exponent in the bottom is subtracted from the exponent in the top.*

4. **Significant figures:** When adding or subtracting, the term with the smallest number of *decimal places* determines the number of *decimal places* in the result. When multiplying or dividing, the factor with the smallest number of *significant figures* determines the number of *significant figures* in the result.

 Connections to *ActivPhysics*

Many of the concepts discussed in Chapter 1, such as estimation, dimensional analysis, and problem solving, are common themes throughout the *ActivPhysics* investigations, although there are no corresponding *ActivPhysics* activities that are specifically related to this chapter. Figure 1-15 shows the icon identifying an *ActivPhysics* activity as one that relates to the material under discussion, and this icon will be found throughout the book.

If you are interested in exploring *ActivPhysics* in order to become familiar with its operation, then you may choose to open Sim 1 of Activity 10.1 *Properties of Mechanical Waves* when you examine Example 1-2, and Activity 9.10 *Pendulum Frequency* if you attempt the accompanying exercise.

CHAPTER 2 MOTION IN A STRAIGHT LINE

This chapter introduces you to kinematics, the quantitative description of motion. We begin by studying the simplest type of motion: motion in a straight line, or one-dimensional motion. Three fundamental quantities (displacement, velocity, and acceleration) are used to describe *any* type of motion.

We then focus our attention on uniformly accelerated straight-line motion and develop several specific equations that predict instantaneous values of position and velocity, applying these to the important case of free-fall motion.

DEFINITIONS

You should know the definition of each of these terms. (The number in parentheses is the text chapter and section in which the term is introduced.)

(2-Intr) *Kinematics* is the quantitative description of motion.

(2-Intr) The term *particle* refers to an object of negligible dimensions. Whether its size is negligible or not depends on the context of the problem. Compared to the size of its orbit around the Sun, the Earth's diameter is negligible, and the Earth can be considered a particle when discussing its orbital motion.

(2-1) The *average speed* of a particle over any time interval is the total distance traveled, divided by the length of the time interval.

(2-1) The *displacement* of a particle is the change in its position.

(2-1) The *average velocity* of a particle over any time interval is the ratio of the particle's displacement to the length of the time interval:

$$\bar{v} \equiv \frac{\Delta x}{\Delta t}.$$

(2-2) The *instantaneous velocity* of a particle is the average velocity, measured over a vanishingly small time interval. Mathematically, this is equivalent to defining instantaneous velocity as the time derivative of position with respect to time:

$$\bar{v} \equiv \lim_{\Delta t \to 0} \frac{\Delta x}{\Delta t} = \frac{dx}{dt}.$$

(2-2) The *instantaneous speed* of a particle at any instant is the magnitude of its instantaneous velocity.

(2-3) The *average acceleration* of a particle over any time interval is the change in its velocity, divided by the length of the time interval:

$$\bar{a} \equiv \frac{\Delta v}{\Delta t}.$$

(2-3) The *instantaneous acceleration* of a particle is defined to be the average acceleration, measured over a vanishingly small time interval. Again, this is equivalent to defining instantaneous acceleration as the time derivative of velocity:

$$a \equiv \lim_{\Delta t \to 0} \frac{\Delta v}{\Delta t} = \frac{dv}{dt}.$$

(2-6) An object acted upon only by the force of gravity is said to be in *free-fall*. (*Note:* This implies that the force of air resistance is negligible. Also note that it says nothing about the initial velocity of the object: Thus, a baseball thrown upward is said to be in free-fall even if it is still on the way up.) Any particle in free-fall has a downward acceleration equal to g, the local acceleration of gravity.

SUMMARY OF EQUATIONS

The first five equations are definitions, and are valid for all types of straight-line motion, whether uniform or variable acceleration.

1. Average speed ·

$$v_{av} \equiv \frac{D}{t} = \frac{D}{\Delta t}$$

The average speed of a particle during any given time interval is defined to be the total distance traveled (D) divided by the length of the time interval (denoted by t or Δt).

2. Average velocity

$$\bar{v} \equiv \frac{\Delta x}{\Delta t} \qquad \text{(Text Eq. 2-1)}$$

In this expression, x is the position of a particle, measured along some axis (here called the x-axis); and $\Delta x (\equiv x_f - x_i)$ is the change in the particle's position during the time interval Δt. (Note: Δx is called the "displacement," and this depends only on the initial and final positions, not on the actual path followed from x_i to x_f.)

3. Instantaneous velocity

$$v \equiv \lim_{\Delta t \to 0} \frac{\Delta x}{\Delta t} = \frac{dx}{dt}. \qquad \text{(Text Eq. 2-2)}$$

The instantaneous velocity of a particle is the time rate of change (i.e., the time derivative) of its position, giving its velocity at a single instant of time, rather than the average over a finite time interval Δt. Note that the instantaneous velocity is written v, whereas the average velocity is written $\bar{v}$.

4. Average acceleration

$$\bar{a} \equiv \frac{\Delta v}{\Delta t} \qquad \text{(Text Eq. 2-4)}$$

The average acceleration is found by dividing the velocity change by the length of a time interval. Like average velocity, the average acceleration depends only on the initial and final values of v, and tells us little about how the velocity actually changed during the time interval. (The average acceleration is not generally as useful a concept as the *instantaneous* acceleration, defined below.)

5. Instantaneous acceleration

$$a \equiv \lim_{\Delta t \to 0} \frac{\Delta v}{\Delta t} = \frac{dv}{dt} \qquad \text{(Text Eq. 2-6)}$$

The instantaneous acceleration describes the rate at which the velocity is changing at a particular instant of time. Note that $v = dx/dt$, so acceleration is the second time-derivative of position: $a = d^2x/dt^2$.

The following equations are specific relations that only apply to one-dimensional motion with uniform (constant) acceleration!

6. Velocity as a function of time

$$v = v_0 + at \qquad \text{(Text Eq. 2-7)}$$

In this expression, v is the velocity of the particle at the time t, v_0 is its initial velocity, and a is its (constant) acceleration.

7. Average velocity in uniform acceleration

$$\bar{v} = \tfrac{1}{2}(v_0 + v) \qquad \text{(Text Eq. 2-8)}$$

This is a very useful expression, telling us that the average velocity during any time interval is found by simply averaging the velocities at the beginning and the end of the time interval. (This *might seem obvious to you*, but remember that average velocity is *defined* to be displacement over elapsed time, and you can only average the initial and final velocities if the acceleration is constant.)

8. Position as a function of time

$$x = x_0 + v_0t + \tfrac{1}{2}at^2 \qquad \text{(Text Eq. 2-10)}$$

In this expression, x is the position of the particle at the time t, given in terms of the initial position of the particle x_0, the initial velocity v_0, and the (constant) acceleration a. (Occasionally, you will see this equation written in the slightly more compact form $\Delta x = v_0t + \tfrac{1}{2}at^2$ when the displacement of the particle is needed, rather than the final position.)

9. Velocity as a function of position

$$v^2 = v_0^2 + 2a(x - x_0) \qquad \text{(Text Eq. 2-11)}$$

Whereas Text Eq. 2-7 gives us the instantaneous velocity at any instant, this expression gives us the instantaneous velocity at a given position. Note this can also be written more compactly as $v^2 = v_0^2 + 2a\Delta x$.

AVOIDING PITFALLS

1. **Acceleration:** Acceleration gives the *rate of change* of velocity, not the magnitude of velocity. An airliner cruising along at a steady 600 mi/h has a zero acceleration, but a child on a tricycle bumping into a tree has a very large (negative) acceleration. Whenever the velocity *changes*, there is an acceleration, even if the velocity happens to be zero at that moment.

2. **Units:** In all but the most complex equations, you should carry the units through the calculations. The extra work is unquestionably worth it! (In working out sample problems for my classes, I often locate an algebraic error by checking the units of each term in an intermediate result. Not carrying the units along makes it much more difficult to find errors.)

   Whenever two expressions are equal, their dimensions must also be equal. Whenever two terms are added or subtracted, their dimensions must be the same. But if two factors are multiplied (or divided), the dimension of the product (or ratio) is the product (or ratio) of the dimensions of the two factors.

3. **g:** The symbol g stands for the *magnitude* of the acceleration of any object in free-fall near the Earth's surface, so the symbol g always has a *positive* value. (Its value actually varies slightly from point to point on the Earth's surface, but it remains within about 0.2% of the average value $g = 9.80$ m/s^2 = 980 cm/s^2 = 32.2 ft/s^2.) If you choose *up* to be positive in solving a problem, then the downward acceleration of an object in free-fall is negative, so $a = -g$. If, instead, you choose the downward direction to be positive, $a = +g$.

4. **Validity of equations:** Note very carefully the distinction between the general definitions (the first five equations in the Summary of Equations at the beginning of this *Study Guide* chapter) and the specific relations for uniformly acceler-

ated motion. The first five can be applied to *any* motion problem, while the last four apply only when the acceleration is constant!

5. **Average velocity vs. average speed:** The average velocity depends only on the initial and final positions, while the average speed depends on the total distance traveled. A salesman who drives 400 miles in an 8-hour day has an average speed of 50 mi/h, but his average *velocity* (defined as the displacement over the time) is zero if he returns home at the end of the day.

6. **Average velocity:** There are two expressions for average velocity presented in this chapter: $\bar{v} \equiv \Delta x/\Delta t$, and $\bar{v} = \frac{1}{2}(v_0 + v)$. The first can be used in any situation, but the second works only if the acceleration is constant.

7. **Quadratic equations:** Often you will encounter quadratic equations in finding the elapsed time in accelerated-motion problems, producing two roots to the equation. Usually only one describes the physical situation you are interested in. You will have to make a choice between the two roots based on physical reasoning and common sense.

8. **Two-car problems:** By "two-car problems," I refer to any problem that involves the motion of two separate objects.

   The easier problem is when the two objects start out at the same instant. Then the time of travel is the same for each, so you can use the same *t* in the equations of motion for both.

   The problem is a little more difficult when one of the two starts out before the other. Then $t_1 \neq t_2$, and you will have to distinguish between the two times of travel.

 Connections to *ActivPhysics*

The 14 investigations found in Unit 1 of *ActivPhysics* can help you overcome many of the common misconceptions and errors students often encounter when beginning the study of physics. An important advantage of physics simulations, especially for these chapters on mechanics, is that you can *see* the motion. For example, if you have never had a course in physics before, it may be difficult to recognize the difference between acceleration and velocity. Activity 1.1 *Analyzing Motion Using Diagrams* allows you to explore the meaning of displacement, velocity, and acceleration by adjusting

initial values for these quantities and seeing the effect on the resulting motion. The simulation attaches arrows to the moving car that represent the velocity and acceleration (as in Figure 2-8), so the relationship between direction for these quantities and algebraic positive and negative signs in equations can be easily understood. Activity 1.4 *Predicting Motion from Equations* is a quick follow-up to Activity 1.1 to check whether you are able to relate initial conditions to equations describing the motion.

Many figures in the text show graphs of position, velocity, or acceleration as functions of time and explain how the slope of a line may correspond to one of these quantities (see Figures 2-1, 2-5, 2-6, and especially Figure 2-9). Activity 1.2 *Analyzing Motion Using Graphs* explores the relationship between kinematics and graphs in great detail, and Activity 1.3 *Predicting Motion from Graphs* is an application problem that will test whether you really understand the concepts in this section of the book. These activities can be very useful if graphical analysis of motion is a course objective.

The main advantage of Unit 1 activities, however, is that they will help you learn how to set up and solve physics word problems. This is the most difficult skill that beginning physics students must learn, and it may take quite a bit of time and a lot of trial and error to be successful *or* to become adept. However, most of the application problems (Activities 1.5–1.14) include full or partial solutions under the Advisor sections, which can help you learn how to think through the construction and solution of a word problem instead of just focusing on a correct answer. The introduction of motion diagrams in Activity 1.1 is especially helpful.

Example 2-5 in the text, *Landing a Jetliner*, is similar to a problem presented in Activity 1.5 *Problem-Solving Strategies for Kinematics*. Example 2-7 *Speed Trap!* is like Activity 1.13 *Car Catches Truck*. (Compare the answer to Question 3 of the activity to Figure 2-13.) And the first part of Activity 1.10 *Pole-Vaulter Lands* corresponds to Example 2-8 *Cliff Diver*, and also to Problem 30.

Activities 1.5–1.8 have only a single equation to solve; Activities 1.9–1.11 have two or more different equations of motion applying to the same object at different times; and Activities 1.12–1.14 compare the motions of two different objects. It may be useful to alternate between these application problems and Problems 40–59 of the text.

The previous chapter developed the mathematical description of straight-line motion. As long as motion was up/down, or right/left, we could adequately describe the two choices by calling one direction positive, and the other direction negative. Now, as we prepare to describe two- and three-dimensional motion, we will need the power of *vector* quantities.

In this chapter, we first study the properties of vectors, themselves, learning two alternative descriptions of vector quantities: the magnitude/direction description, and the component description. We then consider the vector nature of displacement, velocity, and acceleration, concluding with a look at motion from moving frames of reference.

DEFINITIONS

You should know the definition of each of these terms. (The number in parentheses is the text chapter and section in which the term is introduced.)

(3-1) A *vector* is a quantity that requires both a magnitude (number + units) and a direction for its complete specification.

(3-1) A *scalar* is a quantity that is specified completely by its magnitude.

(3-3) A *coordinate system* requires a point in space chosen as the origin, and a set of coordinate axes that (usually) point in perpendicular directions.

(3-3) A *component* of a vector is a signed number that specifies the projection of a vector along a given coordinate axis.

(3-3) A *unit vector* is a vector with magnitude = 1, pointing along one of the coordinate axes. (The Cartesian unit vectors pointing in the x-, y-, and z-directions are $\hat{\imath}$, $\hat{\jmath}$, and $\hat{k}$, respectively.)

(3-5) An *inertial reference frame* is a frame of reference that is not accelerating. (The name comes from the fact that Newton's law of inertia is valid in such a reference frame.)

(3-5) The *principle of Galilean relativity* states that the laws of motion are the same in all frames of reference in uniform motion. (This does not mean that all physical quantities will have the same value in different frames of reference—for example, an object's velocity varies from one frame to the other—but the physical relationships among dynamical quantities like force, mass, momentum, etc., will have the same form no matter which reference frame is used for the measurements.)

SUMMARY OF EQUATIONS

1. Magnitude of a vector

$$A = \sqrt{A_x^2 + A_y^2} \qquad \text{(Text Eq. 3-1)}$$

In this expression, A_x and A_y represent the Cartesian components of a vector $\mathbf{A}$, and A (sometimes written $|\mathbf{A}|$) is the *magnitude* of the vector. (*Note:* In three-dimensional problems, $A = \sqrt{A_x^2 + A_y^2 + A_z^2}$.)

2. Direction of a vector

$$\tan \theta = \frac{A_y}{A_x} \qquad \text{(Text Eq. 3-2)}$$

where θ is the angle between the vector $\mathbf{A}$ and the x-axis. (Positive angles θ are measured counterclockwise; negative angles are measured clockwise, both from the $+x$-axis.)

3. x- and y-components of a vector

$$A_x = A \cos \theta \qquad \text{(Text Eq. 3-3)}$$

$$A_y = A \sin \theta \qquad \text{(Text Eq. 3-4)}$$

Again, θ is the angle between the vector $\mathbf{A}$ and the $+x$ axis.

4. Displacement

$$\Delta \mathbf{r} \equiv \mathbf{r}_2 - \mathbf{r}_1 \qquad \text{(Text p. 48)}$$

where $\Delta \mathbf{r}$ is the vector that represents the change in position of a particle that starts at position $\mathbf{r}_1$ and ends at position $\mathbf{r}_2$.

5. Average velocity

$$\bar{\mathbf{v}} \equiv \frac{\Delta \mathbf{r}}{\Delta t} \qquad \text{(Text Eq. 3-5)}$$

As in one-dimensional motion, average velocity is defined as the ratio of displacement to elapsed time.

6. Instantaneous velocity

$$\mathbf{v} \equiv \lim_{\Delta t \to 0} \frac{\Delta \mathbf{r}}{\Delta t} = \frac{d\mathbf{r}}{dt} \qquad \text{(Text Eq. 3-6)}$$

As the average velocity is computed for shorter and shorter time intervals, it approaches, in the limit, the *instantaneous velocity*.

7. Components of velocity

$$\mathbf{v} = v_x \hat{\imath} + v_y \hat{\jmath} = \frac{dx}{dt} \hat{\imath} + \frac{dy}{dt} \hat{\jmath} \qquad \text{(Text Eq. 3-7)}$$

The x-component of velocity is the time rate of change of its x-coordinate ($v_x = dx/dt$), and the y-component of velocity is the time rate of change of its y-coordinate ($v_y = dy/dt$).

8. Average acceleration

$$\overline{\mathbf{a}} \equiv \frac{\Delta \mathbf{v}}{\Delta t} \qquad \text{(Text Eq. 3-8)}$$

As in one-dimensional motion, average acceleration is defined as the ratio of velocity change to elapsed time.

9. Instantaneous acceleration

$$\mathbf{a} \equiv \lim_{\Delta t \to 0} \frac{\Delta \mathbf{v}}{\Delta t} = \frac{d\mathbf{v}}{dt} \qquad \text{(Text Eq. 3-9)}$$

As the average acceleration is computed for shorter and shorter time intervals, it approaches, in the limit, the *instantaneous acceleration*.

10. Relative velocity

$$\mathbf{v}' = \mathbf{v} - \mathbf{V} \qquad \text{(Text Eq. 3-10)}$$

A particle moves with a velocity $\mathbf{v}$, with respect to a coordinate system S. A second frame of reference (S') moves with a constant velocity $\mathbf{V}$ with respect to S. The velocity of the particle with respect to S' is given by $\mathbf{v}'$.

11. Relative acceleration

$$\mathbf{a}' = \mathbf{a} \qquad \text{(Text Eq. 3-11)}$$

As long as the two frames of reference move with a constant relative velocity, the acceleration of a particle will be the same in both frames of reference.

AVOIDING PITFALLS

1. **Vector quantities:** Don't forget, especially on exams, that any answer that is a vector quantity requires both a magnitude and a direction to be complete. (An equivalent way of completely specifying a vector quantity is to give all of its components.)

2. **Vector equations:** Any vector equation (e.g., $\mathbf{A} = \mathbf{B}$) is a statement that the two quantities have the same magnitude and direction. Equivalently, their components must separately match: $A_x = B_x$, $A_y = B_y$, and $A_z = B_z$. Thus, a vector equation is essentially a shorthand notation for three independent scalar equations.

3. **Finding components:** The familiar equations

$$A_x = A \cos \theta$$
$$A_y = A \sin \theta$$

are correct as written as long as θ is measured from the positive x-axis. (Don't insert a minus

sign with a negative component; the numerical value of $\cos \theta$ or $\sin \theta$ will appear with the proper sign.)

If, instead, you are using the "acute-angle" method, working from

$$\sin \theta = \text{opp/hyp}$$
$$\cos \theta = \text{adj/hyp},$$

then you will have to supply any needed minus signs yourself.

Regardless of which method you use, the first step should *always* be to sketch the vector with its components so you can visualize the direction and approximate the magnitude of the components.

4. **Finding the angle:** If you know the x- and y-components of a vector $\mathbf{A}$, it is a simple matter to find the angle from

$$\theta = \tan^{-1}(A_y/A_x),$$

using the INV TAN keys on a calculator. Keep in mind, however, that your calculator will probably return a value of θ that lies between $+90°$ and $-90°$; any other angle (that is, any vector lying in the second or third quadrants) will require an addition of $180°$ to the displayed value.

5. **Distance vs. displacement:** The distance traveled is *not* just the magnitude of the displacement! (Only in the case of straight-line motion with no reversals in direction, is $D = |\Delta \mathbf{r}|$.)

6. **Speed vs. velocity:** Although the *instantaneous* speed of a particle is the magnitude of its instantaneous velocity ($v = |\mathbf{v}|$), we cannot say that the *average* speed of a particle is the magnitude of its average velocity: $v_{av} \neq |\overline{\mathbf{v}}|$. (This is because we define average speed as the ratio of *distance traveled* to elapsed time, while average velocity is defined as *displacement* over elapsed time, and these are, in general, quite different quantities.)

7. **Relative motion:** If one frame of reference moves relative to the other with a constant velocity, the acceleration of an object is the same in both frames, but the object has a different velocity in the two frames.

ActivPhysics **Connections to *ActivPhysics***

Chapter 3 explains the addition, subtraction, and multiplication of vectors. This is a very important topic and a fundamental mathematical technique that will be used extensively throughout the physics course. For that reason, it is important that every student become proficient in the use of trigonometry for finding vector components. Two activities in particular—Activities 3.5 and 4.1—are extremely helpful for understanding vector quantities and their manipulation.

Activity 3.5 *Initial Velocity Components* shows how to calculate vector components using trigonometry. A hand stretches and turns a vector to different lengths and angles while the x- and y-components of the vector are continually displayed in the upper right-hand corner of the screen. This simulation may be used to find components for almost *any* vector encountered in this or any other chapter. Of course, it's best to use Activity 3.5 as a check of the mathematics and not as a shortcut, since on tests and exams *ActivPhysics* won't be available.

Activity 4.1 *Determining Acceleration Vectors Graphically* is another excellent tutorial for an abstract concept that some students find difficult to grasp. Students are often unclear about the fact that in a vector equation (such as Equation 3-8) both the *magnitude* and the *direction* must be the same on both sides of the equals sign. Therefore, the direction of the acceleration must be the same as the direction of the *change* in velocity. In Activity 4.1, the graphical technique for subtracting vectors is used to find the acceleration of a pendulum bob at different times, with surprising results. Activity 4.2 *Acceleration Direction of a Car* provides more practice with this concept and may be used to check your understanding of these concepts.

CHAPTER 4   MOTION IN MORE THAN ONE DIMENSION

This chapter applies the vector description of motion developed in Chapter 3 to several important situations, including projectile, orbital, and circular motion.

DEFINITIONS

You should know the definition of each of these terms. (The number in parentheses is the text chapter and section in which the term is introduced.)

(4-3) A *projectile* is any particle that is launched into the air and then moves predominantly under the influence of gravity.

(4-3) The *trajectory* of a projectile is the path (usually parabolic) followed by a projectile, and is described by the function $y(x)$.

(4-3) The *horizontal range* of a projectile is the horizontal distance traveled by the projectile, when it has returned to its initial height.

(4-4) A particle follows *uniform circular motion* when it maintains a constant speed around a circular path.

(4-5) Whenever the direction of a particle's velocity changes, there is a *radial acceleration* that points toward the center of curvature of the path followed. The magnitude of this acceleration is given by $a_c = v^2/r$. (*Note:* Another name for this is "centripetal acceleration.")

(4-5) When the *speed* of an object changes, there is a *tangential acceleration* that points along the direction of motion. If the object is speeding up, the tangential acceleration points forward; if the object is slowing down, the tangential acceleration points backward. The magnitude of this acceleration is $a_t = dv/dt$, where v is the *speed*, not the velocity, of the particle.

(*Note:* The particle has, at any instant, *one* single acceleration $\mathbf{a} = d\mathbf{v}/dt$. The radial acceleration is the component of $\mathbf{a}$ that is perpendicular to the object's velocity, and the tangential acceleration is the component that is parallel to the object's velocity.)

SUMMARY OF EQUATIONS

The first set of equations applies to all constant-acceleration motion.

1. Velocity versus time for uniform acceleration

$$\mathbf{v} = \mathbf{v}_0 + \mathbf{a}t \qquad \text{(Text Eq. 4-3)}$$

A particle will have a velocity $\mathbf{v}$ at time $= t$ if it starts with an initial velocity $\mathbf{v}_0$ and moves with a constant acceleration $\mathbf{a}$.

2. Velocity versus position for uniform acceleration

$$v_x^2 = v_{x02} + 2a_x\Delta x \qquad \text{(SG Eq. 4-1)}$$
$$v_y^2 = v_{y0}^2 + 2a_y\Delta y \qquad \text{(SG Eq. 4-2)}$$
$$v_z^2 = v_{z0}^2 + 2a_z\Delta z \qquad \text{(SG Eq. 4-3)}$$

If an object moves with a constant acceleration $\mathbf{a} = a_x\hat{\mathbf{i}} + a_y\hat{\mathbf{j}} + a_z\hat{\mathbf{k}}$, its velocity $\mathbf{v}$ will have the components given above when its displacement is $\Delta\mathbf{r} = \Delta x\hat{\mathbf{i}} + \Delta y\hat{\mathbf{j}} + \Delta z\hat{\mathbf{k}}$. Note that these three equations can be summed to obtain an expression for the object's *speed* as a function of displacement:

$$v^2 = v_0^2 + 2(a_x\Delta x + a_y\Delta y + a_z\Delta z). \quad \text{(SG Eq. 4-4)}$$

3. Position versus time for uniform acceleration

$$\mathbf{r} = \mathbf{r}_0 + \mathbf{v}_0 t + \tfrac{1}{2}\mathbf{a}t^2 \qquad \text{(Text Eq. 4-4)}$$

A particle will be at the position $\mathbf{r}$ at time $= t$ if its initial position is $\mathbf{r}_0$, it has an initial velocity $\mathbf{v}_0$, and it moves with a constant acceleration $\mathbf{a}$.

The following expressions for ideal projectile motion follow directly from the uniform-acceleration equations listed above, with the substitutions $a_x = a_z = 0$, and $a_y = -g$.

4. Velocity components of a projectile versus time

$$v_x = v_{x0} \qquad \text{(Text Eq. 4-5)}$$
$$v_y = v_{y0} - gt \qquad \text{(Text Eq. 4-6)}$$

A projectile is given an initial velocity ($\mathbf{v}_0 = v_{x0}\hat{\mathbf{i}} + v_{y0}\hat{\mathbf{j}}$). As long as air resistance is negligible, the acceleration will be constant ($\mathbf{a} = -g\hat{\mathbf{j}}$). Thus, there is no change in the projectile's horizontal component of velocity, and there is a constant downward acceleration of magnitude $g = 9.8$ m/s^2.

5. Velocity components of an ideal projectile versus position

$$v_x = v_{x0} \qquad \text{(SG Eq. 4-5)}$$
$$v_y^2 = v_{y0}^2 - 2g\Delta y \qquad \text{(SG Eq. 4-6)}$$

6. Position of an ideal projectile

$$x = x_0 + v_{x0}t \qquad \text{(Text Eq. 4-7)}$$
$$y = y_0 + v_{y0}t - \tfrac{1}{2}gt^2 \qquad \text{(Text Eq. 4-8)}$$

7. Trajectory of an ideal projectile

$$y = x\tan\theta_0 - \frac{g}{2v_0^2\cos^2\theta_0}x^2 \qquad \text{(Text Eq. 4-9)}$$

While Text Eqs. 4-7 and 4-8 (the "equations of motion") give the x- and y-coordinates of a projectile as functions of time, this equation gives y as a function of x. The parabolic curve defined by Text Eq. 4-9 is the *trajectory* of an ideal projectile.

The following are general equations that apply to all motion.

8. Radial acceleration

$$a_r = \frac{v^2}{r} \qquad \text{(Text Eq. 4-11)}$$

If the direction of an object's velocity changes, there is a radial (or "centripetal") component of acceleration, perpendicular to the path being followed, and pointing toward the center of the curve. The magnitude of this radial acceleration is given by v^2/r. Note that if the object is following a straight-line path ($r = \infty$), then $a_r = 0$.

9. Tangential acceleration

$$a_t = \frac{dv}{dt} \qquad \text{(Text p. 83)}$$

Whenever the speed of an object changes, there is a component of acceleration tangential to the path being followed (forward if the object is speeding up; backward if the object is slowing down), given by the rate of change of *speed*. Note that if the object's speed is constant ($dv/dt = 0$), then $a_r = 0$.

Thus, the radial and tangential accelerations represent mutually perpendicular components of the acceleration vector of any object.

AVOIDING PITFALLS

1. **Vector equations:** You can use a vector equation in two ways. In one method, you write out the two (or three) separate scalar equations and solve each as an algebraic equation. For example, $\mathbf{v} = \mathbf{v_0} + \mathbf{a}t$ becomes three scalar equations, one for each component:

$$v_x = v_{x0} + a_x t$$
$$v_y = v_{y0} + a_y t$$
$$v_z = v_{z0} + a_z t.$$

The other approach is to treat it as a single (vector) equation, but with each vector quantity expressed in unit-vector notation. Then $\mathbf{v} = \mathbf{v_0} + \mathbf{a}t$ becomes

$$\mathbf{v} = (v_{x0}\hat{\mathbf{i}}) + (v_{y0}\hat{\mathbf{j}}) + (v_{z0}\hat{\mathbf{k}}) + [(a_x\hat{\mathbf{i}}) + (a_y\hat{\mathbf{j}}) + (a_z\hat{\mathbf{k}})]t$$
$$\mathbf{v} = (v_{x0} + a_x t)\hat{\mathbf{i}} + (v_{y0} + a_y t)\hat{\mathbf{j}} + (v_{z0} + a_z t)\hat{\mathbf{k}}.$$

2. **Projectile motion:** The fundamental characteristic of (ideal) projectile motion is that a projectile moves with a constant horizontal component of velocity (equal to v_{x0}), and a constant downward acceleration (equal to $g = 9.8 \text{ m/s}^2$).

3. **Time of flight for a projectile:** If you want to know how much time a projectile will spend in the air, consider its *vertical* motion. The time of rise is just the amount of time it takes v_{y0} to decrease to zero, decreasing at the rate $a_y = -g$ (i.e., losing 9.8 m/s of vertical velocity each second). If the projectile lands at the same elevation that it was launched from, the time to fall is the same as the time to rise.

4. **Symmetry of projectile motion:** Ideal projectile motion is symmetrical. The projectile's speed at any height is the same on the way up as it is on the way back down. If it lands at the same height it was launched from, the time of rise is the same as the time of fall.

5. **Real projectile motion:** Real projectiles (those affected significantly by air resistance) do *not* move with a constant acceleration, so the uniform-acceleration equations we used in this chapter only approximate its motion. In the real world, the acceleration depends on the shape, size, and *speed* of the projectile. Since the acceleration depends on the speed, and the speed depends on the acceleration, the equations must be solved numerically.

6. **Uniform circular motion:** The term "uniform" means that the object's *speed* is constant, not its velocity. Also, although the *magnitude* of an object's acceleration is constant, its direction is continually changing, so the uniform-acceleration equations (e.g., $\mathbf{v} = \mathbf{v_0} + \mathbf{a}t$) don't apply!

7. **Acceleration doesn't just mean speeding up:** The colloquial meaning of "accelerate" is to speed up. In physics, acceleration accompanies *any* change in velocity: speeding up, slowing down, or changing direction. (Just as it's hard to speed up rapidly on ice, it's also difficult to slow down or to change directions.)

8. **Radial acceleration:** Don't think that $a_r = v^2/r$ applies only to uniform circular motion! It describes the radial component of acceleration that appears whenever the direction of an object's velocity changes, so any two- or three-dimensional motion has a radial component of acceleration.

 Connections to *ActivPhysics*

ActivPhysics icons for eight of the nine activities of Unit 3 on Projectile Motion are located in Chapter 4 of the text. The first four activities explore different aspects of projectile motion, but all four of them focus on the same fundamental concept: The motion of a projectile in the vertical direction follows the equations of motion for constant acceleration under gravity, and the motion of a projectile in the horizontal direction is simply constant velocity (Equations 4-5 through 4-8, plus the following sentence). Activities 3.1 *Solving Projectile–Motion Problems* and 3.4 *Projectile x- and y-Accelerations* are particularly effective for visualizing the physical principles of projectile motion.

Unit 3 as a whole is very well constructed. The first four investigations explore the concepts, principles, and relationships of projectile motion in a tutorial fashion; the fifth activity introduces vector components (Chapter 3); and the last four activities are application problems that reinforce the basic concepts. Therefore, one approach to incorporating *ActivPhysics* is to read pages 68–73 of Chapter 4 first and then complete Activities 3.1–3.4 sequentially before continuing in the text. A second possibility is to do the activities first *before* reading the book. The third choice is to open an activity when its icon is encountered in the text, as the simulation is often able to clarify the text explanation or figure. All three study methods can be effective, depending on your personal style.

Chapter 4 also includes the topic of uniform and nonuniform circular motion. The first three activities of Unit 4 on Circular Motion explore these motions. Activity 4.1 *Determining Acceleration Vectors Graphically* was recommended in Chapter 3, and icons for Activities 4.2 *Acceleration Direction of a Car* and 4.3 *Magnitude of Centripetal Acceleration* appear in the text. For these last two sections of the chapter, the most effective approach may be to open and explore each activity when the icon is encountered. The rest of the activities in Unit 4 of *ActivPhysics* include the forces that cause an object to move in a curved path, so it may be best to wait until Chapters 5 and 6 to explore them.

CHAPTER 5   FORCE AND MOTION

Having learned how to describe the motion of an object in terms of its velocity and acceleration, we now turn our attention to the question of *why* it moves in the first place. Two new concepts (force and inertia) are introduced, and they form the basis for the most fundamental laws of all mechanics: Newton's three laws of motion. In this chapter, we concentrate on the ideas expressed in Newton's laws by applying them to somewhat idealized, one-dimensional problems. The following chapter will investigate more complex and realistic situations.

DEFINITIONS

You should know the definition of each of these terms. (The number in parentheses is the text chapter and section in which the term is introduced.) The large number of new terms and laws in this chapter shouldn't intimidate you—this is just your first look at these. Most of these will be discussed in greater detail in succeeding chapters.

(5-Intr) *Dynamics* is the study of motion and its causes.

(5-2) We call whatever it is that changes the state of motion of any object a *force*. Generally speaking, we can think of a force as a push or pull, arising from one object acting on another object.

(5-2) The *momentum* of an object (**p**) is defined to be the product of its mass and velocity: $\mathbf{p} \equiv m\mathbf{v}$.

(5-2) Newton's *first law of motion* (also known as the principle of inertia) states that an object at rest will remain at rest, and an object in motion will continue to move in a straight line with a constant speed, unless acted upon by an external force.

(5-2) Newton's *second law of motion* states that the net force acting on any object is directly proportional to the time rate of change of its momentum: $\mathbf{F}_{net} \propto d\mathbf{p}/dt$. (If the unit of force is chosen properly, we can write this as an equation: $\mathbf{F}_{net} = d\mathbf{p}/dt$.)

Further, if the mass of the object is constant, then $d\mathbf{p}/dt = m(d\mathbf{v}/dt)$, and $\mathbf{F}_{net} \propto m\mathbf{a}$. (Again, with a proper choice of units, we can write this as an equation: $\mathbf{F}_{net} = m\mathbf{a}$.)

(5-2) In the SI system of units, forces are measured in *newtons*. A 1-N force will give a 1-kg mass an acceleration of 1 m/s^2.

(5-3) We give the name *inertia* to the property of matter that causes it to resist any changes in its state of motion.

(5-3) An *inertial frame of reference* is any frame of reference in which the principle of inertia is observed to be valid. (Basically, this implies that the frame of reference is not accelerating.)

(5-3) The *gravitational force* is one of the fundamental forces in nature. It is an attractive force between any two objects, and its strength depends on the mass of the two objects and on their separation. It is by far the weakest of the four forces.

(5-3) The *electroweak force* is another of the fundamental forces in nature. This is a synthesis of three phenomenologically distinct forces (electricity, magnetism, and the weak nuclear force). These three have recently been shown to be manifestations of the same basic interaction, though commonly observed under different environments.

(5-3) The *strong nuclear force* is the force that holds protons and neutrons in proximity to each other within the nucleus of an atom. At very close distances, it is much stronger than either the gravitational or the electroweak forces, but it decreases with distance very rapidly. The strong nuclear force is actually one manifestation of a more fundamental interaction, the color force.

(5-3) The *color force* is still another of the fundamental forces in nature. It is now known that protons and neutrons are themselves made of still smaller particles (called "quarks"), and the force that bonds the quarks together within the proton or neutron is known as the color force. (Just as the gravitational force depends on the masses of the particles and the electroweak force depends on the electric charges of the particles, the color force depends on the "color charge" of the quarks.)

(5-5) *Mass* is a scalar quantity that measures the restistance an object presents to changes in its motion. We can operationally define the mass of an object in the following manner: Apply the same force to the unknown object and to a standard mass (with mass m_S), and measure the resulting accelerations. The mass of the unknown object (m_1) is then defined by $m_1 \equiv m_S(a_S/a_1)$.

(5-5) *Weight* is the gravitational force exerted on an object.

(5-5, 5-8) The *apparent weight* of an object in a particular reference frame is the vertical force needed to keep the body at rest with respect to that frame. If the frame of reference is inertial (i.e., nonaccelerated), the true weight and apparent weight will be the same; if the apparent weight is measured in an accelerated reference frame, they will differ.

(5-6) The *net force* acting on any object is the vector sum of all the forces acting on that object: $\mathbf{F}_{net} = \Sigma \mathbf{F}$.

(5-7) Newton's *third law of motion* (also known as the action-reaction principle) states that whenever one object exerts a force on another object, the second exerts an equal and opposite force on the first. Symbolically, $F_{AB} = -F_{BA}$.

(5-7) When two objects touch each other, they exert a *contact force* on each other. This contact force is usually resolved into two components—one parallel to the surface, called *friction*, and one perpendicular to the two surfaces, called the *normal force*.

(5-7) The *normal force* is the component of the contact force between two surfaces that acts perpendicular to the surface. (The component of the contact force that acts *parallel* to the surface is known as friction, so if there is no friction, the contact force and the normal force are identical.)

(5-8) *Hooke's law* is the empirical statement that many materials will experience a change in length directly proportional to the magnitude of the applied force. Written as a proportion, $F \propto x$; as an equation, $F = -kx$, where k is known as the *spring constant*.

SUMMARY OF EQUATIONS

1. Momentum

$$\mathbf{p} \equiv m\mathbf{v} \qquad \text{(Text Eq. 5-1)}$$

The product of mass and velocity is called *momentum*. Momentum is a vector quantity that points in the direction of the particle's velocity.

2. Newton's second law—general form

$$\mathbf{F}_{net} = \frac{d\mathbf{p}}{dt} \qquad \text{(Text Eq. 5-2)}$$

Newton's second law states that the net force acting on a particle is directly proportional to the net force acting on the particle. When a consistent set of units (like the SI system) is used, we can set the force *equal* to the time rate of change of momentum. Notice that the effect of a force is to *change* the momentum of a particle.

3. Newton's second law—constant mass

$$\mathbf{F}_{net} = m\mathbf{a} \qquad \text{(Text Eq. 5-3)}$$

If the mass of a particle is constant, the only possible change in its momentum is due to its changing velocity, and $d(m\mathbf{v})/dt = m(d\mathbf{v}/dt)$, producing the familiar equation seen above. As before, $\mathbf{F}_{net}$ represents the *net* force acting on the particle.

4. Weight of an object

$$\mathbf{W} = m\mathbf{g} \qquad \text{(Text Eq. 5-4)}$$

The *weight* of an object is defined as the gravitational force exerted on that object, and Newton's second law relates the weight (**W**) to the object's mass m and the free-fall acceleration of gravity **g**.

5. Hooke's law

$$F = -kx \qquad \text{(Text Eq. 5-8)}$$

This is an empirical law stating that the force (F) exerted by an elastic material like a spring is directly proportional to the change in length (x) of the spring. The minus sign indicates that the force exerted by the spring points in the direction opposite the change in length. Also, this law describes the behavior of real springs within their "elastic limit." If stretched beyond its elastic limit, a spring will exhibit permanent deformations, and the force and elongation are no longer proportional.

AVOIDING PITFALLS

1. **Inertia:** When we say that an object at rest remains at rest and an object in motion maintains its motion because of its inertia, it is important to realize that we are not explaining *why* matter behaves this way! "Inertia" is simply the name we give to whatever property it is that makes matter maintain its state of motion in the absence of uncanceled forces. The important point is that it takes a force to *change* the state of motion of any object.

2. **Forces are interactions:** Every force can always be identified as an interaction between two objects, one object pushing or pulling on another object. A falling rock does not "possess" or "contain" any force of its own: it falls because of the gravitational force exerted on it by the Earth, and it exerts a contact force on the ground when it lands, but it does not "have" any force of its own.

3. **Net force:** In Newton's second law, the acceleration of any object is determined by the net force acting *on* the object. Most mistakes in calculating the net force come from inventing nonexistent forces (the "force of inertia," for example), or from including forces exerted by the object *on its surroundings*. The motion of an automobile is determined by the forces exerted *on* the car, and the forces exerted by the car on its surroundings play no direct part in determining the car's motion!

4. **$F \propto ma$ vs. $F = ma$:** In *any* set of units, the net force is directly proportional to the product of mass and acceleration. That is, you must double the force (in any units) to produce twice the acceleration (in any units) for a given mass.

   In the SI system, however, we have defined the unit of force (the *newton*) to make the product of mass and acceleration numerically *equal* to the force, so we can write $F = ma$, not just $F \propto ma$.

Finally, Newton's second law is a vector equation. Since mass is a positive quantity, the acceleration *always* points in the direction of the net force. Also, $\mathbf{F} = m\mathbf{a}$ is a symbolic summary of three independent scalar equations:

$$(F_{net})_x = ma_x$$
$$(F_{net})_y = ma_y$$
$$(F_{net})_z = ma_z.$$

Because of this separation into three independent equations, it is usually most convenient to align one of the coordinate axes with the acceleration.

5. **Action-reaction:** Because the "action-reaction principle" has been (mis?)applied in contexts that Newton never imagined (e.g., economics, marital relations, world politics, etc.), many people have lost sight of its true content.

Newton's third law simply tells us that whenever object A pushes or pulls on object B, then object B always exerts an equal and opposite force on object A. It is simple to identify the reaction to a given force if you first identify the "action" as a force of some object acting on a different object. Once this has been done, the "reaction" is identified by interchanging the two objects. (For example, if the "action" is the force of the floor on my feet, then the reaction is the force of my feet on the floor.)

The terms "action" and "reaction" are unfortunate, since we tend to think of the "action" as the cause, and the "reaction" as the effect. In fact, forces are how we describe the mutual interaction between two objects: each object exerts the same force on the other (in opposite directions), and the two forces appear and disappear together. Which you call the "action" and which the "reaction" is arbitrary.

It is also important to realize that *not every pair of equal and opposite forces forms an "action-reaction pair."* For example, the force of the floor on my feet is equal and opposite to my weight, but it is *not* the action-reaction principle that tells us they are equal. We know they are equal because my acceleration is zero, so the net force acting on my body must be zero: it is the *second* law that makes them equal!

Finally, there are two basic characteristics of action-reaction pairs that should help you identify them:

- Action-reaction pairs *always* act on different objects; they *never* act on the same object.

- Action-reaction pairs are always the same *type* of force: if the action is a gravitational force, then the reaction will be gravitational; if the action is a contact force, then the reaction will also be a contact force.

6. **Mass vs. weight:** Because the two quantities are so intimately connected, it's tempting to use them interchangeably, but they are not the same! The *mass* of an object is a scalar quantity, typically measured in grams or kilograms, that measures how hard it is to change a given object's state of motion: massive objects are hard to start or stop, and objects with little mass are easy to start or stop. The *weight* of an object is the gravitational *force* exerted on the object by the Earth. Since weight is a force, it is a vector quantity (which points toward the center of the Earth), and is typically measured in newtons.

7. **Hooke's law:** Remember that the "x" in $F = -kx$ stands for the *change* in length of the spring, not its actual length.

 Connections to *ActivPhysics*

Newton's three laws of motion completely explain the cause of motion and changes in motion, but they are surprisingly nonintuitive. if not used carefully, they can lead to incorrect (or nonsense) results. The text devotes two chapters to Newton's laws. Chapter 5 introduces the three laws and the Newtonian way of thinking about motion and forces and presents a number of qualitative and simple quantitative examples. Chapter 6 introduces a number of different types of forces (including frictional forces, normal forces, and tension) and two-dimensional problems (including motion on inclined planes and connected masses) that may tax the limits of your algebraic problem-solving skills.

These are not easy topics, but the material in these chapters is fundamental, and understanding it thoroughly will enable you to solve a wide range of problems. Fortunately, just as Unit 1 of *ActivPhysics* helps you learn the basic skills of how to solve physics word problems, Unit 2 on Forces and Motion clarifies the key principles and particular problem-solving techniques for Newton's laws.

The best place to start is to read the first three sections of Chapter 5, then complete all five qualitative questions of Activity 2.1. It isn't necessary to know anything about tension, friction, or air resistance to answer the multiple-choice questions, except to recognize that they are just different kinds of forces. The answers given in the text bar are insightful and are a good check of your understanding of the Newtonian perspective concerning forces and motion.

Section 5-4 provides practice using Newton's second law and linking the law to kinematics equations. Activity 2.11 *Pole-Vaulter Vaults* is similar in style and difficulty level to Example 5-3. The remaining activities explore situations where two or more forces are acting, which is first discussed in Section 5-6. Activities 2.2 *Lifting a Crate* and 2.3 *Lowering a Crate* are a set of paired investigations that compare and contrast results based on a simple change in direction or conditions, and are a good starting point for this section. Most of the remaining activities of this unit examine motion in two dimensions and may be saved for Chapter 6, unless your personal style is to learn by doing and you feel ready to explore vector components of forces in two dimensions, such as on inclined planes.

Activity 2.4 deserves a special comment. Most *ActivPhysics* investigations either introduce concepts through a guided simulation or present an application where the simulation visualizes the written description of the word problem. *Blasting Off* is different from either of these types of investigations. The purpose of this activity is neither to clarify one particular principle nor to find one particular numerical value. It is an authentic exploratory activity, where different sets of initial conditions are suggested and then predictions are made before the results are checked by running the simulation. As with the *Qualitative Questions* of Activity 2.1, the answers may surprise you—which is generally the best way to understand a subject, especially a difficult topic such as Newton's laws.

We now apply Newton's laws of motion to a wider variety of situations. As the problems become more realistic (and more complex), the need for a systematic approach becomes evident, and we build on the procedures we have already been using to develop a general problem-solving strategy.

The forces of friction play a major role in the motion of most objects, and we investigate the behavior of static and kinetic friction. Finally, we consider the forces involved in circular motion.

DEFINITIONS

You should know the definition of each of these terms. (The number in parentheses is the text chapter and section in which the term is introduced.)

(6-1) A *free-body diagram* is a diagram in which a single object has been selected for analysis. The object is drawn floating in space, and an arrow is drawn to represent each force that is exerted on this object.

(6-3) The force acting on an object that causes it to follow a circular arc is sometimes called a *centripetal force.*

(6-4) *Static friction* is the force of friction that acts when two surfaces are in contact, but at rest with respect to each other.

(6-4) The *coefficient of static friction* is the ratio of the *maximum* value of static friction to the normal force: $\mu_s \equiv (F_s)_{max}/N$.

(6-4) *Kinetic friction* is the force of friction that arises when two surfaces are in contact and moving relative to each other.

(6-4) The *coefficient of kinetic friction* is the ratio of kinetic friction to the normal force: $\mu_k \equiv F_k/N$.

(6-5) When an object moves through a fluid, it experiences a *drag* force that opposes its motion relative to the fluid.

SUMMARY OF EQUATIONS

1. Force needed to produce uniform circular motion

$$F = ma = \frac{mv^2}{r} \qquad \text{(Text Eq. 6-1)}$$

In Chapter 4 we saw that any particle following a circular path (even at constant speed) experienced a radial, or centripetal, acceleration $a = v^2/r$. Since any acceleration must be caused by a force, we know that the net force acting on a particle following uniform circular motion must be $F = mv^2/r$.

2. Coefficient of static friction

$$F_s \leq \mu_s N \qquad \text{(Text Eq. 6-2)}$$

When two surfaces are in contact, but no relative motion is occurring, the force of static friction simply equals the force (if any) that is trying to make one surface move relative to the other. There is a *limit* to the force of static friction, and Text Eq. 6-2 states that the limit of static friction is proportional to the force pressing the two surfaces together (the "normal force"). The constant of proportionality (μ_s) is known as the coefficient of static friction, and it is a characteristic of the two particular surfaces.

3. Definition of coefficient of kinetic friction

$$F_k = \mu_k N \qquad \text{(Text Eq. 6-3)}$$

When two surfaces are sliding relative to one another, the force of (kinetic) friction is nearly independent of speed, but it is directly proportional to the force pressing the two surfaces together (the "normal force"). The constant of proportionality (μ_k) is known as the coefficient of kinetic friction.

4. Fluid drag force

$$F_D = \frac{1}{2}C\rho Av^2 \qquad \text{(Text Eq. 6-4)}$$

When an object moves through a fluid (liquid or gas), the fluid exerts a drag force that opposes the object's motion (relative to the fluid). For moderate speeds, experiment shows that this force is proportional to the cross-sectional area A of the object, the density ρ of the *fluid*, and the square of the object's speed through the fluid. The proportionality constant C is known as the drag coefficient, and it depends on the object's shape and surface texture.

AVOIDING PITFALLS

1. **Free-body diagrams:** The crucial first step in all these problems is an accurate free-body diagram. Once the object has been chosen, be sure to include all the forces acting *on* that object. While *all* forces result from an interaction between two separate objects, forces come in two broad types: contact forces (like the normal force, friction, and the tension in a string), and "action-at-a-distance" forces (like the weight of an object).

Be sure to show only the forces exerted *on* the chosen object, not the forces exerted *by* this object on its surroundings!

2. **Ramp problems**: A common problem in this part of the course involves the motion of an object sliding on a ramp. One common source of mistakes is to sketch the ramp at an angle too close to 45°. If this is done, it makes it too easy to put the ramp angle θ in places where its complement belongs. Exaggerate the angle in your sketch if need be, but stay away from the ambiguous case of 45°. (If the ramp angle were 44°, I would sketch it at something like 20° to 30°; if the ramp angle were 46°, I would use the angle of 60° or 70° in the sketch.)

   Second, once the algebra has been completed, you should always see if your results make sense for the two extremes: $\theta = 0°$ (a horizontal surface), and $\theta = 90°$ (a vertical surface).

3. **Choice of coordinate axes**: A properly chosen direction for your coordinate axes can greatly simplify these problems. Generally speaking, it will be most convenient if you align one of the axes with the direction of the object's acceleration.

4. **When to insert negative values**: Often, one or more of the forces will have a component in a negative direction. Don't put minus signs in too soon! You are always *adding* forces and *adding* components—it's just that some of the components may have negative values.

   For example, suppose an object were pulled by four forces:

   $$\mathbf{F_1} = 10 \text{ N, to the right}$$
   $$\mathbf{F_2} = 20 \text{ N, to the left}$$
   $$\mathbf{F_3} = 30 \text{ N, upward}$$
   $$\mathbf{F_4} = 40 \text{ N, downward.}$$

   Newton's second law gives us

   $$\mathbf{F_1} + \mathbf{F_2} + \mathbf{F_3} + \mathbf{F_4} = m\mathbf{a}.$$

   The x- and y-components of this equation become

   $$(F_1)_x + (F_2)_x + (F_3)_x + (F_4)_x = ma_x,$$
   $$(F_1)_y + (F_2)_y + (F_3)_y + (F_4)_y = ma_y.$$

   Notice that, at this time, we have not worried about the actual direction of the individual forces. What we have written here is applicable to *any* object acted upon by four forces, for any choice of axes. Only in the next step will we insert the specific values for each of the components. With the conventional choice of axes (y = up, x = right), the components take on the following values:

   $$(10 \text{ N}) + (-20 \text{ N}) + (0) + (0) = ma_x,$$
   $$(0) + (0) + (30 \text{ N}) + (-40 \text{ N}) = ma_y.$$

5. **Friction**: Both static and kinetic sliding friction are described by similar-looking equations ($F_s \le \mu_s N$, $F_k = \mu_k N$), but they describe quite different situations:

   Static: Since the object is stationary, then the force of static friction simply equals the force trying to make one surface slide over the other. The equation $F_s \le \mu_s N$ gives the *maximum* possible value of static friction; if the applied force exceeds this value, the object moves and then kinetic friction takes over.

   Kinetic: If the object is moving, the force of sliding friction is given by $F_k = \mu_k N$, regardless of the applied force.

6. **Circular motion**: Circular motion does not *produce* a centripetal force! Rather, circular motion is the *result* of any force (friction, gravitational, etc.) that is directed perpendicular to an object's velocity. Remember, it is the force that causes the change in direction, not the direction change that causes the force. The term v^2/r describes the centripetal acceleration of any object following a curve, and Newton's second law tells us that there must be a force that caused this acceleration. The force itself could be friction (when a car rounds a curve), gravitational (when the Earth orbits the Sun), tension (when a ball is whirled around on the end of a string), or any other force.

7. **Drag force**: In the formula for fluid drag force, ($F_D = \frac{1}{2}C\rho A v^2$), remember that ρ represents the density of the *fluid*, not the object. The drag force comes primarily from the fluid's inertia, and this is measured by the *fluid* density.

 Connections to *ActivPhysics*

Chapter 6 tests your ability to find vector components quickly and easily, which was the subject of Chapter 3. Example 6-1 is an excellent place to start. Activity 2.8 *Skier Goes Down a Slope* is a similar problem although the force of friction is included, slowing down the skier, which isn't introduced until Section 6-4 in your book. Activity 2.8 is the same as Example 6-10 *Sledding*. Solving these problems generally requires constructing force diagrams similar to Figure 6-1. Almost all of the text examples include a force diagram, as do most of the Unit 2 activities.

Even though both Activities 2.6 *Pushing a Crate* and 2.7 *Pushing a Crate Up a Wall* include frictional forces, it may be wise to practice constructing force diagrams for these two investigations after completing the first example. Activity 2.10

Pushing a Crate Up an Incline is the third example in this series that is like Example 6-4, except it also includes friction. Other cases of corresponding activities and examples are Example 6-5 *An Alpine Rescue* and Activity 2.14 *Modified Atwood Machine*, and Example 6-9 *Pulling a Trunk* and Activity 2.5 *Truck Pulls Crate*.

Activities 2.8 *Skier Goes Down a Slope* and 2.9 *Skier and Tow Rope* are another example of paired problems. Their advantage lies in the fact that the second activity builds on the first, keeping some attributes the same but changing others. Comparing the results of paired problems and noting when, where, and why a change in a force diagram occurred helps students explore the meaning of physics principles.

Section 6-3 examines the forces involved in circular motion, which is the subject of Unit 4 of *ActivPhysics*. The first three activities were recommended for study in previous chapters; Activities 4.4-4.7 are application problems that include centripetal force, and icons for all four of them appear at different locations in the chapter. Their overall style is the same as the investigations of Unit 2, although Activity 4.5 *Cart Goes Over Circular Hill* may be somewhat more difficult. The last activity of the unit, 4.9 *Bag Hits Bystander*, is an application problem that combines circular motion with projectile motion, and is a good review of both problem types.

CHAPTER 7   WORK, ENERGY, AND POWER

We can study mechanical systems from at least two distinct points of view. In the first six chapters, we developed our understanding of dynamics-the relationship between the forces acting on an object and its resulting motion, emphasizing the relationship between force and acceleration.

We now approach mechanical systems from a different perspective. One of the great triumphs of the past century was the discovery of a set of quantities that are conserved—quantities whose total never changes. Included among these quantities are energy (mechanical and total), momentum (linear and angular), and electric charge.

In this chapter, we begin by developing the concept of work, initially in simple cases, and then generalizing to more complex situations. Following this, we consider the energy possessed by an object due to its motion (its "kinetic energy") and look at the relationship between the work done on an object and its kinetic energy. Finally, we consider the time rate of doing work and define power.

DEFINITIONS

You should know the definition of each of these terms. (The number in parentheses is the text chapter and section in which the term is introduced.)

(7-1) The *work* done by a force $\mathbf{F}$ on a particle is defined as

$$W \equiv \int_{r_1}^{r_2} \mathbf{F} \cdot d\mathbf{r}.$$

(For constant forces, this simplifies to $W = \mathbf{F} \cdot \Delta\mathbf{r} = F\Delta r \cos \theta$.)

(7-2) The *scalar product* (or *dot product*) of two vectors is a scalar quantity, defined by

$$\mathbf{A} \cdot \mathbf{B} \equiv |\mathbf{A}||\mathbf{B}| \cos \theta = AB \cos \theta.$$

(If the two vectors are expressed in their Cartesian components, this becomes $\mathbf{A} \cdot \mathbf{B} = A_xB_x + A_yB_y + A_zB_z$.)

(7-3) A *definite integral* is defined as the difference between the antiderivative of a function evaluated at the final point and the antiderivative evaluated at the initial point. Symbolically, if $dF/dx = f(x)$, then $\int_a^b f dx = F(b) - F(a)$. Geometrically, the definite integral equals the area between the curve $f(x)$ and the x-axis, bounded by $x = a$ and $x = b$.

(7-4) A *line integral* is an integral that is evaluated along a specific path.

(7-5) For our purposes here, we will define *energy* as the ability of a system to perform work.

(7-5) The *kinetic energy* of a particle is the energy it has when in motion that it would not have if at rest. For a particle of mass m, moving with a speed v, the kinetic energy is given by $K \equiv \frac{1}{2}mv^2$.

(7-5) The *work-energy theorem* equates the total work done on a particle (W_{net}) to the change in its kinetic energy:

$$\int_{r_1}^{r_2} \mathbf{F}_{net} \cdot d\mathbf{r} = \frac{1}{2}mv_2^2 - \frac{1}{2}mv_1^2$$

$$W_{net} = \Delta K.$$

(7-5) *joule:* The work done by a 1-newton force, acting parallel to a 1-meter displacement. (SI unit of energy).

erg: The work done by a 1-dyne force, acting over a 1-centimeter displacement. (cgs unit of energy). (1 dyne = 1 g · cm/s²)

foot-pound: The work done by a 1-pound force, acting over a 1-foot displacement. (British unit of energy).

BTU (British thermal unit) is the amount of energy needed to raise the temperature of 1 pound of water by 1 F°.

calorie (cal): The amount of energy needed to raise the temperature of 1 gram of water by 1 C°.

kilowatt-hour: The amount of work done in 1 hour, when performed at the rate of 1 kilowatt (10^3 J/s). (1 kW · hr = 3,600,000 J)

electron-volt: The amount of work done on a particle with a charge equal to that of an electron, when accelerated through a 1-volt potential difference. (1 eV = 1.602×10^{-19} J)

9. *Power* is defined as the time rate at which work is done: $P = dW/dt$.

10. The *watt* is the SI unit of power, defined as 1 joule/second.

SUMMARY OF EQUATIONS

1. Work done in one-dimensional motion-constant force

$$W \equiv F_x \Delta x \qquad \text{(Text Eq. 7-1)}$$

Because the product of force and distance is encountered in so many situations, we give it a name: *work*. In the simplest case, where a particle moves in a straight line and the force is constant, we simply multiply the displacement of the particle (Δx) by the component of the force that acts in the direction of the particle's motion (F_x).

Note that if F_x and Δx have opposite signs, then the work done by the force $\mathbf{F}$ is negative. Also note that this gives only the work done by this particular force; if there are several forces, the work done by each individual force is computed separately.

2. Scalar product

$$\mathbf{A} \cdot \mathbf{B} \equiv AB \cos \theta \qquad \text{(Text Eq. 7-3)}$$

We will repeatedly encounter the product of two vectors' magnitudes and the cosine of their included angle. We now give this particular quantity a name: the *scalar product*, or *"dot"* product. Note that this operation produces a *scalar* quantity, even though it involves two vectors. (Later, in a different context, we will encounter a *vector* product of two vectors.)

If the Cartesian components of these vectors are known, it is more convenient to use the component form of the scalar product:

$$\mathbf{A} \cdot \mathbf{B} = A_x B_x + A_y B_y + A_z B_z. \quad \text{(Text Eq. 7-4)}$$

3. Work done by a constant force—arbitrary displacement

$$W = \mathbf{F} \cdot \Delta \mathbf{r} \qquad \text{(Text Eq. 7-5)}$$

As long as a force acting on a particle is constant (in magnitude and direction), we can compute the work done by this force from the dot product of force and displacement, even if the particle follows a curved path. Note that text Eq. 7-5 is equivalent to the following two forms:

$$W = F \Delta r \cos \theta$$
$$W = F_x \Delta x + F_y \Delta y + F_z \Delta z.$$

Note that it is the *displacement*, not the distance traveled, that appears in these expressions for the work done by a *constant* force.

4. Work done by a variable force—one-dimensional motion

$$W = \int_{x_1}^{x_2} F_x \, dx \qquad \text{(Text Eq. 7-8)}$$

We now consider the case where the particle moves in a straight line, say along the x-axis, from x_1 to x_2. While the particle moves, a force $\mathbf{F}$ acts on the particle. (The force may vary in magnitude and direction from point to point.) The work done by the force $\mathbf{F}$ is found by integrating the x-component of $\mathbf{F}$ from x_1 to x_2. Note that if F_x is constant, then it can be taken out of the integral, leaving the familiar product of force and displacement:

$$W = F_x \int_{x_1}^{x_2} dx = F_x(x_2 - x_1) = F_x \Delta x.$$

5. General definition of work

$$W = \int_{\mathbf{r}_1}^{\mathbf{r}_2} \mathbf{F} \cdot d\mathbf{r} \qquad \text{(Text Eq. 7-11)}$$

Finally, we come to the most general definition of work—one where the particle may follow a curved path and the force may vary. In this expression, $d\mathbf{r}$ represents an infinitesimal displacement of the particle. The work done by $\mathbf{F}$ during that step is $dW = \mathbf{F} \cdot d\mathbf{r} = F \, dr \cos \theta$, where θ is the angle between $\mathbf{F}$ and $d\mathbf{r}$. For computational purposes, Text Eq. 7-11 is written in one of these equivalent forms:

$$W = \int F \, dr \cos \theta, \text{ or}$$
$$W = \int F_x \, dx + \int F_y \, dy + \int F_z \, dz.$$

6. The work-energy theorem

$$W_{\text{net}} = \tfrac{1}{2} m v_2^2 - \tfrac{1}{2} m v_1^2 \quad \text{(Text Eq. 7-14)}$$

$$W_{\text{net}} = \Delta K \qquad \text{(Text Eq. 7-16)}$$

In this theorem, W_{net} stands for the total work done on the object. This can be calculated as the work done by the net force, or as the algebraic sum of the work done by each of the individual forces acting on the object.

The quantity $K = \tfrac{1}{2} m v^2$ is known as the "kinetic energy" of the object, and represents the energy possessed by the object because of its motion. Thus, the work-energy theorem states that the total (or net) work done on any object equals the change in its kinetic energy.

7. Power

$$P = \frac{dW}{dt} \qquad \text{(Text Eq. 7-18)}$$

The power supplied to an object is defined as the time rate at which work is done on the object.

If, however, the power is known and we need the total work done, we can write $dW = P \, dt$ and integrate over time, obtaining

$$W = \int P \, dt. \qquad \text{(Text Eq. 7-20)}$$

8. Power and velocity

$$P = \mathbf{F} \cdot \mathbf{v} \qquad \text{(Text Eq. 7-21)}$$

If a force $\mathbf{F}$ acts on a particle moving with a velocity $\mathbf{v}$, the power delivered to the particle is $\mathbf{F} \cdot \mathbf{v}$.

AVOIDING PITFALLS

1. **Sign of work:** As a quick check on any calculation of work, you should remember that

- a force that acts in the general direction of motion does *positive* work;

- a force that acts in the general direction opposite the motion does *negative* work; and

- a force that acts at right angles to the direction of motion does *no* work.

2. **Variable forces:** Remember that $W = F\Delta r \cos\theta$ only if the force is constant in magnitude *and* direction! (Actually, by constant direction, we mean a constant value of θ, the angle between $\mathbf{F}$ and $\Delta\mathbf{r}$.) If the force changes in magnitude, or changes its direction relative to the direction of motion of the particle, then you must integrate the force over the path followed by the particle.

3. **The angle θ:** In the past, we have generally used θ for the angle between a vector and the x-axis; now, θ denotes the angle between $\mathbf{F}$ and $\Delta\mathbf{r}$.

4. **Sign of the dot product:** Because of the $\cos\theta$ factor in the definition of the dot (or scalar) product, the dot product of any two perpendicular vectors is zero; if the vectors form an acute angle, their dot product will be positive, and if they form an obtuse ($> 90°$) angle, the dot product will be negative.

5. **Work depends on the path:** In general, the work done by a force depends not only on the initial and final positions, but also on the specific path actually followed from $\mathbf{r}_1$ to $\mathbf{r}_2$. (In the next chapter, we will find that certain forces have the remarkable property that their work is path-independent, but this is not true in general.)

6. **Work-energy theorem:** $W_{net} = \Delta K$ is a powerful and concise theorem, but don't forget that W_{net} represents the *total* work done on the object.

7. **Power vs. energy:** If you are asked about the work or energy in a problem, then the time involved in the process makes no difference: The same amount of work is done whether a brick is lifted to a shelf slowly or quickly.

   On the other hand, if you are asked about the *power*, then the time involved is crucial. While the same work is done in both cases, it takes more *power* to lift the brick quickly than it does to lift it slowly.

8. **Units for energy:** Because scientists and engineers were measuring various forms of energy (work, kinetic, potential, thermal energy, etc.) long before they realized they are fundamentally the same thing, we have inherited a whole collection of energy (and power) units. There's no need to memorize the numerical conversions from, say, joules to ergs or kW · hr, but you should have an idea of how the various units are defined.

   Be sure to distinguish between the units that measure the total work or energy (joule, erg, ft · lb, kW · hr, eV, calorie, BTU) and those that measure the *rate* of doing work—the power units (watt, horsepower, ft · lb/s).

ActivPhysics **Connections to *ActivPhysics***

Unit 5 of *ActivPhysics* includes a useful tool for energy problems—the work-energy bar chart. This innovative concept helps students grasp the significance of the conservation of energy principle by visualizing energy transfer through an animated bar chart that shows where energy is located at any given time and shows how it changes throughout the motion. (Figure 15-22 exemplifies this concept in the textbook.)

ActivPhysics takes a very different approach to exploring energy and its transfer than the textbook, making it difficult to determine the best method for incorporating these activities. in Chapters 7 and 8. In this case, *ActivPhysics* is truly a supplement to the text, and an extremely useful one. Instead of merely reinforcing or clarifying concepts presented in the text, *ActivPhysics* presents a new perspective that helps you better understand the meaning and application of the conservation of energy principle.

Because the investigations found in Unit 5 of *ActivPhysics* explore different types of energy transfers, it is probably best to skim Chapters 7 and 8 before beginning so you are familiar with the different forms of energy. Three key topics are emphasized in these two chapters: First; energy comes in many different forms; second, energy is transferred through work; and third, energy is conserved. Many of the different types of energy are defined in the text. When skimming the chapters, focus on Sections 7-1 and 7-2 concerning work; Section 7-5 on kinetic energy; Section 8-2 and particularly the subheadings on gravitational potential energy and spring potential energy; and Section 8-6 on nonconservative forces.

Return to Chapter 7 and complete Activity 5.1 *Work Calculations* immediately after re-reading Sections 7-1 and 7-2. Next complete Activity 5.2 *Ejector Pad* to learn how work-energy bar charts are used. A useful follow-up to Activity 5.2 is Activity 5.4 *Inventing Processes*. At this point you may choose to explore other activities from the unit on your own or to follow the advice of the *ActivPhysics* icons in the text. The investigations are similar in scope, style, and difficulty to Activity 5.2, which should help you decide how many of them you would like to complete while studying these two chapters.

CHAPTER 8   CONSERVATION OF ENERGY

In the previous chapter, we found that the work done by some forces (which we now call "nonconservative") depended not only on the initial and final points, but also on the specific path followed.

Other forces, however, have the remarkable property that their work depends only on the initial and final positions—not at all on the specific path. In this chapter, we will see that there is an elegant method for computing the work done by these forces. For these "conservative" forces, their work can be defined as the change in a potential energy function.

By defining mechanical energy to be the sum of a system's kinetic and potential energy, we find that the mechanical energy changes only if a nonconservative force does work.

DEFINITIONS

You should know the definition of each of these terms. (The number in parentheses is the text chapter and section in which the term is introduced.)

(8-1) A *conservative force* is one that satisfies either of two equivalent criteria:

$$\oint \mathbf{F}_c \cdot d\mathbf{r} = 0, \text{ or}$$

W_{AB} is the same for all paths connecting a given pair of points A and B.

(8-1) A *nonconservative force* is any force for which the work done in moving from A to B depends on the specific path followed from A to B, or equivalently,

$$\oint \mathbf{F}_{nc} \cdot d\mathbf{r} \neq 0.$$

(8-2) The *potential energy* associated with a conservative force $\mathbf{F}_c$ is defined to be the function U that satisfies the relationship

$$\Delta U_{AB} = U_B - U_A = -\int_A^B \mathbf{F}_c \cdot d\mathbf{r}.$$

That is, the change in potential energy equals (−1) times the work done by a conservative force.

(8-3) The *mechanical energy* of a system is defined as the sum of the kinetic energy plus the kinetic energy: $E_{mech} = K + U$, where U represents the total of *all* the potential energies possessed by the system.

(8-3) The *law of conservation of mechanical energy* states that if no work is done by nonconservative forces, then the total mechanical energy of the system is conserved:

$$K_i + U_i = K_f + U_f \qquad (\text{if } W_{nc} = 0).$$

(8-7) The *principle of conservation of total energy* is a statement that the total energy in any isolated system is conserved. In classical physics, "total energy" includes mechanical energy, thermal energy, and electrical potential energy.

(8-7) The *law of conservation of matter-energy* states that the total energy (including *all* forms of energy) of an isolated system is conserved. The law takes its name from Einstein's realization that the total energy of a system is proportional to its mass, according to $E = mc^2$.

SUMMARY OF EQUATIONS

1. Definition of a conservative force

$$\oint \mathbf{F}_c \cdot d\mathbf{r} = 0 \qquad (\text{Text Eq. 8-1})$$

We define a "conservative force" as a force whose work done around any *closed* path is zero. (The circle around the integral sign simply means the path being integrated over is closed.) This is mathematically equivalent to requiring that the work be path-independent.

(A nonconservative force, then, has $\oint \mathbf{F}_{nc} \cdot d\mathbf{r} \neq 0$, which implies the work is path-dependent.)

2. Potential energy change—general case

$$\Delta U_{A \to B} \equiv -\int_A^B \mathbf{F}_c \cdot d\mathbf{r} \qquad (\text{Text Eq. 8-2})$$

A particle moves from point A to point B while a *conservative* force $\mathbf{F}_c$ acts. Since the force is conservative, the work done by this force is the same for any path leading from A to B, and we can define a potential energy function U for this force. The work done by the force is then equal to the difference between the potential energy function evaluated at point B and the potential energy function evaluated at point A. (A minus sign is inserted in this definition to allow us to later define the total mechanical energy as the *sum* of kinetic and potential energy.)

Once the theoretical groundwork has been done and the form of the potential energy function has been derived for the specific force, we can then compute the work done by any conservative force from the change in its potential energy function:

$$W_c = -\Delta U = -(U_2 - U_1).$$

2a. Potential energy—force parallel to motion

$$\Delta U \equiv - \int_{x_1}^{x_2} F_x \, dx \quad \text{(Text Eq. 8-2a)}$$

If a particle moves in the direction of a conservative force, the dot product in Text Eq. 8-2 reduces to the ordinary product of force and displacement (here assumed to be in the x-direction.)

2b. Potential energy—constant force

$$\Delta U = F_x (x_2 - x_1) \quad \text{(Text Eq. 8-2b)}$$

Any constant force is conservative, and its potential energy (change) is the negative product of displacement and component of force along the displacement.

3. Potential energy—uniform gravitational field

$$\Delta U = mg \, \Delta y \quad \text{(Text Eq. 8-3)}$$

In a uniform gravitational field (a region in which the acceleration of a freely falling object has a constant value g), the gravitational potential energy of a particle of mass m is given by $U = mgy$, where y is the vertical coordinate of the particle, measured upward from an arbitrarily chosen origin.

4. Elastic potential energy of a spring

$$U = \tfrac{1}{2}kx^2 \quad \text{(Text Eq. 8-4)}$$

For an ideal spring (one that obeys Hooke's law, $F_x = -kx$), the elastic potential energy stored in the spring is given by $U = \tfrac{1}{2}kx^2$, where x represents the *change* in length of the spring, measured from its relaxed state.

5. The work-energy theorem, with potential energy

$$W_{nc} = \Delta K + \Delta U \quad \text{(Text Eq. 8-5)}$$

In this expression, W_{nc} represents the total work done by all the *nonconservative* forces acting on our system, and U represents the total potential energy of the system. (Recall that the work-energy theorem introduced in Chapter 7 reads $W_{net} = \Delta K$, where W_{net} represents the work done by *all* forces acting on the particle.)

6. Law of conservation of mechanical energy

$$\Delta K + \Delta U = 0, \text{ or} \quad \text{(Text Eq. 8-6)}$$

$$K + U = \text{constant} \quad \text{(Text Eq. 8-7)}$$

The mechanical energy $(K + U)$ of a system is conserved if and only if no work is done by nonconservative forces $(W_{nc} = 0)$. Note that we don't require the *absence* of nonconservative' forces; only that they do no work. Also, don't forget that U represents the total of *all* the forms of potential energy that change in the process.

7. Finding the force from a given potential energy—one dimensional case

$$F_x = - \frac{dU}{dx} \quad \text{(Text Eq. 8-8)}$$

Text Eq. (8-2) defines the potential energy in terms of an integral of the force. With Text Eq. 8-8 we can find the force by taking the derivative of the potential energy function with respect to position.

8. Equivalence of mass and energy

$$E = mc^2 \quad \text{(Section 8-7)}$$

Probably the most famous equation in all of physics, this result from Einstein's special theory of relativity states that energy and matter are fundamentally the same thing. Whenever the energy of a system is increased, its mass increases; if the energy of a system decreases, its mass decreases by a proportionate amount.

AVOIDING PITFALLS

1. **When to use energy?** Although this chapter is devoted to energy-type problems, the problems you will face later won't always be labeled "use the energy approach," or "use the dynamics approach." Knowing which approach to use will save you a lot of time and wasted effort. Generally, problems that involve constant acceleration and ask for velocities or positions at a given *time* are most easily found from the dynamics ($\mathbf{F} = m\mathbf{a}$) approach. When you need the speed at a given *position*, the work-energy approach is generally easier. If you know the system is conservative, then $(E_{mech})_i = (E_{mech})_f$ is the easiest approach, especially when the forces are variable.

2. **Conservative or nonconservative system?** It is crucial in these work-energy problems to know whether you are dealing with a conservative system, where mechanical energy is conserved: $(K + U)_i = (K + U)_f$, or with a nonconservative system, where $(K + U)_i \neq (K + U)_f$.

   Among the familiar conservative mechanical forces are the forces of gravity and ideal springs. Among the familiar nonconservative forces are the forces of kinetic friction, air resistance, and fluid viscosity. Neither list is complete, in that textbook (and study guide) authors are always inventing arbitrary forces for you to analyze, but you should at least recognize that any system in which kinetic friction acts is a nonconservative system, and the mechanical energy will not be conserved.

Finally, keep in mind that the normal force of one surface on the other does no work when the motion is parallel to the surface. Thus, in all the problems where an object moves along some surface, there is no work done by the normal force. (It can do work if there is motion perpendicular to the surfaces, however. As you are lifted by an elevator, it is the normal force of the floor on your feet that changes your kinetic and potential energy.)

3. **Work-energy theorem:** The work-energy theorem appears in two different forms. The original statement (developed in Chapter 7) is

$$W_{net} = \Delta K.$$

Notice that there is no mention of potential energy, and W_{net} represents the *total* work done on the object, by conservative and nonconservative forces together.

In this chapter, we defined the work done by all the conservative forces to be $W_c = -\Delta U$. Writing $W_{net} = W_c + W_{nc}$, the work-energy theorem becomes

$$W_{nc} = \Delta K + \Delta U.$$

The point of this discussion is to emphasize that W_{nc} represents the total work done by all forces *not* included in the potential energy expression, so don't compute the gravitational work as part of W_{nc} *and* include the gravitational potential energy in the right-hand side of the equation. The work from any given force is *either* part of W_{nc} *or* part of the potential energy, but not both!

4. **Gravitational potential energy:** The equation $U_g = mgy$ (or mgh) doesn't care where you put the origin, but it does require that the vertical coordinate (y or h) be measured *upward*.

5. **Elastic potential energy:** The change in the elastic potential energy of a spring as its length is changed from x_1 to x_2 is

$$\Delta U = \tfrac{1}{2}k\, x_2^2 - \tfrac{1}{2}k\, x_1^2$$

and this is *not* the same as $\tfrac{1}{2}k\Delta x^2 = \tfrac{1}{2}k\,(x_2 - x_1)^2$. Also, each value of x in $U = \tfrac{1}{2}kx^2$ must be measured from the rest length of the spring.

6. **Energy is a scalar:** Although energy is defined in terms of vector quantities like force, velocity, and displacement, energy is itself a *scalar* quantity, so there is no such thing as the "x-component of kinetic energy." When the total mechanical energy of a system is computed, it is simply an algebraic sum, not a vector sum.

7. **Force from potential-energy graphs:** If we know how a particle's potential energy varies with position, we can find the force acting on the particle from

$$F_x = -\frac{dU}{dx}$$

If we are given a graph of potential energy versus position, we interpret dU/dx as the slope of the graph, so the force equals the *negative* slope of the graph at any point. (Remember that rocks roll downhill, not uphill!)

Connections to *ActivPhysics*

As for Chapter 7, Unit 5 of *ActivPhysics* on Work and Energy takes a different approach than the textbook. For this reason, it is the new perspective that *ActivPhysics* offers that is of value here, rather than a correlation of specific activities to particular sections of Chapters 7 and 8. Activity 5.4 *Inventing Processes* is designed to familiarize students with the work-energy bar chart, and once this tool is understood, any of these activities can be completed at any time in any order.

CHAPTER 9 GRAVITATION

In this chapter, we study the nature of one of the fundamental forces holding the universe together—gravitation.

In particular, we are studying Newton's law of universal gravitation, first developed to explain the motion of the moon and of Halley's comet, but applied in more recent years to plan the *Apollo* astronauts' trips to and from the moon's surface, and to guide the *Voyager* spacecraft in their 2-½ billion-mile journeys past the outer planets.

Initially, we present Newton's description of the gravitational force between two particles. Since this is a conservative force, we can express the work done by this force in terms of a gravitational potential energy function. Finally, the concept of the gravitational field is introduced as a means of explaining how the force "gets" from the Sun to the Earth.

DEFINITIONS

You should know the definition of each of these terms. (The number in parentheses is the text chapter and section in which the term is introduced.)

(9-2) *Newton's law of universal gravitation* states that every particle in the universe attracts every other particle in the universe with a gravitational force that is directly proportional to the product of the two masses, and inversely proportional to the square of the distance between them. In equation form, $F = Gm_1m_2/r^2$.

(9-3) The *period* of a planet or satellite is the time required for the object to complete one orbit.

(9-3) A *geosynchronous orbit* is one in which the satellite appears to sit at a fixed point in the sky. This requires an equatorial orbit with a period of 24 hours.

(9-4) The *escape speed* is the minimum speed needed for a projectile to completely escape the pull of gravity.

(9-5) The *gravitational field* (**g**) at any point in space is defined as the force per unit mass that would be experienced by any particle at that point: $\mathbf{g} \equiv \mathbf{F}_g/m$. In this description, we say that every particle surrounds itself with its own gravitational field. Then the force exerted on a second particle is a result of the gravitational field (of the first particle) acting on the second particle.

(9-6) The *tidal (or differential) force* experienced by an object in a nonuniform gravitational field is the difference between the gravitational force on its near surface and the gravitational force on its far surface.

(9-7) Einstein's *general theory of relativity* describes gravitational interactions as a warping of space and time. The trajectory of any projectile is then a geodesic (shortest path) in the curved space-time.

(9-7) A *black hole* is an object whose density is so high that the escape velocity near the object exceeds the speed of light.

(9-7) The *equivalence principle* is a statement that the effects of a uniform gravitational field are indistinguishable from those of a uniformly accelerated reference frame.

SUMMARY OF EQUATIONS

1. Magnitude of the gravitational force between two particles

$$F = \frac{Gm_1m_2}{r^2} \qquad \text{(Text Eq. 9-1)}$$

Newton's law of universal gravitation is stated here in equation form, giving the magnitude of the gravitational force between two particles of masses m_1 and m_2, respectively, separated by a distance r.

The constant G is known as the universal gravitational constant, and has the value $G = 6.67 \times 10^{-11}$ N·m²/kg². Thus, two 1-kg masses held 1 m apart would attract each other with a force of $F = 6.67 \times 10^{-11}$ N. Note that this equation gives the force of *either* m_1 on m_2, *or* of m_2 on m_1, since the two forces are always equal, regardless of the relative sizes of m_1 and m_2.

Finally, this equation also gives the gravitational forces between any two spherically symmetric objects of mass m_1 and m_2 if we interpret r as their center-to-center distance.

2. Period of a circular orbit

$$T^2 = \frac{4\pi^2}{GM}r^3 \qquad \text{(Text Eq. 9-4)}$$

If a satellite of mass m orbits a planet of mass M in a circular orbit of radius r, it will complete each orbit in a time T. Note that the period is determined by the mass of the planet, not by the mass of the satellite. (This is strictly true for $M \gg m$).

3. Gravitational potential energy

$$U = -\frac{Gm_1m_2}{r} \qquad \text{(Text Eq. 9-6)}$$

The work done *by* the force of gravity on two particles as they are brought in from an initially infinite separation to a separation r is given by $-U$. In this definition, we have defined the potential energy of the two particles to be zero when they are infinitely far apart. The minus sign tells us that their potential energy has *decreased* (from zero) by this amount as they approach each other.

Put another way, it would take an amount of work $W_{ext} = Gm_1m_2/r$ by an external force to bring the two particles from an initial separation r up to their zero-potential-energy state.

4. Escape speed

$$v_{esc} = \sqrt{\frac{2GM}{r}} \qquad \text{(Text Eq. 9-7)}$$

A particle rests at a point a distance r from the center of a spherically symmetric planet of mass M. If this particle is given an initial speed greater than or equal to v_{esc}, it will eventually escape the gravitational pull of the planet and never return. The direction of its velocity doesn't matter (unless the particle crashes into the planet's surface!).

5. Energy in circular orbits

$$U = -2K$$

$$E = -K = \frac{U}{2} = -\frac{GMm}{2r} \qquad \text{(Text Eq. 9-9)}$$

If a satellite of mass m is orbiting a planet of mass M in a circular orbit, its total mechanical energy ($E = K + U$), which is negative, equals one-half its potential energy, or (-1) times its kinetic energy.

6. Definition of gravitational field

$$g \equiv \frac{F_g}{m}$$

The gravitational field at any point in space is defined as the ratio of the gravitational force experienced by a particle to the mass of the particle. It gives the gravitational force per unit mass that would be experienced by any object that may happen to be placed at that point.

Also note that g and F_g are both vector quantities. Since m is always positive, g always points in the same direction as F_g.

7. Gravitational field near the Earth's surface

$$g = -g\hat{\jmath} \qquad \text{(Text Eq. 9-10)}$$

Near the earth's surface, $F_g = mg$, so the gravitational field is a uniform, downward-pointing field with magnitude $g = 9.8$ m/s^2.

8. Gravitational field of a spherical mass

$$g = -\frac{GM}{r_2}\hat{r} \qquad \text{(Text Eq. 9-11)}$$

In this equation, $\hat{r}$ is a unit vector pointing radially *outward* from the center of the mass M. The gravitational force and gravitational field point radially inward, so the minus sign is needed to give g the proper direction.

AVOIDING PITFALLS

1. **Gravitational forces come in matched pairs:** At first thought, you might assume that the Earth's gravitational force on your body must be much greater than the gravitational force you exert on the Earth, but in fact, the two forces are precisely equal! Newton's third law (the action-reaction principle) holds for *all* forces.

    The Earth has a much more intense gravitational field than your body, but this field only has a small object (your body) to act on. Your body has a very weak gravitational field, but its field has a huge object (the Earth) to attract.

2. **Force vs. potential energy:** The equations for gravitational force ($F = Gm_1m_2/r^2$) and potential energy ($U = -Gm_1m_2/r$) are so similar, it's easy to confuse them. There are two significant differences, though.

    Remember that the gravitational force, like any other force, is a *vector* quantity, so it has x-, y-, and z-components, and forces add as vectors. Potential energy is a *scalar* quantity and adds algebraically. (Don't forget the minus signs, though!)

    Second, note that the force varies as $1/r^2$, while the potential energy varies as $1/r$.

3. **Potential energy of several masses:** When computing the total potential energy of several masses, it's easy to miss one or more pairs. Be sure that you have included the interaction between each mass and *all* of the others, not just its nearest neighbors. Also, check to make sure you haven't included the potential energy of any pair *more* than once (once as U_{12}, and again as U_{21}.)

4. **Mass and orbital motion:** We can calculate the mass of a planet by observing the period and major axis of any of its satellites' orbits, but we learn nothing about the mass of the satellite itself. (Thus, the orbit of the Earth around the Sun tells us the Sun's mass, but not the mass of the Earth.)

5. **Altitude vs. orbital radius:** In orbit calculations, you are frequently given (or asked for) the altitude of a particular orbit. Remember the altitude is measured from the *surface* of the Earth, while the radius of the orbit (in $F = GmM/r^2$, for example) is measured from the *center* of the Earth!

Connections to *ActivPhysics*

Activity 4.8 *Satellite's Orbit* is the only *Activ-Physics* investigation that addresses gravitation. This activity is an effective illustration of the concepts presented in Section 9-3 on Orbital Motion.

The purpose of the first part of the activity is to predict the speed of a satellite that will create a circular orbit; the second part illustrates elliptical orbits. The first simulation animates Figure 9-17 of the text, and the second simulation is similar to Figure 9-15. It is possible to use Equation 9-3 and the data from the circular orbit in the first simulation to calculate the correct speed. The arrow attached to the satellite in the second simulation shows the direction and magnitude of the gravitational force acting on it, demonstrating why the acceleration and therefore the speed of the satellite is continually changing, in accordance with Kepler's laws and Newton's laws of motion.

CHAPTER 10 SYSTEMS OF PARTICLES

In this chapter, we study systems of particles using the concepts of momentum and energy. These laws apply equally to rigid bodies, in which the particles maintain their relative positions, and to loosely bound systems of individual particles, like a swarm of mosquitoes or a spiral galaxy of stars.

One new concept we develop is the idea of center of mass. We also find it useful to distinguish between internal forces and external forces, and we develop the law of conservation of momentum.

DEFINITIONS

You should know the definition of each of these terms. (The number in parentheses is the text chapter and section in which the term is introduced.)

(10-1) The *center of mass* of a system of particles is a point in space determined by the mass-weighted average of the positions of the individual particles in the system:

$$\mathbf{R} = \frac{\sum m_i \mathbf{r}_i}{M}$$

An external force acting at the center of mass of a rigid object causes it to accelerate, but not rotate. Applied anywhere else, both acceleration and rotation occur. Expressed differently, the center of mass is the "balance point" for the system in a uniform gravitational field.

(10-1) An *internal force* is any force exerted on a member of a system by another member of the same system.

(10-1) An *external force* is any force exerted on a member of a system by an object that is not a member of the system.

(10-2) The *law of conservation of momentum* states that, when the external forces acting on a system cancel ($\mathbf{F}_{net\ ext} = 0$), then the total linear momentum of the system is conserved ($\mathbf{P}_i = \mathbf{P}_f$).

(10-2) The *thrust* (T) of a rocket engine is defined as the product of a rocket's mass and its acceleration in empty space, measured in any inertial frame of reference. (*Note:* Since the mass of the rocket is changing as the rocket burns fuel, the thrust is *not* the net force acting on the rocket, even in the absence of gravity.) Expressed in terms of the rate of fuel consumption (dM/dt) and the exhaust velocity of the gases,

$$T = -v_{ex}\frac{dM}{dt}$$

In this expression, v_{ex} is the velocity of the exhaust gases, *relative to the rocket.*

(10-2) The *terminal speed* of a rocket is the maximum speed the rocket can attain in empty space, given a certain total-mass to rocket-mass ratio and exhaust velocity. For a rocket starting from rest,

$$v_{max} = v_{ex}\ln\frac{M_i}{M_f}.$$

In this expression, M_i represents the (initial) total mass of the rocket and fuel; M_f represents the mass of the rocket after all the fuel has been spent.

(10-3) The *internal kinetic energy* of a system of particles is the sum of their individual kinetic energies, each measured in a frame of reference moving with the center of mass of the system:

$$K_{int} = \sum_i \tfrac{1}{2}m_i\bar{v}_i^2.$$

SUMMARY OF EQUATIONS

1. Location of center of mass—finite number of particles

$$\mathbf{R} = \frac{\sum m_i \mathbf{r}_i}{M} \qquad \text{(Text Eq. 10-2)}$$

Consider a system of particles where $\mathbf{r}_i$ represents the position of the ith particle (of mass m_i) relative to the origin of the coordinate system. When each mass is multiplied by its position vector and then summed, and the total is divided by the entire mass of the system, we find the position of the system's center of mass.

Note that any vector equation is actually a condensation of three independent scalar equations, and the actual calculations of the center of mass are usually performed with the scalar equations. The x-, y-, and z-components of $\mathbf{R}$ are:

$$X = \frac{\sum m_i x_i}{M}, \quad Y = \frac{\sum m_i y_i}{M}, \quad Z = \frac{\sum m_i z_i}{M}.$$

2. Location of center of mass of an extended object

$$\mathbf{R} = \frac{1}{M}\int \mathbf{r}\,dm \qquad \text{(Text Eq. 10-5)}$$

If we consider a continuous object as consisting of a large number of tiny particles ("mass elements"), we can compute the center of mass of the elements by summing over each of the elements. In the limit of an infinite number of infinitesimal elements, the summation becomes an integration.

Again, this vector equation represents three independent scalar equations:

$$X = \frac{1}{M}\int x\,dm, \quad Y = \frac{1}{M}\int y\,dm, \quad Z = \frac{1}{M}\int z\,dm.$$

3. Newton's second law for a system of particles

$$\mathbf{F}_{net\ ext} = M\frac{d^2\mathbf{R}}{dt^2} \quad \text{(Text Eq. 10-3)}$$

The total mass of a system of particles is M, and a net external force $\mathbf{F}_{net\ ext}$ acts on the system. The center of mass (located at position $\mathbf{R}$) has an acceleration $\mathbf{A} = d^2\mathbf{R}/dt^2 = \mathbf{F}_{net\ ext}/M$.

4. Momentum of a system of particles

$$\mathbf{P} = M\mathbf{V} \quad \text{(Text Eq. 10-7)}$$

This deceptively simple equation resembles the definition of momentum for a single particle ($\mathbf{p} \equiv m\mathbf{v}$), but the interpretation is very different. The capital $\mathbf{P}$ represents the total momentum of the particles in the system ($\mathbf{P} \equiv \Sigma m_i \mathbf{v}_i$), and M represents the total mass of the system ($M = \Sigma m_i$), but $\mathbf{V}$ represents the velocity of a single point within the system—the center of mass. (In other words, the total momentum of a system of particles is the same as if all the mass of the system were concentrated at, and moved with, the center of mass.)

5. Newton's second law for a system of particles—momentum form

$$\mathbf{F}_{net\ ext} = \frac{d\mathbf{P}}{dt} \quad \text{(Text Eq. 10-8)}$$

Recall that we introduced Newton's second law in Chapter 5 in the form

$$\mathbf{F}_{net} = \frac{d\mathbf{p}}{dt} \quad \text{(Text Eq. 5-2)}$$

There are two differences between Text Eq. 5-2 and 10-8. Equation 5-2 deals with the motion of a single particle, while Eq. 10-8 describes a certain property of the collective motion of an entire *system* of particles. Thus, the capital $\mathbf{P}$ represents the *total* momentum of a system of particles: $\mathbf{P} = \mathbf{p}_i$. Second, the force $\mathbf{F}_{net}$ in Eq. 5-2 represents the vector sum of *all* the forces acting on the single particle, while $\mathbf{F}_{net\ ext}$ in Eq. 10-8 represents the vector sum of the *external* forces acting on the system.

6. Rocket equation

$$M\frac{dv}{dt} = -v_{ex}\frac{dM}{dt} \quad \text{(Text Eq. 10-10b)}$$

This is a special-use equation, which gives the acceleration (dv/dt) of a rocket of total mass M (including fuel), in terms of the exhaust velocity (v_{ex}) of the gas, measured relative to the rocket itself, and the rate of fuel consumption. (Note that dM/dt, a decrease in the total mass of the rocket, is a negative number, so both sides of Text Eq. 10-10 are positive quantities.)

7. Speed of a rocket

$$v_f = v_i + v_{ex}\ln\frac{M_i}{M_f}$$

This is another special-use equation, which gives the speed of a rocket (v_f) in terms of its initial speed (v_i), the exhaust velocity of the fuel (v_{ex}), and the rocket's initial and final mass.

8. Kinetic energy of a system of particles

$$K = K_{cm} + K_{int} \quad \text{(Text Eq. 10-13)}$$

In this expression, K represents the total kinetic energy of the particles in the system. K_{cm} ($=\frac{1}{2}MV^2$) represents the kinetic energy of a single particle with the same total mass, moving with a speed equal to that of the system's center of mass (V). Finally, $K_{int} = \Sigma\frac{1}{2}m_i\tilde{v}_i^2$ represents the kinetic energy of the particles, as measured in a frame of reference *moving with the system's center of mass*.

AVOIDING PITFALLS

1. **Center of mass and symmetry**: The first thing to note in any center-of-mass calculation is that the center of mass must lie on each axis of symmetry of the object. If an object has two (or more) axes of symmetry, then the center of mass must lie at their intersection.

2. **Center of mass of composite objects**: Time is limited during exams, so you generally won't encounter any long integrations. In their place, you will often see objects composed of several rectangles, spheres, or rods. Remember that any object can be treated as a point particle, located at its own center of mass.

   As a variation, you may be asked for the location of the center of mass for something like a rectangle with a hole cut in it. In this case, a trick makes the calculation relatively simple: First, locate the center of mass of the complete rectangle (without the hole). Then treat the hole as a circular object of negative mass, and find the center of mass of this two-mass system.

3. **Newton's second law for systems:** Don't forget that $F_{net\ ext}$ (= dP/dt) represents the net *external* force acting on the system. It really isn't *wrong* to include the internal forces in F; it's just that they cancel pair by pair, so there's no point in including *extra* terms that add nothing to the total.

4. **Center-of-mass momentum and kinetic energy:** The total momentum of a system of particles is the same as if a single particle of mass M moved with the velocity of the center of mass: $P\ (= \Sigma p_i) = MV$.

   However, the total kinetic energy is *not* the same as a single particle of mass M moving with the center-of-mass velocity: $K_{tot} \neq \frac{1}{2}MV^2$. (The correct expression is $K_{tot} = \frac{1}{2}MV^2 + K_{int}$, where K_{int} represents the sum of the particles' kinetic energies, calculated in the center-of-mass frame of reference.)

5. **The rocket equation:** The "rocket equation"

$$M\frac{dv}{dt} = -v_{ex}\frac{dM}{dt}$$

is peculiar in one respect: The velocity v on the left-hand side of the equation is the velocity of the rocket, as measured in any nonaccelerated frame of reference. The v_{ex} on the right-hand side is the velocity of the exhaust gases, *measured in the rocket's own frame of reference.* Thus, the rocket equation relates two velocities that are measured in two different frames of reference, one a constant-velocity frame, and the other an accelerated frame.

 Connections to *ActivPhysics*

The subject matter of Chapter 10, Systems of Particles, and Chapter 11, Collisions, is investigated in Unit 6 on Momentum. The eleven activities of Unit 6 have applications to both chapters, and most of them will be beneficial while studying either chapter.

Center of mass is defined in Section 10-1 of the text and the concept of momentum is introduced in Section 10-2, where the principle of conservation of momentum is shown to be a consequence of center of mass for a system of particles. Activity 6.1 *Momentum and Energy Change* explores the momentum and energy of two pucks with different masses pushed by the same force. Completing this activity should clarify the concept of momentum and also illustrate the similarities and differences between momentum and energy. Completing it may also help prevent simple errors in assigned homework problems for this and the next chapter.

Activity 6.3 Momentum Conservation and Collisions explores conservation of momentum in one and two dimensions in greater depth, and one of the questions found in this investigation is much like Example 10-6 *A Speeding Puck*. Activity 6.4 *Collision Problems* is a follow-up application activity where final velocities are calculated for different types of collisions acting in two dimensions. Problems 20, 21, 22, 26, and 33 in the text are also two-dimensional momentum problems, and the two *ActivPhysics* activities may serve as useful tutorials before attempting the problems. Because both activities allow for the possibility of two objects rebounding off each other (e = 1.0) or sticking together (e = 0) when acting in one dimension, Problems 19, 30, and 31 also relate to these activities.

Two investigations that are recommended by *ActivPhysics* icons in Chapter 10 are Activities 6.6 *Saving an Astronaut* and 6.7 *Explosion Problems*; however, any or all of the first seven activities of the unit will familiarize you with the basic concepts and methods of solution for momentum and collision problems, whether covered in this chapter or the next.

CHAPTER 11 COLLISIONS

In this chapter, we focus on collisions—short-duration interactions between particles. The total linear momentum of the interacting particles is nearly always conserved during a collision, but the system may lose anywhere between 0 and 100% of its initial mechanical energy, depending on the specific nature of the collision process.

We have two fundamental relations to guide us in analyzing collisions. In all collisions, the momentum will be (nearly) conserved. Since momentum is a vector quantity, there is a corresponding scalar equation for each component. The other relation depends on the nature of the collision. In some collisions (which we call "elastic"), the total kinetic energy is conserved. In other collisions, some of the kinetic energy is lost, and in totally inelastic collisions (in which the two objects stick together), their final velocities are identical.

DEFINITIONS

You should know the definition of each of these terms. (The number in parentheses is the text chapter and section in which the term is introduced.)

(11-Intro) A *collision* is a short-duration interaction between two or more particles in which the collision forces are much greater than the uncanceled external forces.

(11-1) An *impulsive force* is any force that acts on an object for a short time interval.

(11-1) The *impulse* produced by any given force is defined as the time integral of the force: $I = \int F\, dt$. (For a constant force, this reduces to $I = F\Delta t$.)

(11-2) An *elastic collision* is any collision that conserves the mechanical energy of the system.

(11-2) An *inelastic collision* is any collision in which the mechanical energy of the system changes. A *totally inelastic collision* is one in which the particles stick together after the collision.

(11-4) The *impact parameter* of a collision is distance by which the center of one particle would miss the center of the other particle, if there were no interaction between the two particles.

SUMMARY OF EQUATIONS

1. Definition of impulse

$$I \equiv \int F\, dt \qquad \text{(Text Eq. 11-1)}$$

Earlier (in Chapter 7), we gave the name "work" to the integral of force over displacement ($W \equiv \int \mathbf{F} \cdot d\mathbf{r}$). We now turn our attention to the integral of force over *time*, which we call "impulse." Note that impulse, unlike work, is a vector quantity, and so has three components:

$$I_x \equiv \int F_x\, dx, \quad I_y \equiv \int F_y\, dy, \quad I_z \equiv \int F_z\, dz.$$

2. Impulse-momentum theorem

$$\Delta \mathbf{p} = \int \mathbf{F}_{net}\, dt \qquad \text{(Text Eq. 11-1)}$$

From Newton's second law ($\mathbf{F}_{net} = d\mathbf{p}/dt$), we can write $d\mathbf{p} = \mathbf{F}_{net}dt$. If we integrate over a finite time interval, the impulse produced by the net force equals the change in an object's momentum.

Again, Text Eq. 11-1 corresponds to three independent scalar equations, one for each component of force and momentum:

$$\Delta p_x = \int F_x\, dt, \quad \Delta p_y = \int F_y\, dt, \quad \Delta p_z = \int F_z\, dt.$$

3. a. Totally inelastic collision

$$\mathbf{v}_{1f} = \mathbf{v}_{2f} \qquad \text{(Section 11-3)}$$

A totally inelastic collision is one in which the two objects stick together after the collision, so they have the same final velocity.

3. b. Final velocity in a totally inelastic collision

In any collision, the total linear momentum is conserved, so we find for the final velocity in a totally inelastic collision,

$$\mathbf{v}_f = \frac{m_1\mathbf{v}_{1i} + m_2\mathbf{v}_{2i}}{m_1 + m_2}. \qquad \text{(Text Eq. 11-4)}$$

Again, remember that there are three independent scalar equations corresponding to this vector equation, one for each component of velocity. Unlike momentum, which is conserved in all collisions, the mechanical energy in an inelastic collision is *not* conserved.

4. a. Perfectly elastic collision

$$(K_{tot})_i = (K_{tot})_f \qquad \text{(Section 11-4)}$$

A (perfectly) elastic collision is one in which the total kinetic energy of the objects involved does not change.

4. b. Final velocities in a one-dimensional elastic collision

$$v_{1f} = \frac{m_1 - m_2}{m_1 + m_2}v_{1i} + \frac{2m_2}{m_1 + m_2}v_{2i} \qquad \text{(Text Eq. 11-9a)}$$

$$v_{2f} = \frac{2m_1}{m_1 + m_2}v_{1i} + \frac{m_2 - m_1}{m_1 + m_2}v_{2i} \qquad \text{(Text Eq. 11-9b)}$$

These equations give the final velocities of two particles after a head-on, perfectly elastic collision. Each of the v's in these equations represents the x-component of the particle's velocity, and may have a positive or negative value. These results follow from the law of conservation of momentum ($\mathbf{P}_i = \mathbf{P}_f$), and from the elastic nature of this collision ($K_i = K_f$.).

AVOIDING PITFALLS

1. **Momentum as a vector quantity:** Since momentum is a vector, there is a change in momentum when *either* the magnitude *or* the direction of **p** changes. Also, note that a particle experiences a smaller change in its momentum if it is simply brought to a stop than if it rebounds backwards.

2. **Conservation of momentum:** There are two situations that commonly preserve the momentum of a system. The first, and most obvious, is when all the external forces acting on the system exactly cancel. Then $\mathbf{P}_i = \mathbf{P}_f$, exactly.

   The other case is when the external forces don't exactly cancel, but the impulsive forces acting during the collision are very much greater than any external forces. During the brief duration of the collision process itself, the external forces are dwarfed by the internal forces, and we can set $\mathbf{P}_i \approx \mathbf{P}_f$.

3. **Elastic collisions:**
   (a) When a collision conserves mechanical energy, the interaction is said to be elastic. Assuming no change in potential energy, then $K_i = K_f$.
   (b) In a two-dimensional *elastic* collision, the angle between the final velocities will always be 90° *if* one of the particles was initially at rest.

4. **Momentum changes during collisions:** A direct consequence of Newton's third law (the action-reaction principle) is that both objects involved in the collision experience the *same* change in momentum, apart from a minus sign difference. Thus, when a bug splatters on the windshield of your car, the momentum of the bug changes by *exactly* the same amount as the momentum of your car! (There's a vast difference in their changes of *velocity*, however.)

 Connections to *ActivPhysics*

As we noted for Chapter 10, the activities of Unit 6 *Momentum* apply equally well to Chapters 10 and 11. Activities 6.2 *Collisions and Elasticity*, 6.3 *Momentum Conservation and Collisions*, and 6.5 *Car Collision: Two Dimensions* are recommended by icons at various points in the chapter. You may have already completed them while studying the previous chapter, or you may have waited to explore them with the appropriate section of this chapter. Whichever approach is taken, any or all of the first seven activities of Unit 6 will familiarize you with the basic concepts and methods of solution for momentum and collision problems. The only activity that needs particular comment here is 6.2 *Collisions and Elasticity*. This investigation in particular is strongly recommended because it does a wonderful job of visualizing the nature of elasticity and demonstrating the difference between elastic and inelastic collisions.

The topic of impulse introduced in Section 11-1 is included in Activity 6.1 *Momentum and Energy Change*. A different version of Example 11-2 *The Ballistic Pendulum* is explored in Activity 6.9 *Skier and Cart*, but it is still true that both momentum and energy changes must be included to complete the problem. Example 11-3 *A Fusion Reaction* is similar to one of the questions of Activity 6.4 *Collision Problems*, and Figures 11-8 and 11-11 are animated in Activity 6.3 *Momentum Conservation and Collisions*. A similar situation to Figure 11-9 (b) is animated in Activity 6.10 *Pendulum Bashes Box* and Figure 11-9 (a) can also be re-created by the simulation found in Activity 6.4.

CHAPTER 12 ROTATIONAL MOTION

In this chapter, we study the motion of rotating objects. Much of this chapter parallels material we have already developed for linear motion.

We begin by learning how to describe rotational motion in terms of angular displacement, angular speed, and angular acceleration. Then we investigate the relationship between torque and angular acceleration, finding that the rotational inertia of an object depends not only on its mass, but also on the distribution of mass relative to the axis of rotation. Finally, we extend the concepts of work and energy to rotational motion.

DEFINITIONS

You should know the definition of each of these terms. (The number in parentheses is the text chapter and section in which the term is introduced.)

(12-1) The *average angular velocity* $\bar{\omega}$ is defined as the change in angular position ($\Delta\theta$), divided by the elapsed time (Δt): $\bar{\omega} \equiv \Delta\theta/\Delta t$.

(12-1) The *instantaneous angular velocity* is defined as the average angular speed, taken over a vanishingly small time interval:

$$\omega \equiv \lim_{\Delta t \to 0} \frac{\Delta\theta}{\Delta t} = \frac{d\theta}{dt}$$

(12-1) The *radian* is a measure of angle, defined as the ratio of subtended arc length (s) to radius:

$$\theta(rad) \equiv \frac{s}{r}.$$

(12-1) The angular acceleration describes the rate at which angular speed (actually, angular velocity) is changing. The *average angular acceleration* is the ratio of angular velocity change to elapsed time ($\bar{\alpha} \equiv \Delta\omega/\Delta t$) for a finite time interval Δt.

(12-1) The *instantaneous angular acceleration* is the rate of change of angular velocity, at a single instant of time: $\alpha = d\omega/dt$.

(12-2) The *torque* produced by a force about a chosen point, called the "torque axis," is defined as the product of the force and its "moment arm," which is the perpendicular distance from the torque axis to the *line of action* of the force:

$$\tau \equiv d\,F.$$

The moment arm (denoted by d or r_i) can itself be expressed in terms of r, the distance from the torque axis to the *point of application* of the force $\mathbf{F}$ by $d = r \sin\theta$, giving $\tau = rF \sin\theta$.

(12-3) The *moment of inertia* of a rigid object is the constant of proportionality between the net torque and the angular acceleration:

$$\tau = I\alpha.$$

This turns out to have the form $I = \Sigma m_i\, r_i^2$ for point particles, and $I = \int r^2 dm$ for extended objects.

(12-3) The *parallel-axis theorem* relates the moment of inertia (I_{cm}) of an object rotating about its center of mass to I, its moment of inertia when rotating about a parallel axis displaced a distance h from the center of mass:

$$I = I_{cm} + Mh^2.$$

(12-3) The *rotational work-energy theorem* states that the work done by the net torque acting on an object ($W_{rot} \equiv \int \tau_{net}\, d\theta$) equals the change in the object's rotational kinetic energy (where $K_{rot} = \frac{1}{2}I\omega^2$):

$$W_{rot} = \Delta K_{rot}.$$

SUMMARY OF EQUATIONS

1. Definition of average angular velocity

$$\bar{\omega} \equiv \frac{\Delta\theta}{\Delta t} \qquad \text{(Text Eq. 12-1)}$$

If the angular position of an object changes by an amount $\Delta\theta$ in a time interval Δt, the object's average angular velocity is defined as the ratio of angular displacement ($\Delta\theta = \theta_f - \theta_i$) to elapsed time.

2. Definition of instantaneous angular velocity

$$\omega \equiv \lim_{\Delta t \to 0} \frac{\Delta\theta}{\Delta t} = \frac{d\theta}{dt} \qquad \text{(Text Eq. 12-2)}$$

If we measure the (average) angular velocity over shorter and shorter time intervals, we approach, in the limit, the *instantaneous* angular velocity.

3. Definition of instantaneous angular acceleration

$$\alpha \equiv \lim_{\Delta t \to 0} \frac{\Delta\omega}{\Delta t} = \frac{d\omega}{dt} \qquad \text{(Text Eq. 12-5)}$$

Angular acceleration is defined as the time rate of change of angular velocity. If the angular velocity is decreasing, then $d\omega$ and α are negative; if the angular velocity increases, then $d\omega$ and α are positive.

4. Relationship between linear distance and angular displacement

$$s = r\theta \qquad \text{(Text Eq. 12-3)}$$

In this expression, s represents the distance traveled around a circle of radius r, and θ (or $\Delta\theta$) is the angular displacement, measured in *radians*.

5. Relationship between linear speed and angular speed

$$v = r\omega \qquad \text{(Text Eq. 12-4)}$$

The linear speed (v) of a particle while moving in a circle of radius r is the product of the radius and the angular speed, when ω is measured in *radians per unit time*.

6. Relationship between tangential acceleration and angular acceleration

$$a_t = r\alpha \qquad \text{(Text Eq. 12-6)}$$

The tangential acceleration (a_t) of a particle moving in a circle of radius r is the product of the radius and the angular acceleration, with α measured in *radians per unit time squared*. (This is the "speeding-up" or "slowing-down" acceleration, due to the change in the *magnitude* of the particle's velocity.)

7. Relationship between radial acceleration and angular speed

$$a_r = \frac{v^2}{r} = \omega^2 r \qquad \text{(Text Eq. 12-7)}$$

The radial (or centripetal) acceleration is caused by the changing *direction* of the particle's velocity, and points radially inward. (When using the second form above, ω must be expressed in *radians* per unit time.)

8. Equations for uniformly accelerated circular motion

$$\bar{\omega} = \tfrac{1}{2}(\omega_0 + \omega) \qquad \text{(Text Eq. 12-8)}$$

$$\omega = \omega_0 + \alpha t \qquad \text{(Text Eq. 12-9)}$$

$$\theta = \theta_0 + \omega_0 t + \tfrac{1}{2}\alpha t^2 \qquad \text{(Text Eq. 12-10)}$$

$$\omega^2 = \omega_0^2 + 2\alpha(\theta - \theta_0) \qquad \text{(Text Eq. 12-11)}$$

In these equations, the angles can be measured in any convenient unit as long as a consistent choice is made within each equation. For example, if we are using Text Eq. 12-10 to find θ in revolutions, we need $[\theta_0]$ = rev, $[\omega_0]$ = rev/time, and $[\alpha]$ = rev/time^2.

9. Definition of torque

$$\tau \equiv rF\sin\theta \qquad \text{(Text Eq. 12-12)}$$

The *torque* produced by a force is defined as the product of the magnitude of force, distance from the torque axis to the point of application of the force, and the sine of the angle between the direction of **F** and the direction of the line drawn from the torque axis to the point of application of **F**.

(Torque can also be expressed in terms of the "moment arm," or "lever arm," which is the perpendicular distance from the torque axis to the line of action of the force. Letting d represent the moment arm, $d = r\sin\theta$, and $\tau = Fd$.)

10. Newton's second law for rotations: Constant rotational inertia

$$\tau = I\alpha \qquad \text{(Text Eq. 12-14)}$$

The angular acceleration is directly proportional to the net torque applied to the object. The constant of proportionality (I) is known as the moment of inertia of the object. The moment of inertia is itself directly proportional to the total mass of the object, but it also depends on the distribution of mass relative to the axis of rotation.

Recall that **F** = m**a** is a special case (for constant mass) of the more general statement **F** = d**p**/dt. Similarly, $\tau = I\alpha$ only if the moment of inertia of the object is constant. If the moment of inertia changes, we must use a more general form of this law (Text Eq. 13-5), expressed in terms of angular momentum.

11. Rotational inertia, or moment of inertia

$$I = \Sigma\, r_i^2 m_i \qquad \text{(Text Eq. 12-15)}$$

$$I = \int r^2\, dm \qquad \text{(Text Eq. 12-16)}$$

The first form is used to compute the moment of inertia of a collection of point particles, where the ith particle (of mass m_i) lies at a distance r_i from the axis of rotation. The integral form is used for a continuous, extended object.

12. The parallel-axis theorem

$$I = I_{cm} + Mh^2 \qquad \text{(Text Eq. 12-20)}$$

This provides an easy way to find the moment of inertia of an object for off-center rotations. In this theorem, I_{cm} represents the moment of inertia about an axis through its center of mass, and I represents its moment of inertia when rotated about a *parallel* axis, displaced by a distance h from the center of mass.

13. Rotational kinetic energy

$$K_{rot} = \tfrac{1}{2}I\omega^2 \qquad \text{(Text Eq. 12-21)}$$

If we add the kinetic energy of each of the particles in a rigid object that rotates around a fixed axis, the total kinetic energy turns out to have this familiar form. (Compare to $K = \tfrac{1}{2}mv^2$ for linear motion.)

14. Work done by a torque

> constant torque: $W = \tau\,\Delta\theta$ (Text Eq. 12-22a)

> variable torque: $W = \int \tau\,d\theta$ (Text Eq. 12-22b)

When a torque acts on an object that undergoes a rotation, work is done. If the torque acts in the direction of rotation, positive work is done; if the torque opposes the rotation, negative work is done.

15. The work-energy theorem for rotation

$$\int \tau\,d\omega = \tfrac{1}{2}I\omega_f^2 - \tfrac{1}{2}I\omega_0^2 \quad \text{(Text Eq. 12-23)}$$

$$W_{\text{rot}} = \Delta K_{\text{rot}}$$

where W_{rot} represents the work done by the *net* torque acting on the object.

16. Kinetic energy of a rolling object

$$K_{\text{roll}} = \tfrac{1}{2}Mv^2 + \tfrac{1}{2}I_{\text{cm}}\omega^2 \quad \text{(Text Eq. 12-24)}$$

A rolling object is both translating (with a translational kinetic energy $K_{\text{tr}} = \tfrac{1}{2}Mv^2$) and rotating (with rotational kinetic energy $K_{\text{rot}} = \tfrac{1}{2}I_{\text{cm}}\omega^2$). As v represents the velocity of the object's center of mass, I_{cm} represents its moment of inertia for rotations about its center of mass.

AVOIDING PITFALLS

1. **Radians:** Any equation in this chapter that relates rotational quantities (θ, ω, α) to linear quantities (s, v, a) or to dynamical quantities (F, τ, K_{rot}) requires the angles to be expressed in *radians*, (not degrees or revolutions).

   Also, because the radian is a dimensionless unit, it has a mystifying (to the beginning student) habit of appearing and disappearing in these equations. For example, with $\omega = 5$ rad/s and $r = 2$ m, the linear speed of a point on the rim of a wheel is $v = r\omega = 10$ rad $\cdot$ m/s $= 10$ m/s.

2. **Rolling:** When an object rolls without slipping along a surface, there is a simple relationship between its angular velocity and the velocity of its center: $v_{\text{center}} = R\omega$. This relationship does not hold if the object slips while it rolls.

   Also, a rolling object is constantly rotating about the point of contact with the ground with an angular velocity $\omega = v_{\text{center}}/R$.

3. **Parallel-axis theorem:** Remember that this theorem only relates the moments of inertia about *parallel* axes, one of which must pass through the center of mass.

4. **Fixed axis of rotation:** Keep in mind that this chapter discusses a special case of rotational motion—motion in which the axis of rotation doesn't change directions. (The axis may *translate*, as in the case of a rolling object, but if the axis changes its orientation, we have to consider the vector nature of these quantities, which will be discussed in the next chapter.)

 Connections to *ActivPhysics*

Chapter 12 begins with the definitions of angular velocity and angular acceleration in Section 12-1, and Activity 7.8 *Rotational Kinematics* visualizes both of these concepts using spinning disks; it also includes a careful explanation of the vector nature of these quantities. Section 12-2 presents the definition of torque, and even though Activity 7.1 *Calculating Torques* is primarily concerned with static equilibrium (Chapter 14), the equations given in the text bar and the method shown for calculating torque are presented clearly and thoroughly.

Section 12-3 explores rotational inertia, which is also the subject of Activity 7.7 *Rotational Inertia*. The investigation applies Equation 12-15 to four balls lying along a line with adjustable positions and different choices for the center of torque; it concludes with two videos that demonstrate the effect of the location of mass on angular acceleration. Both the simulations and the videos should convince you of the significance of moment of inertia and the placement of masses when considering rotational dynamics.

Section 12-3 of the text notes that Activities 7.10 *Rotoride: A Dynamics Approach* and 7.12 *Woman and Flywheel Elevator: A Dynamics Approach* are examples of application problems using rotational dynamics, as are Activities 7.9 *Car Peels Out* and 7.11 *Falling Ladder*. The methods used for solving rotational dynamics problems mirror those of linear dynamics, and each of these problems may be solved as a sequence of steps following the instructions given in the text bar.

Section 12-4 introduces rotational energy, which is also the subject of Activities 7.13–7.15. Activity 7.13 *Race Between a Block and a Disk* is similar to Example 12-14, and it may be instructive to examine the two problems together. Activities 7.14 *Woman and Flywheel Elevator: An Energy Approach* and 7.15 *Rotoride: An Energy Approach* repeat the investigations of Activities 7.12 and 7.10, respectively, but are solved using energy conservation instead of torque and moment of inertia. One possibility is to complete each set of problems as a

CHAPTER 13 ROTATIONAL VECTORS AND ANGULAR MOMENTUM

This chapter extends our analysis of rotational motion beyond the fixed-axis cases studied in Chapter 12. We will now make use of the vector nature of torque and angular quantities, and we will consider angular momentum.

DEFINITIONS

You should know the definition of each of these terms. (The number in parentheses is the text chapter and section in which the term is introduced.)

(13-1) The *angular velocity* (ω) is a vector that points along the axis of rotation in a right-hand sense, with a magnitude equal to the angular speed $\omega = d\theta/dt$.

(13-1) The *angular acceleration* (α) is defined as the time rate of change of angular velocity. It is a vector that points in the direction of the *change* in ω. (If the axis of rotation is fixed, and the angular *speed* is changing, then α is parallel to ω if the angular speed is increasing, but points in the opposite direction from ω if the angular speed is decreasing. If the angular speed is constant, but the axis of rotation is changing its orientation, then α is perpendicular to ω.)

(13-2) The *cross-product* of two vectors **A** and **B** is defined to be a vector with magnitude equal to $AB \sin\theta$, where θ is the angle between **A** and **B**. The direction of their cross-product is perpendicular to the plane containing **A** and **B**.

(13-2) The *torque* exerted by a force **F** about a point O is defined as $\tau = \mathbf{r} \times \mathbf{F}$, where **r** is the vector drawn from O to the point of application of **F**. This torque vector has a magnitude given by $\tau = rF \sin\theta$.

(13-3) The *angular momentum* of a single particle about the point O is defined as $\mathbf{L} = \mathbf{r} \times \mathbf{p}$, where $\mathbf{p} = m\mathbf{v}$ is the particle's linear momentum, and **r** is the position vector of the particle, relative to point O.

For a symmetric object with moment of inertia I, the angular momentum becomes $\mathbf{L} = I\boldsymbol{\omega}$.

(13-3) *Newton's second law for rotations* follows from the definition of angular momentum given above:

$$\tau = \frac{d\mathbf{L}}{dt}.$$

In this expression, τ represents the net external torque acting on the object. If the moment of inertia of the object is constant, then we can write $d\mathbf{L}/dt = I\,d\boldsymbol{\omega}/dt$, obtaining $\tau = I\alpha$.

(13-4) The *law of conservation of angular momentum* states that, if the external torque acting on any system is zero, then the angular momentum of the system is constant.

(13-5) If a torque acts on an object with a nonzero angular momentum, the component of the torque that acts perpendicular to **L** causes a change in the *direction* of the angular momentum. This change in the orientation of the axis of rotation is known as *precession*.

SUMMARY OF EQUATIONS

1. Definition of angular acceleration

$$\alpha \equiv \frac{d\omega}{dt} \qquad \text{(Text Eq. 13-1)}$$

The angular acceleration (vector) is defined as the time rate of change of the angular *velocity*. The angular velocity is itself a vector whose magnitude is the angular speed ($\omega = d\theta/dt$), and the direction of ω points along the rotation axis, in a right-hand sense. (Wrap the fingers of your right hand around the axis of rotation, with the fingers pointing in the direction of rotation. Your thumb points in the direction of ω.)

Note that ω can change either in magnitude or in direction. In either case, α points in the direction of the *change* in ω.

2. Vector definition of torque

$$\tau = \mathbf{r} \times \mathbf{F} \qquad \text{(Text Eq. 13-2)}$$

The torque τ produced by a force **F** is defined as the-cross product of **r** and **F**. In this expression, **r** is the position vector drawn from the point chosen as the "torque axis" to the point of application of the force.

(If all the forces and radius vectors lie in the same plane, we can combine torques as scalar quantities, using the magnitude of the cross-product:

$$\tau = rF \sin\theta. \qquad \text{(Text Eq. 12-12)}$$

To distinguish between clockwise and counterclockwise torques, we usually treat counterclockwise torques as positive quantities, and clockwise torques as negative quantities.)

3. Definition of angular momentum—point particle

$$\mathbf{L} = \mathbf{r} \times \mathbf{p} \qquad \text{(Text Eq. 13-3)}$$

The angular momentum (L) of a particle of momentum $\mathbf{p} = m\mathbf{v}$, relative to an arbitrarily chosen point (relative to which the particle's position vector is $\mathbf{r}$), is defined as the cross-product of the particle's position vector and its linear momentum. Note that the angular momentum thus depends on the point chosen as the origin.

4. Definition of angular momentum—symmetric extended object

$$\mathbf{L} = I\boldsymbol{\omega} \qquad \text{(Text Eq. 13-4)}$$

By summing the angular momenta from each of the particles that together comprise a rigid object that is symmetric around the rotation axis, we find that the angular momentum is just the product of its moment of inertia and its angular velocity, in direct analogy with $\mathbf{p} = m\mathbf{v}$.

5. Newton's second law for rotations: General form

$$\boldsymbol{\tau}_{net} = \frac{d\mathbf{L}}{dt}. \qquad \text{(Text Eq. 13-5)}$$

The net torque acting on any object equals the time rate of change of its angular momentum. Recall that both $\boldsymbol{\tau}$ and $\mathbf{L}$ depend on which point is chosen as the axis. Just be sure to use the same axis for both $\boldsymbol{\tau}$ and $\mathbf{L}$.

6. Rate of precession

$$\Omega = \frac{\tau}{L}. \qquad \text{(Text Eq. 13-7)}$$

Just as an external force acting perpendicular to an object's linear momentum causes the direction of $\mathbf{p}$ to change, an external torque $\boldsymbol{\tau}$ acting perpendicular to the angular momentum of a rotating object causes a change in the direction of $\mathbf{L}$. Thus, the axis of rotation *precesses* with an angular speed Ω.

AVOIDING PITFALLS

1. **Order of cross-product factors:** The cross-product is not commutative (i.e., $\mathbf{A} \times \mathbf{B} \neq \mathbf{B} \times \mathbf{A}$), so you have to be careful that you write $\boldsymbol{\tau} = \mathbf{r} \times \mathbf{F}$ and $\mathbf{L} = \mathbf{r} \times \mathbf{p}$, *not* $\mathbf{F} \times \mathbf{r}$ or $\mathbf{p} \times \mathbf{r}$. (Actually, if you reverse the order, you will still get the proper magnitude, but the direction will be 180° off.)

2. **Cross-product of perpendicular vectors:** The magnitude of the cross-product includes $\sin\theta$, so $\mathbf{A} \times \mathbf{B} = 0$ if $\mathbf{A}$ and $\mathbf{B}$ are parallel or antiparallel. On the other hand, $\mathbf{A} \times \mathbf{B}$ is a maximum ($= AB$) if $\mathbf{A}$ and $\mathbf{B}$ are perpendicular.

3. **Cross-product of unit vectors:** The unit vectors are perpendicular to each other, so the cross-product of any two *different* unit vectors pro-duces (± 1) times the third unit vector. On the other hand, the cross product of any vector with itself is zero (e.g., $\hat{\mathbf{i}} \times \hat{\mathbf{i}} = 0$).

4. **Choice of torque axis:** Remember that the torque and angular momentum both depend on the point you choose as the axis. Thus, the question "What torque does a given force produce?" has no answer unless the torque axis has been specified. (There is one exception that you should be aware of. If two equal and oppositely directed forces act on the same object, their net torque is the same for any choice of axis.)

5. **L isn't just for rotations:** The angular momentum of *any* particle (or system of particles) can be computed from $\mathbf{L} = \mathbf{r} \times \mathbf{p}$, even if the particle is moving in a straight line. As long as no uncanceled torque acts, the angular momentum will be conserved.

Connections to *ActivPhysics*

Two *ActivPhysics* investigations explore angular momentum concepts: Activities 7.16 *Ball Hits Bat* and 7.17 *Scattering*. Although Activity 7.1 *Calculating Torques* focuses on the conditions of static equilibrium, the first part of the activity introduces torque, which may be a useful investigation for Section 13-2. The vector nature of angular velocity is also thoroughly explained in Activity 7.8 *Rotational Kinematics* (Section 13-1).

Activity 7.16 shows a ball striking a rotating bat fixed at its center. The initial vertical position of the ball and the elasticity of the collision are adjustable, resulting in different motions of the two objects after collision. The activity explores conservation of angular momentum and shows how to calculate it either as a cross-product (Equation 13-3) or as the product of moment of inertia and angular velocity (Equation 13-4). Observing the motion of the bat before and after collision may help you better understand the concepts of angular velocity and angular acceleration.

Activity 7.17 allows for an adjustable position and initial speed of a particle passing through an attractive force field. The x- and y-coordinates of the particle are given so the path of the particle may be plotted, as well as the x- and y-components of its velocity vector. The purpose of the investigation is to show that angular momentum is conserved using the matrix form of the cross-product. The final question, asking *why* angular momentum should be conserved in this case, is an important one to answer and may serve as a check of your conceptual understanding of the relationship between torque and angular momentum.

CHAPTER 14 STATIC EQUILIBRIUM

In this chapter, we study objects that aren't moving—objects in static equilibrium. *Two* conditions are necessary for equilibrium: The net force acting on the object must be zero, and the net torque must be zero.

One of the forces acting on any object is its weight, and we find that an object's weight is a vertical force acting at its center of gravity. Finally, we express the three types of equilibrium (stable, unstable, and neutral) in terms of potential energy.

DEFINITIONS

You should know the definition of each of these terms. (The number in parentheses is the text chapter and section in which the term is introduced.)

(14-1) An object in *equilibrium* has no linear acceleration ($a = 0$) and no angular acceleration ($\alpha = 0$). Two conditions must be met for an object to be in equilibrium:

(1) The net force acting on the object must be zero: $\Sigma \mathbf{F} = 0$.

(2) The net torque acting on the object must be zero, with any point chosen as the axis: $\Sigma \tau = 0$.

(14-1) An object in *static equilibrium* also has no linear or angular velocity (i.e., the object is at rest).

(14-2) The *center of gravity* of an object is that point at which the weight of an object can be considered to be concentrated. More formally, it is defined by these equivalent descriptions:

- The total gravitational torque on an extended object will be zero if the center of gravity is chosen as the axis.

- If the combined gravitational force on any extended object is represented by a single force ($\mathbf{W} = \Sigma \mathbf{w}_i$), the combined *torque* of all the individual forces of gravity will be the same as if that single force acted through the center of gravity.

(14-4) *Stable equilibrium* results if any displacement of an object from its equilibrium position produces a restoring force, trying to return it to the equilibrium point. At a point of stable equilibrium, the potential energy of the system is at a minimum.

(14-4) If any small displacement from equilibrium results in a force that tends to move the system farther from its equilibrium point, the equilibrium is *unstable*. A point of unstable equilibrium is a point of maximum potential energy.

(14-4) If the net force on an object remains zero even if the object is displaced from its equilibrium position, it is said to be in *neutral equilibrium*.

(14-4) *Metastable equilibrium (or conditional eauilibrium)* results if small displacements produce a restoring force, but larger displacements produce a force that carries the system away from equilibrium. At metastable equilibrium, the potential energy of the system is at a local minimum.

SUMMARY OF EQUATIONS

1. First condition for equilibrium: Force

$$\Sigma \mathbf{F}_i = 0 \qquad \text{(Text Eq. 14-1)}$$

This follows directly from Newton's second law ($\mathbf{F}_{net} = m\mathbf{a}$), since any object in translational equilibrium has no acceleration. Again, this condition requires that the sum of the components in *each* direction be zero:

$$\Sigma F_x = 0, \quad \Sigma F_y = 0, \quad \Sigma F_z = 0.$$

2. Second condition for equilibrium: Torque

$$\Sigma \tau_i = 0 \qquad \text{(Text Eq. 14-2)}$$

The torque about a point O (called the torque axis) is defined by $\tau_i = \Sigma (\mathbf{r}_i \times \mathbf{F}_i)$, where $\mathbf{r}_i$ is the vector from O to the point of application of the force $\mathbf{F}_i$.

If an object is in equilibrium, then $\tau_{net} = 0$ for *any* choice of torque axis.

3. Condition for equilibrium: Potential energy

$$\frac{dU}{dx} = 0 \qquad \text{(Text Eq. 14-3)}$$

In this expression, U represents the total potential energy of the system, and x stands for any variable that describes the position or configuration of the system. From your study of calculus, you should recognize this as the condition for U to be at a local extremum. See the next paragraph for more on this point.

4. Stability of equilibrium

$$\text{[stable]} \quad \frac{d^2U}{dx^2} > 0 \qquad \text{(Text Eq. 14-4)}$$

$$\text{[unstable]} \quad \frac{d^2U}{dx^2} < 0 \quad \text{(Text Eq. 14-5)}$$

$$\text{[neutral]} \quad \frac{d^2U}{dx^2} = 0$$

Remember that in any equilibrium position, the *first* derivative of the potential is zero. It is the sign of the second derivative that determines the *stability* of the equilibrium position.

AVOIDING PITFALLS

1. **Free-body diagrams:** It is essential to start each of these problems with a free-body diagram. In the free-body diagram, you must include each force acting *on* the object you have chosen. The forces exerted *by* the object on its surroundings should *not* be included!

2. **Direction of common forces:**

   - The force of gravity acting on any object is a force that points vertically downward, through its center of gravity.

   - The tension in a rope or cable is a force that acts along the length of the rope. (There are no transverse components.)

   - The contact force exerted on an object by a frictionless surface is always normal to the surface. (Remember that friction is the parallel component of a contact force, so a frictionless surface can only exert a normal force.)

   - Forces exerted by hinges and pivots can, in general, have both vertical and horizontal components. It is usually easiest to represent these in the form of two separate forces (F_v and F_h) acting at the pivot point. Note that the force exerted by a hinge does not necessarily point along the hinged object.

3. **Moment arm:** By thinking of the torque as the product of a force and its lever arm ($\tau = r_\perp F$), it becomes easy to identify zero-torque forces. Remember that the lever arm is the *perpendicular* distance from the axis to *the line of action* of the force. Thus, any force whose line of action passes exactly through the axis has a zero torque for that axis.

4. **Choice of torque axis:** For an object in equilibrium, the sum of the torques about *any* point must be zero. Thus, we may choose any point at all as the axis for the torque calculation. Even an inappropriate choice will eventually lead to the correct answer, but it will require a longer calculation. In general, try to pick an axis that lies on the line of action of one or more unknown forces *that you are not interested in.* (If you are solving for the tension in a guy wire, don't put the axis on the guy wire. If you do, the tension will disappear from the equations!)

5. **Torque: Vector or scalar?** The torque is always given by $\tau = \mathbf{r} \times \mathbf{F}$, but when all the torque vectors point in the same direction (i.e., when the forces and moment arms all lie in the same plane), then torques can be treated as signed numbers (CCW = +, CW = -) and added as scalars.

6. **Three-force members:** This is a useful fact to know: If any member in equilibrium is acted upon by three (nonparallel forces), the lines of action of these forces must intersect at a single point. (Proof: If they didn't, choosing the intersection of two of them as our torque axis would leave the third force with a nonzero moment arm, preventing equilibrium.)

Connections to *ActivPhysics*

The conditions of static equilibrium require that both vector forces and torques add to zero. The first six activities of Unit 7 integrate these principles in a tutorial approach using realistic statics problems as examples. The textbook and *ActivPhysics* complement each other well, and the best method for studying the material may be to alternate between the example problems of the chapter and the *ActivPhysics* activities.

Activity 7.1 *Calculating Torques* shows a brick on a horizontal beam held to a vertical wall by a wire. (This set-up is very similar to Problem 41 of the text.) The algebraic equations for calculating torques from knowledge of position, force, and angle are thoroughly explained in the text bar. One advantage of this activity is that when the position and mass of the brick are changed, the magnitudes of all the forces in the problem are automatically adjusted. Consequently, this simulation helps you visualize the relationships between position, force, and the magnitude of the resulting torque.

Activity 7.2 *A Tilted Beam: Torques and Equilibrium* shows a weight hanging from a tilted beam, much like the equilibria of Problems 31 and 42, and Activity 7.4 *Two Painters on a Beam* investigates the effect of mass and position on normal forces in an equilibrium system. (Other examples of objects on boards include Problems 12, 13, 16, and 18). As with the first activity, each of these problems is constructed as a sequence of smaller problems, where each equilibrium condition is treated separately. The last static equilibrium problem, Activity 7.6 *Lecturing from a Beam*, is an interesting example of a connected system.

An important application of torques and statics, especially for health sciences majors, is body mechanics. Activity 7.3 *Arm Levers* explores the mechanics of the bicep and tricep. The same bicep problem is given in Example 14-5, and another body mechanics problem in the text is Problem 19, on the deltoid muscle. Activity 7.5 *The Back* is a slightly more difficult problem concerning the back and, as shown in the text, it is similar to Example 14-3.

CHAPTER 15 OSCILLATORY MOTION

When an object is near a point of stable equilibrium, a small displacement will result in a restoring force that tends to pull the object back toward the equilibrium point. If energy losses are small, oscillations about the equilibrium point will then result.

If, as often happens, the restoring force is proportional to the displacement, a special type of oscillation (called "simple harmonic motion") occurs, and most of the chapter discusses this type of motion.

We begin by defining the terms (frequency, amplitude, etc.) that we will use to describe oscillations, and we then examine the physical factors that determine the characteristics of a particular system's oscillations. Finally, we extend our analysis into the important cases of damped and driven oscillations, encountering the phenomenon of resonance.

DEFINITIONS

You should know the definition of each of these terms. (The number in parentheses is the text chapter and section in which the term is introduced.)

(15-1) The *amplitude* of an oscillation is the maximum displacement from the equilibrium position.

(15-1) The *period* of oscillatory motion is the time that elapses between successive occurrences of the same configuration.

(15-1) The *frequency* of oscillatory motion is defined as the number of oscillations that occur per unit time. (This is also known as the *linear frequency*, to distinguish it from the angular frequency ω.) The frequency is the reciprocal of the period.

(15-2) *Simple harmonic motion* is a special type of oscillatory motion. SHM results from a restoring force (or torque) that is directly proportional to the displacement from equilibrium. SHM is characterized by solutions that involve the "harmonic functions" (sine and cosine), and a period that is independent of amplitude.

(15-2) The *angular frequency* (ω) is defined as the linear frequency multiplied by 2π rad/cycle. Angular frequency is measured in radians per second.

(15-2) The *phase constant* (ϕ) is a constant that is determined by the initial state of the system, and it appears in the argument of the cosine (or sine) function used to describe the motion of the particle: $x(t) = A \cos(\omega t + \phi)$.

(15-3) A *simple pendulum* consists of a point particle of mass m, swinging from a massless string of length ℓ.

(15-3) If the rotational inertia of the pendulum differs from that of a point particle, we have a *physical pendulum*.

(15-6) If dissipative forces (friction, fluid viscosity, etc.) act on an oscillating system, the oscillations will decrease with time as the mechanical energy of the system is gradually converted into thermal energy. Oscillations with a decreasing amplitude constitute *damped harmonic motion*.

(15-7) To maintain a constant amplitude if damping forces are present, a periodic driving force is necessary to replenish the mechanical energy of the system. The resulting oscillations are known as *driven harmonic motion*.

(15-7) If the frequency of the driving force matches the natural frequency of oscillation of the system, the system is in *resonance* and the amplitude of the oscillations reaches a maximum.

SUMMARY

1. Relationship between period and frequency

$$f = \frac{1}{T} \qquad \text{(Text Eq. 15-1)}$$

where T represents the time required for one complete oscillation. The SI units for period are $[T]$ = sec/osc = s. f represents the frequency (or linear frequency), and is defined as the number of oscillations per unit time. Thus, $[f]$ = osc/sec = s^{-1} = hertz = Hz.

Note that the number of seconds per oscillation and the number of oscillations per second are reciprocals of each other.

2. Condition for simple harmonic motion

$$F_x = -kx \qquad \text{(Text Eq. 15-2)}$$

In this expression, x represents the displacement of an object from its equilibrium position. If a force such as this acts on a particle, it will undergo simple harmonic motion (SHM).

3. Motion of object in SHM

$$x = A \cos(\omega t + \phi) \qquad \text{(Text Eq. 15-9)}$$

The sinusoidal motion of an object in SHM is described by this equation where A represents the maximum displacement of the object from its equilibrium position, and ω is the "angular frequency" of the motion (described below). ϕ is known as the "phase constant" and essentially determines what fraction of an oscillation has already been completed when the clock is started. If $\phi = 0$, then

$$x = A \cos(\omega t), \qquad \text{(Text Eq. 15-5)}$$

which describes the oscillations of an object that starts at $x = A$ at time $t = 0$.

4. Relationship between linear and angular frequency

$$\omega = 2\pi f \qquad \text{(Text Eq. 15-7)}$$

Because of the close connection between uniform circular motion and SHM (see text section 15-4), it's useful to think of one oscillation as equivalent to 360° or 2π radians. Thus, with $[\omega]$ = rad/s, the "angular frequency" of SHM is simply 2π times the linear frequency, in osc/sec.

5. Angular frequency and spring constant

$$\omega = \sqrt{\frac{k}{m}} \qquad \text{(Text Eq. 15-8a)}$$

For a mass m subject to a force $F = -kx$, the angular frequency of the resulting oscillations is determined by the mass and the spring constant. (Note that this immediately leads to $f = (\frac{1}{2\pi})\sqrt{k/m}$ and $T = 2\pi\sqrt{m/k}$.)

6. Angular frequency and torsional constant

$$\omega = \sqrt{\frac{k}{I}} \qquad \text{(Text Eq. 15-14)}$$

If an object with a moment of inertia I is subject to a torque $\tau = -\kappa\theta$, the angular frequency of the resulting oscillations is determined by the moment of inertia and the torsional constant.

7. Angular frequency of a physical pendulum

$$\omega = \sqrt{\frac{mgL}{I}} \qquad \text{(Text Eq. 15-16)}$$

If an object is pivoted at a distance L from its center of mass and allowed to swing, the angular frequency for small oscillations is given by Text Eq. 15-16 where I is the moment of inertia for rotations about the pivot.

8. Angular frequency of a simple pendulum

$$\omega = \sqrt{\frac{g}{\ell}} \qquad \text{(Text Eq. 15-17)}$$

If a particle hangs from a massless string of length ℓ, the frequency of small oscillations does not depend on the amplitude of the oscillations or on the particle's mass. The frequency depends only on the length of the string and the acceleration of gravity.

9. Energy in simple harmonic motion

$$E = K + U = \tfrac{1}{2}kA^2 \qquad \text{(Text Sect. 15-5)}$$

The mechanical energy of a particle oscillating in simple harmonic motion is constant in time, even though the kinetic energy and potential energy both separately oscillate in time.

10. Equation of damped harmonic motion

$$x = Ae^{-bt/2m}\cos(\omega t + \phi) \qquad \text{(Text Eq. 15-20)}$$

When a dissipative force of the form $F_d = -bv$ reduces the mechanical energy of an oscillating system, the amplitude of oscillations decreases exponentially with time.

11. Amplitude of driven, damped harmonic motion

$$A = \frac{F_0}{m\sqrt{(\omega_d^2 - \omega_0^2)^2 + b^2\omega_d^2/m^2}} \qquad \text{(Text Eq. 15-23)}$$

Text Eq. 15-23 gives the amplitude of the steady oscillations that result when an oscillating force (with frequency ω_d) drives a system with a natural frequency of oscillation $\omega_0(\approx\sqrt{k/m})$. The important feature of this expression is that when the driving frequency matches the natural frequency of oscillation of the system, the denominator takes on its smallest value and the maximum amplitude results.

AVOIDING PITFALLS

1. **Angles in radians**: The expressions in this chapter presume that the argument of the cosine (or sine) function is an angle *in radians*. Be sure you have your calculator set to RADIANS when working these problems.

2. **Acceleration is *not* constant**: In oscillatory motion, the acceleration is continually changing in response to the time-varying forces. Thus, you *cannot* use the kinematic equations (e.g., $x = x_0 + v_0t + \tfrac{1}{2}at^2$) that were derived for uniform acceleration.

3. **Finding v(x)**: If you are asked for the velocity of an object in SHM at a particular *position*, it is easiest to use conservation of energy:

$$\tfrac{1}{2}kA^2 = \tfrac{1}{2}kx^2 + \tfrac{1}{2}mv^2.$$

4. **Finding v(t)**: If you are asked for the velocity or position of an object in SHM at a particular *time*, you will have to work from the equations of motion for SHM:

$$x = A \cos(\omega t + \phi)$$
$$v = -\omega A \sin(\omega t + \phi).$$

5. **Angular and linear frequency**: Be sure to note whether you are asked for (or given) the *linear* frequency (*f*, in osc/sec or Hz), or the *angular* frequency (ω, in rad/s). Note that ω is larger than *f* by a factor of 2π.

6. **Maximum values:** Common exam questions ask for the maximum values of displacement (x), velocity (v), and acceleration (a). These are usually rather simple if you remember that the maximum displacement is just the amplitude of the motion (A), the maximum speed is ω times the amplitude ($v_{max} = \omega A$), and the maximum acceleration is ω times the maximum speed ($a_{max} = \omega^2 A$).

7. **Reconstructing the equation of motion:** If you are asked to fill in the numerical values for A, ω, and ϕ in the equation of SHM from a graphical or verbal description of a system, the simplest quantity is the amplitude (A). It is usually easy to find the period (T) of the motion from the graph, and from this the angular frequency can be computed: $\omega = 2\pi/T$. Obvious values of the phase constant ($\phi = 0, \pm\pi/2, \pi$) can be read from the graph, but the odd values of ϕ must be computed from $\cos\phi = x(0)/A$.

 Connections to *ActivPhysics*

Chapter 15 on Oscillatory Motion and Unit 9 of *ActivPhysics* on Vibrations are similar in their approach. Sections 15-1 and 15-2 introduce the concepts and terms of simple harmonic motion and Activities 9.1 *Position Graphs and Equations* and 9.2 *Describing Vibrational Motion* visualize the same material. Activity 9.1 begins with Equation 15-4 (where $\phi = 2\pi f$), and one effective study aid is to run Activity 9.1 while reading the text. Sim 2 of the activity corresponds to the first topic encountered in the reading-that is, frequency; Sim 1 illustrates the second topic, vibrational amplitude; and Sim 3 is an excellent visualization of the third topic, phase angle.

Section 15-2 concludes with velocity and acceleration graphs for simple harmonic motion. The last Advisor section of Activity 9.1 provides the full derivation of the velocity and acceleration equations for two different vibrating blocks introduced in Sim 4. Compare these results with Equations 15-9, 15-10, and 15-11. After completing Activity 9.1, it may be useful to immediately explore Activity 9.2 in which all three equations of motion are deduced for two particular oscillating blocks, especially if Problems 4, 5, 10, 53, 54, or 62 have been assigned as homework.

Section 15-3 examines three different types of vibrating systems: a vertical spring; a torsional oscillator; and a pendulum. Activities 9.4 *Two Ways to Weigh Young Tarzan* and 9.5 *Ape Drops Tarzan* are examples of problems involving vertical springs. Activity 9.5 considers the effect of changing mass on the properties of the vibrating system. (Activities 9.6 and 9.7 explore similar issues for horizontal springs.) Activity 9.4 is another vertical spring application problem; however, it includes energy relationships which aren't introduced until Section 15-5. Activity 9.9 *Vibro-Ride* is a quantitative problem for a horizontal spring similar in style and difficulty level to Activity 9.4; be sure not to miss this one if Problem 69 has been assigned. Activities 9.10–9.14 investigate the behavior of pendulums. Activity 9.10 *Pendulum Frequency* could be completed before reading about the pendulum in Section 15-3 of the text, then follow up that part of the section (i.e., before attempting Example 15-4) with Activity 9.11 *Pendulum Timer*, which is quite short. Activity 9.11 relates directly to Problems 17, 18, and 21.

Activity 9.13 *Physical Pendulum* covers this topic of the same name at the end of Section 15-3 in great depth. This investigation is worth completing, especially if Problem 20, in particular, or Problems 21, 28, or 29–33 have been assigned as homework. On the other hand, Activity 9.8 *One- and Two-Spring Vibrating Systems* will be helpful if Problems 34 or 35 are assigned.

Section 15-5 considers conservation of energy in vibrational motion. *ActivPhysics* presents a thorough examination of the same topic in Activity 9.3 *Vibrational Energy*; in particular, compare Figure 15-22 to Sim 3 of the activity. It will be worth the time and effort to at least skim through this investigation, and it will definitely help with all eight problems on this topic, Problems 39–46.

CHAPTER 16 WAVE MOTION

If an elastic substance is disturbed and then released, the energy in the initial disturbance propagates through the medium in a collective motion of the particles known as a wave. In this chapter, we study the nature of wave motion, beginning with the common characteristics of waves, and defining the terms that we will use to specify the exact form of a particular wave (terms like wavelength, frequency, amplitude, etc.).

We then examine the factors that govern the propagation of waves, and we consider the transport of energy by waves. Finally, we examine the result of superimposing two or more waves, encountering constructive and destructive interference, and beats.

DEFINITIONS

You should know the definition of each of these terms. (The number in parentheses is the text chapter and section in which the term is introduced.)

(16-Intr) A *wave* is a disturbance that moves through a medium, carrying energy but not matter.

(16-2) The *amplitude* of a wave is defined as the maximum displacement from equilibrium that occurs during any cycle of the wave.

(16-2) In *longitudinal waves*, the particles in the medium oscillate parallel to the direction of the wave propagation.

(16-2) In *transverse waves*, the particles in the medium oscillate perpendicular to the direction of the wave propagation.

(16-2) The *wavelength* of a periodic wave is the distance from any point on one wave to the corresponding point on the next wave. (For example, it is the distance from one wave crest to the next crest.)

(16-2) The *period* of a wave is the length of time it takes a wave to travel a distance equal to its wavelength. (Equivalently, it is the time required for any particle in the medium to complete one oscillation as the waves pass.)

(16-2) The *frequency* of a wave is defined as the number of waves passing any fixed point per unit time. (Equivalently, it is the number of oscillations per unit time completed by any of the particles in the medium.)

(16-3) A *simple harmonic wave* is one in which the oscillations that make up the wave are simple harmonic oscillations. These give rise to sinusoidal wave functions.

(16-3) The *wave number* is defined as 2π radians, divided by the wavelength: $k = 2\pi/\lambda$.

(16-5) The *intensity* of a wave is defined as the power per unit area flowing through a surface oriented perpendicular to the wave velocity. (For waves traveling along a two-dimensional surface, the linear intensity [power per unit length] is used.)

(16-6) The *superposition principle* states that when two waves meet, each continues, undisturbed by the presence of the other, with its original velocity. Where the two waves are both present, their resultant is the point-by-point algebraic sum of the individual waves' displacements.

(16-6) *Constructive interference* results when two waves arrive at the same point in phase with each other. In this case, the amplitude of their resultant is the sum of the individual amplitudes.

(16-6) *Destructive interference* results when two waves arrive at the same point 180° out of phase with each other. In this case, the amplitude of their resultant is the *difference* of the two individual amplitudes. (If the component waves have equal amplitudes, total cancellation can result.)

(16-6) *Dispersion* is the name given to the property of certain materials in which the wave speed depends on the frequency of the waves.

(16-6) When two waves travel in the same direction with slightly different frequencies, their resultant has an amplitude that oscillates in time with a frequency equal to the difference in the two frequencies. The oscillating loudness (for sound waves) is known as *beats*.

SUMMARY OF EQUATIONS

1. Wave speed

$$v = \frac{\lambda}{T} = \lambda f \qquad \text{(Text Eq. 16-1)}$$

The period (T) is just the time required for a wave to travel a distance of one wavelength, so $v = d/t$ becomes $v = \lambda/T$. The speed with which a wave propagates is determined predominantly by the medium through which the wave is traveling, not the characteristics of the wave itself. Thus, with a constant wave speed, any change in the period will produce a proportionate change in the wavelength.

Since $f = 1/T$, we can also write $v = f\lambda$, showing that the wavelength is *inversely* proportional to the frequency. (High-frequency waves have short wavelengths, and low-frequency waves have long wavelengths.)

2. a. Basic description of a harmonic wave

$$y(x, t) = A \cos\left[2\pi\left(\frac{x}{\lambda} \pm \frac{t}{T}\right)\right]$$

Waves can have almost any imaginable shape, but the simplest and most fundamental is the "harmonic wave," or sinusoidal wave. This equation describes a harmonic wave traveling along the x-axis with an amplitude A, wavelength λ, and period T. (The *minus* sign describes a wave moving in the $+x$ direction, and the *plus* sign describes a wave moving in the $-x$ direction.)

2. b. Description of a harmonic wave—wavelength and wave speed

$$y(x, t) = A \cos\left[\frac{2\pi}{\lambda}(x \pm vt)\right] \quad \text{(Text Eq. 16-2)}$$

By using $v = \lambda/T$ to replace T in the basic equation, we can describe a harmonic wave in terms of its wavelength λ and speed of propagation v.

3. Definition of angular frequency

$$\omega \equiv 2\pi f = \frac{2\pi}{T} \quad \text{(Text Eq. 16-3)}$$

Because the linear frequency is always multiplied by 2π (radians) in the description of harmonic waves, it is convenient to define the "angular frequency" as $2\pi f$. Note that $[\omega] = $ rad/s.

4. Definition of wave number

$$k \equiv \frac{2\pi}{\lambda} \quad \text{(Text Eq. 16-4)}$$

The "wave number" is defined as 2π (radians), divided by the wavelength, so $[k] = $ rad/m. Note the similarity between ω (measured in rad/s, sometimes called the *temporal frequency* of a harmonic wave) and k (measured in rad/m, sometimes called the *spatial frequency*). The advantage in defining these two quantities lies in the simplicity of the following form of the harmonic wave.

2. c. Description of a harmonic wave—wave number and angular frequency

$$y = A \cos(kx \pm \omega t) \quad \text{(Text Eq. 16-5)}$$

The equations given above describe a harmonic wave with a positive maximum at the origin at $t = 0$; if the wave is in any other initial state, we need to add a phase constant in the argument of the cosine function: e.g., $y = A \cos(kx \pm \omega t + \phi)$.

5. Wave speed and wave number

$$v = \frac{\omega}{k} \quad \text{(Text Eq. 16-6)}$$

This relation follows immediately from the definitions of angular frequency and wave number ($\omega = 2\pi/T$ and $k = 2\pi/\lambda$).

6. Speed of transverse waves in a stretched cord

$$v = \sqrt{\frac{F}{\mu}} \quad \text{(Text Eq. 16-7)}$$

When a flexible cord (of linear mass density μ) is stretched by a force F, the speed of propagation of small-amplitude waves equals the square root of the tension divided by the linear mass density.

7. Power in stretched-cord waves

$$\overline{P} = \tfrac{1}{2}\mu\omega^2 A^2 v \quad \text{(Text Eq. 16-8)}$$

The time-averaged rate at which energy passes a fixed point on a stretched string is proportional to the speed of propagation, and to the squares of the wave frequency and the wave amplitude.

8. Definition of intensity

$$I \equiv \frac{P}{A} \quad \text{(Text Eq. 16-9)}$$

The power per unit area (oriented perpendicular to the direction of propagation) is known as the *intensity* of the wave at that point.

9. The wave equation

$$\frac{\partial^2 y}{\partial x^2} = \frac{1}{v^2}\frac{\partial^2 y}{\partial t^2} \quad \text{(Text Eq. 16-11)}$$

Any function $y(x, t)$ whose x and t partial derivatives are related in this way describes a wave traveling with a speed v in the $\pm x$-direction. For a transverse wave traveling along a rope, y represents the transverse displacement of the rope at the point x at the time t. For a sound wave, y represents the pressure difference (above or below atmospheric pressure) at the point x.

It is important to note that sinusoidal waves are only one type of solution to this equation. In general, any function of the form $y = f(x \pm vt)$ will satisfy the wave equation.

AVOIDING PITFALLS

1. **Radians:** As in Chapter 15, remember that all the trig functions in this chapter are written with their arguments in *radians*. Set your calculator to RADIANS when you start this chapter!

2. **Angular vs. linear frequency:** Again, be sure to distinguish between the angular frequency (ω), given in radians per second, and the linear frequency (f), given in waves/sec, or hertz.

3. **Speed of waves:** The speed of propagation (the "wave speed") is generally determined by the properties of the medium (density, elasticity, etc.), not the properties of the wave itself (frequency, amplitude, etc.).

   (In dispersive media, there is a slight dependence of wave speed on frequency, but we will not deal with such systems in this chapter. The phenomenon of dispersion will be considered in Chapter 35 when we study prisms and rainbows. Also, for very large amplitude waves, there may be some amplitude dependence as well.)

4. **Direction of wave travel:** If, in the wave function, the x and t terms have the same sign $[y = f(x+vt)$, or $y = f(-x - vt)]$, the wave travels in the *negative* x-direction. If they have opposite signs $[y = f(x - vt)$, or $y = f(-x + vt)]$, then the wave travels in the *positive* x-direction.

 Connections to *ActivPhysics*

The *ActivPhysics* investigations of Unit 10 are useful demonstrations of physical principles of wave motion, which are examined in Chapters 16 and 17 of the text. The best way to begin exploring wave motion is to open Activity 10.1 *Properties of Mechanical Waves* and view the first simulation. Each term introduced in Section 16-2 of the text is visualized in this simulation. These models of transverse waves on a string or in water and longitudinal waves in a gas should be helpful as the different wave properties are discussed in the text.

Section 16-4 presents the relationship between wave speed on a string and its mechanical properties. Equation 16-7 is explored in greater detail in Activity 10.2 *Speed of Waves on a String*. This activity may be helpful for Problems 21-32, 58, and 64. Two other topics that are investigated in *ActivPhysics* are beat frequency and complex waves, both found in Section 16-6. Activity 10.7 *Beats and Beat Frequency* not only animates Figure 16-23, it also includes two audio examples of beats and changes in beat frequency as the two frequencies approach each other. (Problems 49, 61, and 62 require calculations based on the beat frequency principle.) In the same way, the square wave of Figure 16-20, as well as the triangular wave of Problem 48, can be built in Activity 10.10 *Complex Waves: Fourier Analysis*. The animations of these activities in Unit 10 make the wave concepts of Chapter 16 more understandable.

CHAPTER 17   SOUND AND OTHER WAVE PHENOMENA

This chapter applies the description of waves just developed to one of the most familiar types of waves-sound. While discussing sound waves, we will also examine several additional general wave phenomena (the Doppler effect, standing waves, and wave reflection) that occur in any type of wave.

DEFINITIONS

You should know the definition of each of these terms. (The number in parentheses is the text chapter and section in which the term is introduced.)

(17-1) The *pressure* at any point is the force exerted per unit area. Pressure is measured in SI units of N/m^2, which are called *pascals* (Pa).

(17-3) The *intensity level* of a sound wave is normally measured in decibels (dB), defined by the equation

$$\beta \equiv 10 \log \frac{I}{I_0}$$

where I_0 is an arbitrarily chosen reference intensity of 10^{-12} W/m^2.

(17-6) A *standing wave* is the result of superimposing identical waves traveling in opposite directions. It consists of a series of oscillating loops, separated by stationary points of zero motion where the two component waves always cancel.

(17-6) The points of no motion in a standing wave are called *nodes*.

(17-6) The locations of the maximum-amplitude oscillations in a standing wave are known as *antinodes*.

(17-7) When a source of waves moves through the medium, or when the detector of the waves moves, a change in frequency and wavelength is observed. This frequency or wavelength shift is known as the *Doppler effect*.

(17-8) A *shock wave* is a large-amplitude wave caused by a wave source moving through a medium faster than the speed of wave propagation.

(17-8) The *Mach number* is the ratio of the speed of a wave source to the speed of sound in that medium.

SUMMARY OF EQUATIONS

1. Speed of sound in gases

$$v = \sqrt{\frac{\gamma P}{\rho}}$$ (Text Eq. 17-1)

The speed of sound waves through a gas is proportional to the square root of the ratio of pressure to density. The value of the constant

γ depends on the molecular structure of the gas: $\gamma = 5/3$ for monatomic molecules (e.g., He, Ar); $\gamma = 7/5$ for diatomic molecules (e.g., N_2, O_2), and $\gamma = 4/3$ for CO_2.

2. Average intensity of sound waves

$$\bar{I} = \frac{1}{2} s_0 \omega \Delta P_0$$ (Text Eq. 17-3a)

The intensity (power per unit area) of a sound wave, averaged over any number of complete cycles, is proportional to the displacement amplitude s_0, the (angular) frequency ω, and the pressure amplitude ΔP_0.

By expressing the displacement and frequency in terms of the density ρ and the speed of propagation v, we obtain

$$\bar{I} = \frac{\Delta P_0^2}{2\rho v}.$$ (Text Eq. 17-3b)

Finally, the pressure amplitude can be eliminated, obtaining

$$\bar{I} = \frac{1}{2} \rho \omega^2 s_0^2 v.$$ (Text Eq. 17-3c)

3. Intensity level of a sound wave

$$\beta \equiv 10 \log \frac{I}{I_0}$$ (Text Eq. 17-4)

The intensity level (in decibels) is determined by the logarithm of the ratio of the sound intensity being measured to a standard intensity, chosen to be $I_0 = 10^{-12}$ W/m^2.

4. Equation for standing waves

$$y(x, t) = 2A \sin(kx) \sin(\omega t)$$ (Text Eq. 17-7)

When identical waves traveling in opposite directions are superimposed, standing waves are produced. If the two component waves are $y_1 = A \cos(kx - \omega t)$ and $y_2 = -A \cos(kx + \omega t)$, their superposition is described by Text Eq. 17-7.

If these waves result from reflections from two fixed ends separated by a distance L, the possible wavelengths are given by

$$\lambda = \frac{2L}{m}, \text{ where } m = 1, 2, 3, \ldots$$

5. The Doppler effect

(moving source) $f' = \dfrac{f}{1 \pm u/v}$ (Text Eq. 17-10)

(moving observer) $f' = f(1 \mp u/v)$ (Text Eq. 17-11)

In each equation, the number of waves per second emitted by the source is f; the number of waves per second reaching the observer is f'. The speed of the waves through the medium is v, and the speed of the source or observer relative to the medium is u. If the two approach each other, use the upper sign; if they are moving away, use the lower sign.

6. Half-angle of shock wave

$$\sin \theta = \frac{v}{u} \quad \text{(Text Section 17-8)}$$

When a source of waves moves through a medium faster than the speed of wave propagation, a conical shock wave is formed (a V-shaped shock wave for surface waves), and the angle formed at the vertex of the shock wave is 2θ.

AVOIDING PITFALLS

1. **Intensity and amplitude:** For all waves, the intensity (power per unit area) is proportional to the *square* of the amplitude of the waves. For sound waves, we have three ways of expressing this dependence:

$$\bar{I} \propto s_0^2; \quad \bar{I} \propto \Delta P_0^2; \quad \bar{I} \propto s_0 \Delta P_0$$

2. **Intensity level and intensity:** The "intensity level" (β) is measured in decibels (dB) and is proportional to the (base-10) logarithm of the ratio of the sound intensity to a standard intensity. Thus, a fixed *increase* in intensity level (e.g., $\Delta\beta = \beta_2 - \beta_1 = +20$ dB) implies a fixed *ratio* of intensities ($I_2/I_1 = 100$).

3. **Standing waves:** Standing waves occur when identical waves traveling in opposite directions are superimposed. Remember that the distance between adjacent nodes in a standing wave pattern is *half* the wavelength, but the amplitude of oscillation at the antinodes is *twice* the amplitude of each of the component waves.

4. **Standing waves in pipes:** The fundamental and overtone frequencies are the same in pipes that are open at both ends and pipes that are closed at both ends. Pipes open at one end and closed at the other differ in two ways from symmetric pipes: The fundamental frequency in an open/closed pipe is *half* the fundamental frequency of a symmetric (closed/closed or open/open) pipe of the same length. Also, the open/closed pipe produces only the odd-numbered multiples of the fundamental frequency, while the symmetric pipes produce *all* integer multiples of the fundamental.

5. **Reflection:** When a pulse is reflected from a *fixed* end (or from a boundary where the inertia of the medium increases), the reflected pulse will experience a 180° phase change (i.e., it will be inverted).

If a pulse is reflected from a *free* end (or from a boundary where the inertia of the medium decreases), the reflected pulse will be in phase with the incident pulse (i.e., it will be erect).

(In both cases, the *transmitted* pulse will be in phase with the incident pulse.)

6. **Frequency at boundaries:** When a wave passes from one medium into another, the number of waves leaving the boundary per second is the same as the number of waves reaching the boundary per second. In other words, the *frequency* of the wave does not change at the boundary.

Since the frequency is constant, then the wavelength and wave speed are directly proportional. Thus, if the wave speeds up, the wavelength increases; if the wave slows down, the wavelength decreases.

Connections to *ActivPhysics*

The first four sections of Chapter 17 review the nature and behavior of sound waves; the last four sections examine some general properties of waves: reflection, standing waves, and the Doppler effect. Figure 17-1 of the text is animated in Activity 10.1 *Properties of Mechanical Waves*; Sections 17-2 and 17-4 are explored in greater depth by Activity 10.3 *Speed of Sound in a Gas*. The equation for the speed of sound in a gas is slightly different from Equation 17-1, but the results are equivalent. Problems 31–37 all deal with the propagation of sound through different materials.

Three different activities explore standing wave motion, and I recommend completing Activity 10.4 *Standing Waves on a String* before beginning Section 17-6. The first video shows students creating standing wave patterns; the second video shows standing wave patterns associated with corresponding sound frequencies. The activity includes introductory material on the relationship between the mechanical properties of a string and wave speed that was introduced previously in Section 16-4. Activities 10.5 *Tuning a Stringed Instrument* and 10.6 *String Mass and Standing Waves* expand on these relationships by calculating the correct tension on a string or its mass per unit length to create a particular standing wave pattern. These investigations will be useful if Problems 39, 40, 42, 44, or 45 are assigned.

A complementary discussion of the Doppler effect, Sections 17-7 and 17-8, is found in Activities 10.8 and 10.9. The first investigation encourages the student to test different initial conditions and to develop the Doppler equation based on the observed results. In the second investigation, frequency shifts are calculated using the Doppler equation for particular sets of conditions. Both of these activities may be useful if any Doppler effect problems are assigned.

CHAPTER 18   FLUID MOTION

Fluids include liquids, gases, and plasmas. Unlike solids, fluids cannot maintain their own shape, and their behavior is determined by the shape of the vessel and the external pressures exerted on the fluid.

We begin by studying systems involving fluids at rest, concentrating on pressure transmittal (Pascal's principle) and buoyancy (Archimedes' principle).

We then consider fluid dynamics. In the simple cases we will study, fluids in motion can be described by two principles: the equation of continuity (conservation of matter) and Bernoulli's principle (conservation of energy).

DEFINITIONS

You should know the definition of each of these terms. (The number in parentheses is the text chapter and section in which the term is introduced.)

(18-Intr.) A *fluid* is a substance that cannot maintain its own shape. Gases, liquids, and plasmas are fluids.

(18-1) The *density* of a substance is defined as the mass per unit volume: $\rho \equiv m/V$. SI units of density are $[\rho] = kg/m^3$.

(18-1) The *pressure* exerted on a surface is defined as the perpendicular component of the force exerted on the surface, per unit area: $P \equiv F_{\perp}/A$. The SI unit of pressure is $[P] = N/m^2 =$ pascal, but several other units [e.g., lb/in² (psi), atmospheres (atm), mm of mercury (torr), etc.] are still in common use.

(18-2) *Hydrostatic equilibrium* is the condition that every element in a fluid at rest is in equilibrium.

(18-2) The *gauge pressure (or over pressure)* is the difference between the (absolute) pressure at a point and atmospheric pressure:

$P = P_{ga} + 1$ atm.

(18-2) *Pascal's law* states that if an external pressure is applied to an enclosed fluid at any point, the pressure at *every* point in the fluid increases by the same amount.

(18-3) The difference between the pressure on the bottom surface and the top surface of an object immersed in a fluid gives rise to a net upward force on the object, known as the *buoyant force*.

(18-3) *Archimedes' principle* states that the buoyant force on any object equals the weight of the displaced fluid.

(18-4) A *streamline* can be thought of as a continuous line that follows the motion of any single fluid particle in steady flow.

(18-4) A *flow tube* is a bundle of streamlines that encloses the path of an element of a fluid in steady flow. The significant idea is that all the fluid entering one end of a flow tube must leave through the far end, since no fluid passes through the (imaginary) walls of the tube.

(18-4) The *continuity equation* states that the mass entering any flow tube per unit time ($\rho_1 v_1 A_1$) must equal the mass leaving the flow tube per unit time ($\rho_2 v_2 A_2$): $\rho_1 v_1 A_1 = \rho_2 v_2 A_2$. If the fluid is incompressible, the density is constant, and we have the simpler form, $v_1 A_1 = v_2 A_2$, generally applicable to liquids.

(18-4) *Bernoulli's equation* states that the energy per volume is constant along any flow tube, assuming no viscous or frictional energy losses, and no work done by the surroundings. Since a fluid can do work (and therefore possesses energy) because of its gravitational potential energy, its kinetic energy, or its pressure, Bernoulli's equation takes on the form

$P + \frac{1}{2}\rho v^2 + \rho g y =$ constant along any flow tube.

(18-5) Bernoulli's equation predicts that if the speed of a fluid (in level flow) increases, the pressure of that fluid must correspondingly decrease. This decrease in pressure with flow velocity is known as the *Bernoulli effect*.

(18-6) In *viscous flow*, the layers of fluid do not slide frictionlessly over each other, but there are energy losses associated with this internal friction. The *viscosity* is a number that measures the "thickness" of a fluid—i.e., its fluid friction.

SUMMARY OF EQUATIONS

1. Variation of pressure with depth: Hydrostatic equilibrium

$$\frac{dP}{dh} = \rho g \qquad \text{(Text Eq. 18-2)}$$

In a fluid at rest, the pressure increases with depth at a rate equal to the weight density of the fluid. Keep in mind that h in this equation is the depth below the surface, and is measured in the *downward* direction.

If the fluid has a uniform density, then $\Delta P = \rho g \, \Delta h$, and the pressure at a depth h becomes $P = P_0 + \rho g h$, where P_0 is the pressure applied to the surface of the fluid.

2. Equation of continuity

$$\rho v A = \text{constant along} \atop \text{any flow tube} \qquad \text{(Text Eq. 18-4b)}$$

If we follow along any tube of flow (a set of streamlines following the flow of a particular element of the fluid), we find that the product of fluid density (ρ), velocity (v), and cross-section area (A), which gives the mass flow rate in kg/s, is constant.

For a fluid with constant density, the velocity is then inversely proportional to the cross-sectional area (vA = constant).

3. Bernoulli's equation

$$P + \tfrac{1}{2}\rho v^2 + \rho g y = \text{constant along any tube flow} \qquad \text{(Text Eq. 18-6b)}$$

The energy of a fluid (its ability to do work) arises from three aspects: It can have gravitational potential energy (mgy), kinetic energy ($\tfrac{1}{2}mv^2$), or it can do work because of its pressure (PV). The energy per unit volume is then $E/V = P + \tfrac{1}{2}\rho v^2 + \rho g y$.

If there are no mechanical energy losses (viscosity, friction, etc.), then the energy of this fluid is constant, and we obtain Bernoulli's equation.

AVOIDING PITFALLS

1. **Density of water:** Remember that the density of water in SI units is $\rho = 1000 \text{ kg/m}^3$ (*not* 1 kg/m^3!)

2. **Gauge vs. absolute pressure:** The gauge pressure is defined as the *difference* between the (absolute) pressure and atmospheric pressure:

$$P_{ga} = P_{abs} - 1 \text{ atm.}$$

(Remember that a tire gauge will read zero when connected to a flat tire, but that doesn't mean there's a perfect vacuum inside the tire!)

The equations in this chapter are written for the *absolute* pressure. (If you watch carefully, however, the 1 atm often cancels from both sides of an equation, leaving only the gauge pressure.)

3. **Velocity vs. flow rate:** Be sure to notice whether you are asked for the fluid velocity (v, in m/s), or the flow rate ($\Delta V/\Delta t$, in m^3/s). Also, note that V (volume) and v (velocity) often show up in the same equation.

4. **h is positive downward:** In Text Eq. 18-2 ($dP/dh = \rho g$), h represents the *depth* beneath the fluid surface, so it is measured *downward*.

5. **y is positive upward:** In Text Eq. 18-6 (Bernoulli's equation), y represents the *elevation* of the fluid (appearing in the term mgy), and is positive *upward*.

6. **Buoyant force:** Archimedes' principle states that the buoyant force exerted by a fluid equals the weight of the displaced fluid.

A submerged object displaces a volume of fluid equal to its own *volume*, but a floating object displaces an amount of fluid that *weighs* the same as the object itself.

7. **Area $\propto$ (diameter)^2:** Many of these problems involve fluid flow through pipes with a nonuniform cross-sectional. Any cylindrical pipe has a cross-section area given by $A = \pi r^2 = (\pi/4)d^2$. Thus, the area is proportional to the *square* of the diameter or radius. If the diameter is doubled, the area quadruples.

8. **Radius $\neq$ diameter:** When computing the actual flow rate from Av, remember that the area of a circle is π times the square of the *radius*, while most pipes are sized by their diameters.

 Connections to *ActivPhysics*

Chapter 18 explores the concepts of pressure and its measurement, Pascal's principle, Archimedes' principle, and Bernoulli's equation. There are no *ActivPhysics* activities corresponding to the material covered in this chapter.

CHAPTER 19   TEMPERATURE AND HEAT

In this chapter, we begin our investigation of the general area of heat, temperature, and thermodynamics.

We start by defining the concept of thermodynamic equilibrium. From this we assign equality of temperature as the necessary condition for existence of thermal equilibrium. We then operationally define the Kelvin temperature through the constant-volume gas thermometer, and the other scales (Celsius, Fahrenheit, and Rankine) are defined in terms of the Kelvin scale.

We then introduce the concept of heat, define its unit of measure, and, through the specific heat of a substance, consider the relationship between heat and temperature. Finally, we consider the mechanisms by which heat can be transferred from place to place.

DEFINITIONS

You should know the definition of each of these terms. (The number in parentheses is the text chapter and section in which the term is introduced.)

(19-1) *Thermodynamics* is the study of heat, temperature, thermal energy, and their relationship to work.

(19-2) If the addition of heat to one system results in a change in the macroscopic properties of a second system, then the two systems are said to be in *thermal contact*.

(19-2) If the macroscopic properties of two systems in thermal contact do not change with time, then the two systems are in *thermodynamic equilibrium*.

(19-2) If the thermodynamic properties of one system can change without affecting the corresponding properties of another system, the two systems are *thermally insulated*.

(19-2) The *zeroth law of thermodynamics* states that if system A is in thermodynamic equilibrium with system C, and system B is also in thermodynamic equilibrium with system C, then it will be found that systems A and B are in thermodynamic equilibrium with each other.

(19-3) A *thermometer* is any system with a conveniently observed macroscopic property that changes with temperature.

(19-3) The *triple point* of a substance is the unique pressure and temperature at which all three phases (solid, liquid, and gas) coexist in equilibrium. For water, this occurs at a pressure of 4.58 torr, and is assigned the temperature $T_{tr} = 273.16$ K.

(19-4) *Heat* is energy transferred from one object to another because of temperature differences alone. Essentially, heat is thermal energy in transit.

(19-5) The *heat capacity (C)* of an object is the ratio of heat transferred to temperature change: $C \equiv \Delta Q / \Delta T$.

(19-5) The *specific heat (c)* of a substance is defined as the heat capacity per unit mass, according to $\Delta Q = m\, c\, \Delta T$.

(19-5) The *calorie* is a unit of heat (or any other form of energy), defined as the amount of heat needed to raise the temperature of 1 gram of water by 1 Celsius degree. (*Note:* Since this amount of heat depends slightly on the temperature of water, there are a number of slightly different calories in use. Most common is the *thermochemical calorie*, defined as exactly 4.184 J.)

(19-5) The *British thermal unit (Btu)* is defined as the amount of heat needed to raise the temperature of 1 pound of water by 1 Fahrenheit degree: 1 Btu = 1055 J.

(19-6) In the process known as *conduction*, thermal energy is transmitted through a substance by molecule-to-molecule collisions.

(19-6) The *thermal conductivity (k)* of a substance is defined as the constant of proportionality between the rate of heat flow (*H*) and the product of cross-sectional area and temperature gradient (*dT/dx*):

$$H = -kA\frac{dT}{dx}.$$

(19-6) The *thermal resistance (R)* of an object is defined as

$$R = \frac{\Delta x}{kA}$$

where Δx represents the distance heat has to travel, and *A* is the cross-sectional area of the object, measured perpendicular to the direction of heat flow.

(19-6) The *R-factor* of an object is defined as the product of thermal resistance and cross-sectional area, measured in British units: $\Re \equiv RA$.

(19-6) In *convection*, thermal energy is carried by the movement of a fluid.

(19-6) *Radiation* is the propagation of thermal energy in the form of electromagnetic waves, particularly in the infrared region.

(19-6) The *Stefan-Boltzmann law* relates the power radiated by an object to its surface area, emissivity, and temperature: $P = e\sigma A T^4$.

SUMMARY OF EQUATIONS

1. Definition of absolute temperature

$$T \equiv 273.16\frac{P}{P_3} \qquad \text{(Text Eq. 19-1)}$$

The Kelvin temperature (T) of a substance is defined in terms of the operation of a constant-volume gas thermometer. The thermometer (enclosing a fixed volume of an ideal gas) is first placed in thermal contact with a system at the triple point of water, when the thermometer gas shows a pressure P_3. Then the thermometer is placed in thermal contact with the system whose temperature is to be measured, and the gas shows a pressure P. The Kelvin temperature of the system is *defined* to be the value given by Text Eq. 19-1.

2. Celsius, Fahrenheit, and Rankine temperature scales

$$T_C = T - 273.15 \qquad \text{(Text Eq. 19-2)}$$
$$T_F = (9/5)T_C + 32 \qquad \text{(Text Eq. 19-3)}$$
$$T_R = (9/5)T$$

The Celsius and Kelvin temperature scales use the same size degree, but the Celsius scale places 0°C at the normal (1 atm) freezing point of water (273.15 degrees above absolute zero).

The Fahrenheit and Rankine scales both use a smaller degree (5/9 as large as the kelvin). The Rankine scale starts at absolute zero (like the Kelvin scale), and the Fahrenheit scale defines the normal freezing point of water to have a temperature of 32°F.

3. Definition of specific heat

$$\Delta Q = m\, c\Delta T \qquad \text{(Text Eq. 19-5)}$$

A sample of mass m absorbs a small amount of heat ΔQ, which raises its temperature by an amount ΔT. The specific heat c of the substance is then defined by Text Eq. 19-5. The SI units of specific heat are $[c] = \text{J/kg} \cdot \text{C}°$, although $\text{cal/g} \cdot \text{C}°$, $\text{J/g} \cdot \text{C}°$, and $\text{Btu/lb} \cdot \text{F}°$ are also in common use.

Note: If the temperature changes by a large amount, it is likely that the specific heat itself may vary with temperature. Then the specific heat at a particular temperature is defined by the ratio of infinitesimal quantities:

$$dQ = m\, c\, dT.$$

From this, the heat required to raise the temperature of an object from T_1 to T_2 is given by the integral

$$Q = \int dQ = \int_{T_1}^{T_2} mc\, dT.$$

4. Rate of heat conduction

$$H = -kA\frac{\Delta T}{\Delta x} \qquad \text{(Text Eq. 19-8)}$$

Experiment shows that the rate of heat flow ($H = dQ/dt$) is directly proportional to the cross-sectional area A through which the heat is flowing, and to the temperature gradient ($\Delta T/\Delta x$). The constant of proportionality (k) is known as the *thermal conductivity* of the material. Note that it is not just the temperature difference that determines the rate of heat flow, but how rapidly the temperature changes with distance (the "temperature gradient"). It is often convenient to describe heat flow in terms of the "thermal resistance," defined as $R = \Delta x/kA$. Written in terms of thermal resistance, Text Eq. 19-8 becomes

$$H = \frac{\Delta T}{R}.$$

6. Definition of R-factor

$$\mathfrak{R} \equiv RA = \frac{\Delta x}{k} \qquad \text{Text Eq. 19-11}$$

The R-factor is defined as the product of thermal resistance and area, with all quantities expressed in *British* units: $= [\mathfrak{R}] = \text{ft}^2 \cdot \text{F}° \cdot \text{h/Btu}$.

7. Stefan-Boltzmann law

$$P = e\sigma AT^4 \qquad \text{(Text Eq. 19-12)}$$

The rate at which thermal energy is radiated by an object is known as its (radiant) power, and is measured in watts (J/s). The radiant power is found to be proportional to the surface area and to the *fourth* power of the (absolute) temperature.

The quantity σ is a universal constant, known as the Stefan-Boltzmann constant, and has the value

$$\sigma = 5.67 \times 10^{-8} \text{ W/m}^2 \cdot \text{K}^4.$$

The actual power radiated at a given temperature depends on the composition and surface texture of the radiating object, and this dependence is described by an empirical constant (e), known as the emissivity of the object. The emissivity ranges from 0 (for an absolute nonradiator) to 1 (for a perfect radiator).

Interestingly, the emissivity of any object equals its absorptivity. That is, a perfect radiator ($e = 1$) is also a perfect absorber (i.e., it is perfectly black), and an absolute nonradiator ($e = 0$) is also an absolute nonabsorber (i.e., it is a perfect reflector).

AVOIDING PITFALLS

1. **Temperature conversions:** Be sure to note whether you are working with specific temperatures, or with temperature *intervals*. That is, $\Delta T_k = \Delta T_c$ because the Kelvin and Celius scales use the same size degree. However, $T_k = T_c + 273.15$ because the zero point is different on the two scales.

2. **Specific heat calculations:** If the temperature range is moderate, you can use the familiar equation $\Delta Q = mc\,\Delta T$. However, if the specific heat changes appreciably over the temperature range, then you must integrate: $\Delta Q = \int m\,c\,dT$.

3. **Units of specific heat:** You may encounter several possible units for the specific heat of a substance: $cal/g \cdot C°$, $J/g \cdot C°$, $J/kg \cdot C°$, or $kJ/kg \cdot C°$. (Also, the $C°$ may be replaced with K.) Don't forget that 1 joule = $1\ kg \cdot m^2/s^2$, so the mass must be expressed in kilograms when using this relation.

4. **Radiation:** For emission of thermal radiation, $P = -e\sigma A T^4$, where T is the Kelvin temperature of the emitting object. Note that the rate of emission is determined only by the temperature of the radiating object, and is independent of the temperature of the surroundings.

    The same equation also describes the *absorption* of thermal radiation ($P = +e\sigma A T^4$), but T now represents the temperature of the *surroundings*. The rate of absorption depends on the temperature of the surroundings, but *not* on the temperature of the absorbing object itself.

5. **H or P?** When discussing heat flow by conduction, the symbol used for the rate of heat transfer is H. When discussing heat transfer by radiation, the symbol P is used to represent the same physical quantity. Both H and P represent the energy transferred per second ($\Delta Q/\Delta t$), and both are measured in SI units of joules/second, or watts.

 Connections to *ActivPhysics*

Chapter 19 introduces temperature and its measurement, explains the relationship between heat and temperature, and explores the three methods of heat transfer, while Unit 8 of *ActivPhysics* focuses on the theoretical aspects of thermodynamics. The activities thus do not correlate with the approach used in the text, although the first part of Activity 8.6 *Heat, Internal Energy, and the First Law of Thermodynamics* does explore the relationship between heat and the microscopic behavior of matter. Note that Activity 8.7 *Heat Capacity* is **not** the same concept as the one presented in Section 19-5, even though the titles appear to represent the same thing.

CHAPTER 20   THE THERMAL BEHAVIOR OF MATTER

This chapter begins with a review of the ideal gas law. Then we study on a microscopic scale the manner in which gases respond to a temperature change, first for ideal gases, and then for a more realistic model of gases. From a very simple model of gases, we find that temperature is a measure of the average kinetic energy of the molecules.

We then turn to a macroscopic description as we discuss the physical processes accompanying phase changes, identifying the critical and triple points, and the latent heats of transformation.

Finally, we consider the thermal expansion of solids, liquids, and gases.

DEFINITIONS

You should know the definition of each of these terms. (The number in parentheses is the text chapter and section in which the term is introduced.)

(20-1) The *ideal gas law* states that the product of pressure and volume is directly proportional to the product of the number of molecules and the absolute temperature of the gas, and that the proportionality constant is the same for all gases: $PV = NkT$.

(20-1) The *kinetic theory of ideal gases* is a simple model that explains many of the macroscopic properties of gases. The model is based on the following assumptions:

1. The gas consists of a large number of identical point particles of mass m.

2. The particles do not interact with each other.

3. The particles move in random directions with a range of speeds.

4. The particles make perfectly elastic collisions with the walls of the container.

(20-1) The *Maxwell-Boltzmann distribution* is an expression that predicts the number of molecules in a given sample of gas that have speeds in a certain narrow range.

(20-1) The *thermal speed* (also known as the *root-mean-square*, or *rms speed*) is the speed of a molecule whose kinetic energy is $3/2 kT$. (This is found by taking the square root of the average value of v^2, averaged over all molecules in the sample.)

(20-1) The *van der Waals force* is a weak electrical force of attraction that appears only when two molecules are in close proximity.

(20-2) In this context, *phase* refers to a distinct state of matter. Most commonly, the three phases are solid, liquid, and gas. (In addition to these three, plasmas comprise a fourth distinct phase,

and many substances display more than one distinct solid or liquid phase.)

(20-2) The *critical temperature* is the maximum temperature at which the liquid and vapor phases are distinct.

(20-2) The *triple point* is the unique condition of pressure and temperature at which all three phases of a substance can coexist in equilibrium.

(20-2) The *heat of fusion* is the heat per unit mass required to melt a substance: $L_f = Q/m$.

(20-2) The *heat of vaporization* is the heat per unit mass required to vaporize a substance: $L_v = Q/m$.

(20-3) If a substance is heated, it normally expands. If it is prevented from expanding, *thermal stresses* can occur.

SUMMARY OF EQUATIONS

1. The ideal gas law

$$PV = NkT \qquad \text{(Text Eq. 20-1)}$$

The response of a gas to changing conditions of temperature (T), volume (V), pressure (P), and number of molecules (N) is summarized in the ideal gas law. While strictly true only in the limit of low pressures and high temperatures (i.e., low particle densities), this equation very closely describes the behavior of most gases under normal conditions.

The constant k is known as Boltzmann's constant, and has the value $k = 1.38 \times 10^{-23}$ J/K · molecule. (Usually, we don't write "molecule" in the denominator, but it's a good reminder that this is related to the energy *per molecule* at a given temperature.)

If we express the ideal gas law in terms of the number of *moles (n)* of a gas, then we obtain

$$PV = nRT, \qquad \text{(Text Eq. 20-2)}$$

where $R = (6.02 \times 10^{23} \text{ molecules/mole}) k = 8.314$ J/K · mol. (Note that *mol* is the SI symbol for *mole*, not molecule!)

2. Kinetic-molecular interpretation of temperature

$$\tfrac{1}{2} m \overline{v^2} = \tfrac{3}{2} kT \qquad \text{(Text Eq. 20-4)}$$

The left-hand side of this equation is simply the average value of the kinetic energy of a single molecule. Thus, we could equally well write $\overline{K} = \tfrac{3}{2} kT$, and we see that the average kinetic energy of the gas molecules is determined solely by the temperature of the gas, and is independent of the mass of the molecules.

3. Maxwell-Boltzmann distribution

$$N(v)\Delta v = 4\pi N \left(\frac{m}{2\pi kT}\right)^{3/2} v^2 e^{-mv^2/2kT}\Delta v$$

(Text Eq. 20-6)

We have a sample of N gas molecules, each of mass m, at a temperature T. The Maxwell-Boltzmann distribution, $N(v)\Delta v$, gives the number of these molecules that have a speed between v and $v + \Delta v$.

4. The van der Waals equation

$$\left(P + \frac{n^2 a}{V^2}\right)(V - nb) = nRT \quad \text{(Text Eq. 20-7)}$$

The ideal gas equation predicts that all substances obey the same simple gas law all the way down to absolute zero. The van der Waals equation is an attempt to produce a more realistic model. In this equation, a is a constant that depends on the strength of the short-range electrical forces of attraction that molecules exert on each other when in close proximity, and b is related to the volume occupied by each molecule.

5. Heat of transformation

$$L = \frac{Q}{m} \qquad \text{(Text Eq. 20-8)}$$

When a substance undergoes a transformation from one phase to another, a certain amount of heat is absorbed or released. If Q represents the heat absorbed or released in melting or freezing, L is the *heat of fusion*, L_f. If Q represents the heat absorbed or released in boiling or condensing, L is the *heat of vaporization*, L_v.

6. Coefficient of volume expansion

$$\beta \equiv \frac{\Delta V/V}{\Delta T} \qquad \text{(Text Eq. 20-9)}$$

The volume coefficient of expansion is defined as the relative change in volume ($\Delta V/V$) per degree of temperature change.

7. Coefficient of linear expansion

$$\alpha \equiv \frac{\Delta L/L}{\Delta T} \qquad \text{(Text Eq. 20-10)}$$

The linear coefficient of expansion is defined as the relative change in length ($\Delta L/L$) per degree of temperature change. Finally, there is a simple relation between the volume and linear coefficients of expansion:

$$\beta = 3\alpha. \qquad \text{(Text Eq. 20-11)}$$

AVOIDING PITFALLS

1. **Ideal gas law:** You can save a lot of time (and aggravation) if you think in terms of proportions, rather than plugging numbers into the gas law and solving for explicit values of n, T, etc. For example, if the absolute temperature is doubled, then the volume will double (at constant n, P). If the temperature triples while the pressure is halved, then the pressure must increase by a factor of 6, and so on.

Also, be sure to distinguish between N (the number of molecules) and n (the number of moles). If you get an outlandish answer (a temperature of 298×10^{23} K, for example), you can assume that you are off by a factor of Avogadro's number.

2. **Mean square vs. square of the mean:** In the kinetic molecular theory of gases, you may encounter two similar expressions:

mean-square speed: $\overline{v^2}$,

square of the mean speed: $(\overline{v})^2$.

These are *not* the same! In the first case, the individual speeds are first squared, and then the average of these squared values is computed. (It is this quantity that appears in the mean kinetic energy of the molecules, and the "thermal speed" is the square root of the mean-square speed.)

In the second case, the individual speeds are first averaged, and then this average value is squared.

Since an average of the squared values weights the high speeds more heavily than the low speeds, the thermal speed is higher than the mean speed.

3. **Temperature and kinetic energy:** The most significant result of the kinetic molecular theory is that the mean kinetic energy of the gas molecules is directly proportional to the temperature: $\overline{K} = \frac{3}{2}kT$. This says that all gas molecules at a given temperature (*regardless of mass*) have the same kinetic energy. Thus, in a mixture of gases at a single temperature, the lighter gas molecules will be moving more rapidly, in order to have the same kinetic energy as the heavy molecules.

4. **Heat of transformation:** When heat is added to a substance and it remains in the same phase (solid, liquid, or gas), the effect is to produce a temperature rise, according to $Q = m\,c\Delta T$.

When a heat transfer produces a phase change (melting, freezing, boiling, or condensing), there is *no* temperature change, but there is a transfer of heat nonetheless: $Q = \pm mL$. The

± sign is to remind you that heat is *absorbed* during melting and boiling, while heat is released during condensing and freezing.

5. **Thermal expansion:** When an object of uniform composition is heated, *every* dimension (height, width, depth, diameter, etc.) increases according to $\Delta L = \alpha L \Delta T$. It's the same as if a photograph of the object were enlarged. Thus, not only do the outside dimensions increase, but the size of a hole or cavity also increases.

Also, if each of the linear dimensions of an object increases by 1%, the area will increase by about 2% and the volume will increase by about 3%.

 Connections to *ActivPhysics*

The first four activities of Unit 8 and the first section of Chapter 20 explore the microscopic nature of gases. The simulation of Activity 8.1 *Characteristics of a Gas* follows the path of a single particle in a model of an ideal gas. Adjusting the temperature of the model will show the relationship between temperature and average speed of the atoms of the gas. It is worthwhile to view this simulation before starting the chapter so that you will have this animated model in mind while reading the text.

I recommend stopping at Example 20-2 and completing Activity 8.4 *State Variables and the Ideal Gas Law* next. The text will have provided a good introduction to the state variables of pressure, volume, and temperature. The advantage of the activity is that changes in state variables are demonstrated in the second simulation, and graphical relationships between the state variables are covered in depth through a series multiple choice questions. The activity concludes with definitions of, and simulations showing, constant pressure (isobaric), constant volume (isochoric), and constant temperature (isothermal) processes.

The relationship between the statistical distribution of particle speeds in a gas and temperature are shown in Activities 8.2 and 8.3 *Maxwell–Boltzmann Distribution*. Both exercises explore the meaning of the curve and the connection between microscopic states and temperature. Even if understanding the Maxwell–Boltzmann distribution is not a course objective, it may be very useful to examine these activities, especially before beginning the next chapter on the First Law of Thermodynamics, or if any of problems 14–18, 20-22, or 74 have been assigned as homework.

CHAPTER 21   HEAT, WORK, AND THE
FIRST LAW OF THERMODYNAMICS

The central idea in this chapter is the concept of internal energy. The internal energy of a system can be increased by adding heat to the system, or by performing work on the system. Conversely, if a system performs work on its surroundings, then its internal energy must have decreased by the same amount.

In this chapter, we continue to interpret temperature as a measure of the (translational) kinetic energy of the molecules, but we now recognize that rotations and vibrations are additional forms of internal energy (ones that do not show up in the temperature, however).

Finally, we encounter the equipartition theorem, which states that the internal energy of a system is equally shared by the various degrees of freedom available to the system. From this, and from some ideas borrowed from quantum mechanics, we understand why the specific heat of gases increases in steps as the temperature rises.

DEFINITIONS

You should know the definition of each of these terms. (The number in parentheses is the text chapter and section in which the term is introduced.)

(21-1) In this chapter, we generalize the concept of *work* to include any transfer of energy that does not require a temperature difference.

(21-1) The *first law of thermodynamics* states that the change in the internal energy of a system is equal to the heat added to the system minus the work done by the system: $\Delta U = Q - W$.

(21-1) A *thermodynamic state variable* is a property of a system that does not depend on the actual process used in getting the system into that state.

(21-2) A *quasi-static process* is one in which the system is nearly in equilibrium at every instant. A minute change in the conditions of the surroundings would be sufficient to reverse the direction of the process.

(21-2) A *reversible process* is just another name for a quasi-static process.

(21-2) An *irreversible process*, on the other hand, is typically a sudden change in the condition of the system. In an irreversible process, different parts of the system will have very different properties during the process, and will only settle into a unique, single state at the end of the process.

(21-2) An *isothermal process* is one carried out at a constant temperature.

(21-2) A *constant-volume (or isochoric, or isovolumic) process* is one in which the volume of the system is held constant.

(21-2) An *isobaric process* is a constant-pressure process.

(21-2) An *adiabatic process* is one in which there is no transfer of heat to or from the system.

(21-2) The *constant-volume molar specific heat* of a substance is defined as the heat capacity per mole of the substance, for a constant-volume process. With n = number of moles, $C_V = (1/n)$ dQ/dT.

(21-2) The *constant-pressure molar specific heat* of a substance is defined as the heat capacity per mole of the substance, for a constant-pressure process. With n = number of moles, $C_P = (1/n)$ dQ/dT.

(21-2) The ratio of constant-pressure molar specific heat to the constant-volume molar specific heat is known as "gamma": $\gamma = C_P/C_V$.

(21-3) The number of *degrees of freedom* possessed by a system equals the number of independent spatial coordinates that appear in the expression for the system's energy.

(21-3) The *equipartition theorem* states that the total internal energy in a system with a large number of particles divides itself equally among the various degrees of freedom available to the system. Specifically, the energy of each molecule will be $\frac{1}{2}kT$ per degree of freedom.

SUMMARY OF EQUATIONS

1. The first law of thermodynamics

$$\Delta U = Q - W \qquad \text{(Text Eq. 21-1)}$$

Consider a process that takes a system from an initial state *i* to a final state *f*. Experiment shows that the difference between the heat added to the system (*Q*) and the work performed by the system (*W*) is the same for *all* processes that take the system from state *i* to state *f*. The difference between the heat added and the work done is interpreted as the change in the system's internal energy (ΔU).

2. Work done by a gas during a change in volume

$$W = \int_{v_1}^{v_2} P \, dV \qquad \text{(Text Eq. 21-3)}$$

where P represents the pressure exerted by a gas enclosed within a volume V. The work done by this gas (on its surroundings) is found by integrating the pressure over the change in volume.

Note that if the volume increases ($V_2 > V_1$), the work is positive; if the volume decreases ($V_2 < V_1$), the work done by the gas is negative; and if the volume doesn't change ($V_2 = V_1$), no work is done.

3. Constant temperature expansion of an ideal gas

$$Q = W = nRT \ln \frac{V_2}{V_1} \quad \text{(Text Eq. 21-4)}$$

If the temperature of an ideal gas is held constant, then its internal energy is constant. Thus, the work done by the gas equals the heat added to the gas, and this is calculated from $W = \int P \, dV$, with P replaced by its ideal gas law equivalent, $P = nRT/V$.

4. Definition of molar specific heat

$$C \equiv \frac{1}{n} \frac{dQ}{dT}$$

The *molar* specific heat is defined as the heat capacity (dQ/dT) per mole. For gases especially, this quantity depends on the nature of the process. Thus, we distinguish between C_P (the molar heat capacity for a constant-pressure process) and C_V (the molar heat capacity for a constant-volume process), because they are not the same, even for the same gas.

5. Molar specific heat: constant volume

$$C_v = \frac{1}{n} \frac{dU}{dT} \quad \text{(Text Eq. 21-8)}$$

When heat is added to a system at constant volume, no work is done, so the additional thermal energy simply increases the internal energy of the system ($dQ = dU$).

6. Constant-pressure and constant-volume molar specific heats

$$C_P = C_V + R \quad \text{(Text Eq. 21-12)}$$

When heat is added to an ideal gas in a constant-pressure process, the work done by the gas increases the amount of heat needed to produce a given temperature rise. Thus, the constant-pressure molar specific heat is larger than the constant-volume molar specific heat.

6. Adiabatic expansion of an ideal gas

$$PV^\gamma = \text{constant} \quad \text{(Text Eq. 21-13a)}$$

In an adiabatic expansion (in which no heat transfer occurs), the product PV^γ remains constant. In this expression, $\gamma = C_P/C_V$ is the ratio of

the two molar specific heats of the gas. (We can also obtain similar expressions involving $\{T,V\}$ or $\{P,T\}$ by solving the ideal gas law for P or V.)

AVOIDING PITFALLS

1. **Work and heat:** In this chapter (and the next), heat is positive when it *enters* a system, but work is positive when the system does work on its surroundings. (Thus, if work is done *on* the system, it is considered negative.) Also, don't forget that heat and work must be expressed in the same units (usually, joules). You can't add calories to foot-pounds and get joules!

2. **Heat and work depend on path:** The amount of heat (and the amount of work) needed to transform a system from some given initial state to a given final state depends on the specific process that is used. (Is it isothermal, adiabatic, isobaric, etc.?) Thus, Q and W are *path-dependent*.

   However, the *difference* between these two quantities ($Q - W = \Delta U$) gives the change in the system's internal energy, and this is the same for *all* paths connecting a given initial state i and a given final state f. Thus, ΔU is *path-independent*.

3. **$U(T)$ for ideal gases:** The internal energy of an ideal gas is determined solely by its temperature (and the number of molecules). Thus, all states at the same temperature (even though they may have different pressures and volumes) have exactly the same internal energy and $U_f = U_i$ for any process that returns an ideal gas to its initial temperature.

4. **Iso- processes:** The prefix "iso-" means "constant." Thus, isobaric means constant pressure (remember, a barometer measures air pressure!); isovolumic means constant volume (isochoric is an older term that also means constant volume); isothermal means constant *temperature*, not constant heat. Finally, a process in which no heat is transferred is called *adiabatic*. For a given sample of an ideal gas,

   $PV = \text{constant}$ in an isothermal process,

   $PV^\gamma = \text{constant}$ in an adiabatic process.

5. **Monatomic vs. diatomic gases:** Many of the thermodynamic properties of gases depend on whether the molecules are monatomic (like the rare gases He, Ne, Ar, etc.), diatomic (O_2, N_2, CO, etc.), or polyatomic gases (H_2O, CO_2, etc.). A homework or exam question may not explicitly state that nitrogen gas is diatomic, so be sure you notice this.

6. **Energy in degrees of freedom:** The equipartition theorem and the kinetic-molecular theory of gases tell us that a molecule will have an aver-

age energy of $\frac{1}{2}kT$ for each degree of freedom. However, the temperature of the gas depends only on the energy in the *translational* kinetic energy, so the energy that goes into rotational or vibrational motion does not increase the temperature.

 Connections to *ActivPhysics*

ActivPhysics offers a complete and thorough set of animations and simulations of every major concept presented in Chapter 21 except for quantum effects. For this reason, the activities will be useful for just about all of the textbook problems and examples.

Activities 8.1 and 8.4 present a model and an equation of state for an ideal gas. Activities 8.5 and 8.6 introduce work and heat as forms of energy transfer that may change the internal energy of a gas, and Activities 8.8–8.11 analyze in depth four particular types of processes: isobaric (constant pressure); isochoric (constant volume); isothermal (constant temperature); and adiabatic (no heat transfer). Activities 8.12 and 8.13 show how these types of processes can be combined to create cyclic processes. The depth of your involvement in these investigations, whether you complete all parts of each one or you only use some of the simulations to visualize a process, will depend to a large part on course objectives and the priorities of your instructor.

An excellent place to begin studying this topic is with Activity 8.5 *Work Done by a Gas* before you read any part of the chapter. The investigation presents an expanded version of the information given in Section 21-2 under the heading *Work and Volume Changes*. This should be followed up with Activity 8.6 *Heat, Internal Energy, and the First Law*

of Thermodynamics, which continues with an exploration of heat as a form of energy transfer and the development of the first law. The last section of Activity 8.6 shows how work, heat, and internal energy change for the four processes mentioned above, which are introduced in the last section of Activity 8.4 *State Variables and the Ideal Gas Law*. Activity 8.7 *Heat Capacity* expands on the principles developed on pages 523 and 524 of the text showing that temperature changes on heating will depend on the conditions of the gas, such as constant-volume or constant-pressure conditions.

The four constant-variable processes are explored in greater depth in Activities 8.8–8.11. These same processes are introduced and described in Section 21-2. Each activity follows the same form: equations for heat, work, and internal energy are given for that type of process; a prediction is made for how these quantities might change for the model simulation; and particular values of all three quantities are recalculated based on simulation data. A summary of equations and relationships is also given in Table 21-1 of the text.

The significance of these processes will become evident in Chapter 22; however, the concept of a cyclic process is introduced on page 514 and in Example 21-5, and they are explained in much greater depth in Activities 8.12 and 8.13. Activity 8.12 *Cyclic Process-Strategies* presents a simple box on a pressure-volume graph and has you calculate work, heat, and internal energy at each of the four corners, in order to see how each quantity changes. The three videos at the end of Activity 8.12 shouldn't be missed; they will help you understand the importance of cyclic processes. Activity 8.13 *Cyclic Process—Problems* repeats a similar set of calculations for differently shaped cyclic processes—Figure 21-27 is one of them.

CHAPTER 22   THE SECOND LAW OF THERMODYNAMICS

We conclude our study of mechanics, and thermo-dynamics in particular, with the second law of thermodynamics—considered by many to be the most significant result in all of classical physics.

The major part of this chapter is devoted to a study of heat engines and their efficiency, with particular attention paid to the Carnot engine—an ideal process that has the greatest theoretical efficiency. From the impossibility of a perfect conversion of thermal energy into work, we are led to two similar statements of the second law, one stating that an ideal heat engine cannot exist, and the other stating that an ideal refrigerator cannot exist.

Finally, we develop the concept of entropy as a measure of the quality of energy, and state the second law of thermodynamics one last time, now as a statement that the entropy of the universe never decreases.

DEFINITIONS

You should know the definition of each of these terms. (The number in parentheses is the text chapter and section in which the term is introduced.)

(22-2) A *heat engine* is a device that extracts heat from a reservoir and converts some of that energy to useful work.

(22-2) a. *The "engine" statement of the second law (by Kelvin and Planck):* It is impossible to construct a heat engine operating in a cycle that extracts heat from a reservoir and delivers an equal amount of work.

(22-2) b. *The "refrigerator" statement of the second law (by Clausius):* It is impossible to make a refrigerator, operating in a cycle, whose sole effect is the transfer of heat from a cooler object to a hotter object.

(22-5) c. *The "entropy" statement of the second law:* The entropy of a closed system can never decrease.

(22-2) The *efficiency* of a thermodynamic cycle is defined to be the ratio of the work done (W) to the heat transferred at the high temperature (Q_h):

$$e \equiv \frac{W}{Q_h}$$

(22-2) The *Carnot cycle* is a cycle of four reversible steps, consisting of

    isothermal expansion;

    adiabatic expansion;

    isothermal compression;

    adiabatic compression.

(The cycle may begin with any of these steps. If the cycle operates in the sequence shown above, it is operating as a heat engine. If the steps are reversed in sequence [read up the list rather than down], the cycle becomes a refrigerator.)

(22-2) A *reversible engine* is an engine (or refrigerator) that is always infinitesimally close to equilibrium throughout its cycle. Thus, the direction of the heat flows can be reversed by making an infinitesimal change in the temperatures.

(22-2) *Carnot's theorem* states that all reversible engines operating between two given temperatures have the same efficiency, and that all irreversible engines have a lower efficiency.

(22-3) The *coefficient of performance* of a refrigerator is defined as the ratio of the heat transferred from the low-temperature reservoir to the work needed to run the cycle:

$$\mathrm{COP} \equiv \frac{Q_c}{W}$$

(22-4) The *thermodynamic temperature* is the temperature (T) of a reservoir, determined from the efficiency of a system operating reversibly between the unknown reservoir and another reservoir of known temperature (T_0). In terms of heat transfers,

$$\frac{T}{T_0} = \frac{Q}{Q_0}$$

(22-4) The *third law of thermodynamics* states that it is impossible to cool any object to absolute zero in a finite number of steps.

(22-5) The *entropy* of a system is a measure of the disorder of the system, or of the inability of the system's energy to perform work. The change in the entropy of any system can be computed from the heat that would be required (in a reversible process) to produce the given change in state:

$$\Delta S \equiv \int \frac{dQ_{rev}}{T}$$

SUMMARY OF EQUATIONS

1. Definition of efficiency

$$e \equiv \frac{W}{Q_h}$$

$$e = 1 - \frac{Q_c}{Q_h} \qquad \text{(Text Eq. 22-1)}$$

The efficiency of any cyclic thermodynamic process is defined as the ratio of work to heat transferred to (or from) the high-temperature reservoir ($e = W/Q_h$). For a heat engine, the efficiency is essentially "what you get" divided by "what you pay for."

In any cyclic process, the system is returned to its initial state, so $\Delta U = 0$, and $W = Q_h - Q_c$, the *net* heat transferred into the system. In terms of heat transfers, the efficiency becomes $e = 1 - Q_c/Q_h$.

(Note that a positive value of Q_h represents a heat flow *into* the system, while a positive Q_c represents a heat flow *out* of the system, and W again represents the work done by the system on its surroundings.)

2. Efficiency of a reversible cycle

$$e = 1 - \frac{T_c}{T_h} \qquad \text{(Text Eq. 22-3)}$$

For any *reversible* process operating between temperatures T_h and T_c, the efficiency is determined solely by the ratio of the two (absolute) temperatures.

3. Coefficient of performance

$$\text{COP} \equiv \frac{Q_c}{W}$$

$$\text{COP} = \frac{Q_c}{Q_{h-Q_c}} \qquad \text{(Text Eq. 22-4)}$$

The coefficient of performance of a refrigerator is defined, like the efficiency of a heat engine, as "what you get" divided by "what you pay for." In a refrigerator, what you get is the heat removed from the (cool) interior of the refrigerator (Q_c), and what you pay for is the work needed to run the process (W).

If the refrigerator is a reversible process, then the COP is determined solely by the two temperatures involved:

$$(\text{COP})_{\text{rev}} = \frac{T_c}{T_h - T_c}. \qquad \text{(Text Eq. 22-5)}$$

4. Entropy change in a reversible process

$$dS_{\text{rev}} \equiv \frac{dQ}{T}$$

We define the entropy change of a system during a reversible process to be the ratio of heat transfer to Kelvin temperature. If a system is taken from a temperature T_1 to a temperature T_2 by the *reversible* transfer of heat, the total change in the system's entropy can be computed by summing the entropy change that occurs with each infinitesimal heat transfer, each at a slightly different temperature:

$$\Delta S_{\text{rev}} = \int_1^2 \frac{dQ}{T}. \qquad \text{(Text Eq. 22-8)}$$

The entropy change that occurs during an *irreversible* process is *not* dQ_{irrev}/T. However, since entropy is a state variable, if we can invent a *reversible* process that takes the system from the given initial state to the given final state, we can set

$$\Delta S_{\text{irrev}} = \int_1^2 \frac{dQ_{\text{rev}}}{T}.$$

AVOIDING PITFALLS

1. **Sign of heat transfers:** We are retaining the point of view that work is positive when performed *by* the system, and the net heat is positive when added *to* the system. However, in a cyclic heat engine, heat (Q_h) enters the system from a high-temperature reservoir, and heat (Q_c) leaves the system to a low-temperature reservoir. *Both* of these heat transfers are treated as positive quantities, so $Q_{\text{net}} = Q_h - Q_c$.

2. **Definition of efficiency:** The efficiency of a thermodynamic cycle is *defined as*

$$e = \frac{W}{Q_h},$$

where Q_h represents the total of all heat transfers from the high-temperature reservoir(s). Note that this is different from Q_{net}.

Since the work performed in any cycle is the difference between the total heat brought in to the system and the total heat taken away from the system, we can equally well write

$$e = 1 - \frac{Q_h}{Q_h}.$$

(These two expressions are valid for *any* thermodynamic cycle, reversible or irreversible.)

3. **Efficiency of a reversible cycle**: If a *reversible* cycle absorbs heat Q_h at a single temperature T_h and exhausts heat Q_c at a single temperature T_c, then its efficiency is given by the Carnot efficiency:

$$e = 1 - \frac{T_h}{T_h}.$$

The temperatures must both be *absolute* temperatures. Also, this expression is usually derived for the ideal-gas Carnot cycle (four alternating isothermals and adiabatics), but it is equally valid for *any* reversible cycle operating between the two temperatures T_c and T_h.

If a reversible cycle draws heat in at a number of different temperatures, or exhausts heat at a number of different temperatures (as would happen in a constant-pressure cooling, for example), then the efficiency will be a thermal average of the Carnot efficiencies computed for each infinitesimal step in the entire cycle.

4. **Efficiency vs. coefficient of performance**: The thermodynamic efficiency (defined as W/Q_h) of a Carnot cycle is the same ($e = 1 - T_c/T_h$) whether it is operating as a heat engine (positive work) or as a refrigerator (negative work).

However, the goal of a heat engine (high efficiency, producing maximum work for a given heat input Q_h) is different from that of a refrigerator (high coefficient of performance, producing maximum heat input Q_c for a given amount of work). Thus, a refrigerator with a high efficiency (W/Q_h) has a *low* coefficient of performance (Q_c/W)!

5. **Entropy change in irreversible processes**: The entropy change for a *reversible* process is defined as

$$\Delta S_{\text{rev}} = \int \frac{dQ_{\text{rev}}}{T}.$$

For an *irreversible* process, $\Delta S_{\text{irrev}} \neq \int dQ_{\text{irrev}}/T$. However, we can compute the entropy change in an irreversible process by inventing a *reversible* process that takes the system from the same initial state to the same final state as the actual (irreversible) process. Then we can write

$$\Delta S_{\text{irrev}} = \int \frac{dQ_{\text{rev}}}{T}$$

 Connections to *ActivPhysics*

The field of thermodynamics arose from practical concerns about the efficiency of engines during the Industrial Revolution, and all practical engines follow some type of cycle through the state variables for that system. Examples of three different types of realistic and workable engines are shown as video clips at the end of Activity 8.12 *Cyclic Process—Strategies.*

Both Activities 8.12 and 8.13 were recommended for the previous chapter. If these investigations weren't completed before, they should be done now. (Activity 8.12 is the same as Problem 54.) These two activities plus Activity 18.14 *The Carnot Cycle* (Example 22-1 and Problem 25) should assist you if either of these problems or Problems 43, 61, 65, or 67 have been assigned.

PART II

Guide to *ActivPhysics*

CHRISTOPHER WOZNY

The traditional general physics course begins with the subject of mechanics, and the first topic of mechanics is kinematics, or the study of how things move.

This unit is extremely important for students because the majority of the homework assignments and often all the exam questions in a physics course are word problems. *ActivPhysics* can help you understand how to set up and successfully solve word problems, not only in kinematics but in the rest of physics as well.

A typical word problem will have more than one unknown value. To successfully solve the problem, you will have to apply at least some of the following skills:

1. Interpret the word problem correctly to determine the physical setting and which quantities are unknown.

2. Divide the problem into two or more sequential steps.

3. Determine which physics equations are applicable to the problem at hand.

4. Create new equations relating physical quantities based on the description of the particular problem (such as a relationship between two different times or distances).

5. Solve two or more equations simultaneously in order to calculate values for all unknown quantities.

Kinematics has only three or four fundamental equations describing motion. Later units will add more equations and also trigonometry, but the basic approach to solving physics word problems will remain the same.

Most students underestimate the difficulty of solving physics word problems. One reason for this may be that the textbook and instructor make it appear so easy. Here is a classic, medium-level-difficulty word problem in kinematics:

A speeder in a car is traveling at a constant rate of 60 mi/h when he passes a motorcycle policeman hiding behind a sign. The policeman starts from rest and begins to accelerate at a constant rate of 2 m/s^2 exactly 1 s after the speeder passes him. How long does it take the policeman to catch up to the speeder from the time the speeder passes the sign, and how far away are the policeman and speeder from the sign at that time?

The equations of motion needed to solve this problem are $v = v_0 + at$ and $d = d_0 + v_0t + at^2$

where t is time, d is distance, v is velocity, a is acceleration at time t, and the subscript 0 means the initial value of the quantity at time $t = 0$. This information is all that is required to solve this word problem.

It is certainly unfair to ask you to solve a kinematics problem before any instruction has been given, but it is my experience as a physics teacher that, no matter what the quality of a lecture or the amount of instruction or the number of examples presented in class, students always have trouble solving word problems at first on their own. This unit of *ActivPhysics* is not a magic bullet that will spare you the frustration of trying to figure out how to do physics, but it may gently guide you down the correct path.

GAME PLAN

The activities in this unit can help you solve kinematic word problems in three important ways. First, because kinematics is the study of how things move, it is extremely useful to *see* the motion described in a word problem. Although that will not be the case on an exam, it may enable you to interpret the meaning of standard phrases found in these types of problems.

Second, the motion diagram is introduced in Activity 1.1 with instructions on how to construct them. Motion diagrams are an effective way to visualize problems, and you will find that they assist you in correctly interpreting the physical situation presented in the activity and in identifying the known and unknown quantities.

Third, most of the *ActivPhysics* activities are written as a series of steps with full or partial solutions given in the Advisor section accompanying a simulation. This format provides for immediate feedback and guidance as you attempt to complete a problem.

You will get the greatest benefit from these activities if you think about *what* you did and *how* you did it before moving on to a new problem, so that after three or four sample problems you will begin to see the connections. In particular, what did you learn from the solution that will help you with the next one? Also, imagine that the next problem is an exam question: would you be able to complete it unassisted? If not, then you probably need to do more problems until you are confident you understand the methods used to solve physics word problems.

Your approach to this unit will depend on three factors: your personal learning style, your background in physics, and the instructor's course objectives.

If you are naturally methodical in your approach to academics or if your background in physics is minimal, then it would be worth while to begin with the first five simulations. From them you will begin to see connections between physics words (such as velocity and acceleration) and their physical meaning. However, this will take extra time, so plan for it. Activity 1.4 *Predicting Motion from Equations* is particularly useful and it is short. If you can't correctly match the motion of the car by the last example, then it's important that you ask for assistance from your instructor as soon as you can. It's no use attempting word problems if you cannot see how the variables relate to the equations of motion.

If you are more intuitive, if you like figuring things out on your own, or if you need quick results to keep you going, then start with Activity 1.6 *Skier Races Downhill.* Try Activity 1.4 *Predicting Motion from Equations* next, since it shouldn't take much time at all if you are able to convert word problems into mathematics easily. Activity 1.5 *Problem-Solving Strategies for Kinematics* presents a careful step-by-step explanation of the problem-solving technique used in Activities 1.6–1.14. Your personal evaluation of how well you understood Activity 1.6 will determine how much time you should spend working through it. Finally, work sequentially from Activities 1.7–1.13 and return to the first five activities as necessary to pick up missing concepts.

If the relationship between kinematics and graphical analysis is *not* a course objective, then Activities 1.2 *Analyzing Motion Using Graphs* and 1.3 *Predicting Motion from Graphs* and the graphical parts of Activities 1.6-1.14 can be skipped. But if you do not feel very confident in your ability to understand physics, I recommend doing them anyway because the graphical method should help you develop important thinking skills that will lead to later success in the course.

Finally, if homework is assigned and collected, then it may be wise to alternate between the text problems and the application problems in *ActivPhysics.* You will then see how the simulations help you understand the assigned problems, and it will give you confidence to know that the assignment is being completed.

One last strong recommendation. Do not wait until later to work on physics problems. The best time to start, if possible, is immediately after the lecture.

THE DETAILS

1.1 Analyzing Motion Using Diagrams

A car with adjustable initial conditions moves along a line to demonstrate concepts of position, velocity, and acceleration. Questions 1–6, relating to the first simulation, explore the effect of positive, negative, and zero velocities and accelerations on the motion of the car. Question 7 asks you to set initial position, velocity, and acceleration for four different simulations so that the motion of a green dot matches the pre-set motion of a car.

Layout Introductory activity; five simulations.

Pointers This activity is extremely important for understanding how to set up and solve word problems, so treat it with respect. Reserve about an hour of time without interruptions and work through all seven questions sequentially. You will spend most of your time working through the first example, but it will be time well spent. Do all four simulations for Question 7—don't stop until you are done! Follow the instructions step-by-step. It may help to do this activity with another student so you can trade ideas and discuss items that may confuse you.

1.2 Analyzing Motion Using Graphs

The same car as in Activity 1.1 moves along a line to show concepts of position, velocity, and acceleration, but in addition, position-vs.-time, velocity-vs.-time, and acceleration-vs.-time graphs are plotted as the car moves. Different curves are traced out on the graphs as initial conditions change with positive, negative, or zero initial position, velocity, and acceleration.

Layout Introductory activity; four matched simulations. Sim 1 graphs position vs. time as a green line; Sim 2 adds a graph of velocity vs. time to the same axes as a red line; and Sim 3 includes a graph of acceleration vs. time with the other two as a blue line. Sim 4 tracks the position of the car at different times, as in a motion diagram.

Pointers Graphical analysis isn't always a course objective, but if you have a weak background in physics, it can be very helpful for grasping the concepts of position, velocity, and acceleration, and recognizing their differences. The simulations and graphs clearly demonstrate the relationship between kinematic quantities and the shapes, slopes, and positions of the graphed variables. If this activity or the next one confuses you, then it may be a sign that you need extra tutoring from a knowledgeable person.

1.3 Predicting Motion from Graphs

For each of five particular motions that include a position-vs.-time graph, predict the corresponding velocity-vs.-time and acceleration-vs.-time graphs and construct a motion diagram.

Layout Application activity; 10 simulations in 5 matched sets. The first simulation shows a particular position-vs.-time graph and the second simulation adds the correct velocity-vs.-time and acceleration-vs.-time graphs.

Pointers This investigation checks your understanding of the concepts explored in Activities 1.1 and 1.2. Recall that initial position is the value of x when $t = 0$ and velocity is the slope of the line at a point in time. The accelerations are held constant, so acceleration-vs.-time graphs should be just horizontal lines. If acceleration is constant, and if acceleration is the value of the slope on a velocity-vs.-time graph, then what should the velocity-vs.-time curve look like?

1.4 Predicting Motion from Equations

Initial conditions of a white dot are set to match the motion of a car with a written equation of motion of a car. This process is applied to four particular cases.

Layout Application activity; four simulations each showing a car, a white dot, the equation of motion for the car, and including adjustable parameters for the dot.

Pointers This activity is quick and simple, but it reinforces the basic skill of relating the physical quantities in a word problem to the constants in a kinematic equation of motion (such as $x = x_0 + v_0 t + \frac{1}{2}at^2$ in this problem).

1.5 Problem-Solving Strategies for Kinematics

The time of travel and the final position of a car are predicted as it comes to a stop. Two follow-up questions ask you to evaluate the meaning of the motion with respect to the values of the kinematics quantities at various times.

Layout Introductory activity; five matched simulations. Sim 1 shows the motion; Sim 2 adds a list of initial conditions; Sim 3 adds the motion diagram; Sim 4 adds kinematic graphs; and Sim 5 presents the full solution to the problem.

Pointers This investigation and Activity 1.1 lay the foundation for problem-solving techniques in physics. The purpose here is not just to calculate the final values but to construct a step-by-step solution of a kinematics problem. For both of these activities, I recommend reading through the text bar word for word and doing what is asked immediately without skipping ahead to the next section.

1.6 Skier Races Downhill

Find the constant acceleration and time of travel of a skier moving down an incline given her initial and final speeds and the total distance traveled. The last question is a qualitative prediction of the skier's velocity at a certain time given her velocity at a different time and the known constant acceleration.

Layout Application activity; two matched simulations. Sim 1 shows the motion, Sim 2 adds kinematic graphs.

Pointers If the Advisor's solution to Question 1 is confusing, then try Activities 1.4 and 1.5. If you still don't understand the solution after completing those investigations, then get help immediately. DO NOT be satisfied with simply finding the numerical answer to the problem. Physics is not about calculating a number but about understanding how the universe works. Don't count on algebraic luck—it will ultimately fail you.

1.7 Balloonist Drops Lemonade.

Find the time it takes an object to reach a given position from its known initial conditions and its speed at that time.

Layout Application activity; four matched simulations. Sim 1 shows the motion; Sim 2 adds a list of initial conditions; Sim 3 adds a motion diagram; Sim 4 adds graphs and presents the full solution to the problem.

Pointers Initial conditions are found in the text bar. Note that acceleration and velocity are not necessarily acting in the same direction. The questions asked in this investigation (Questions 2, 3, and 7, and the set after Sim 4) demonstrate why doing well on a physics exam takes more than finding equations; it is also about understanding what the equations mean and knowing how to use them correctly.

1.8 Seat Belts Save Lives

The deceleration of a flatbed truck moving at constant speed is found as it hits a bush. The initial speed is changed and the calculation is repeated. Next, a crate is added to the simulation, and its motion is compared to that of the truck.

Layout Application activity; three simulations, the first two matched; five audio clips, three video clips. Sim 1 shows the motion; Sim 2 includes acceleration; Sim 3 (with an audio clip) adds a crate to the truck and tracks both objects' velocities and accelerations.

Videos: Crate on a Truck—1, Crate on a Truck—2, Egg Hits Windshield The first two video clips demonstrate the behavior of a real crate in a real truck, and the last video clip shows the behavior of an egg in a decelerating vehicle both with and without seat belts.

Pointers The equation needed for Question 1 must relate acceleration to position and speed but not time. Be sure to reset the speed from 20 m/s to 10 m/s in Sim 2 in order to see the answer to Question 1 before completing Question 2. Question 4 and the videos are fun and instructive, and they can be viewed without doing any calculations.

1.9 Screeching to a Halt

Two different motions (one unaccelerated and the other with a constant acceleration) are examined in order to find the full stopping distance when screeching to a halt.

Layout Application activity; four matched simulations; one audio clip. Sim 1 shows the motion; Sim 2 adds a list of initial conditions; Sim 3 adds the motion diagram; Sim 4 adds graphs and presents the full solution to the problem.

Pointers This investigation shows the practical realities of applying physics to real life through a discussion of reaction time. It shows how to divide a motion into parts and then how to combine those parts to achieve a final answer. This is the first activity that has two equations of motion, and the next five activities also have more than one equation of motion in the exercise. Even if you successfully completed the previous activities, these new problems may be difficult for you—don't assume that solving them will be easy!

1.10 Pole-Vaulter Lands

Two different accelerated motions are calculated in order to find the deceleration of a pole-vaulter striking a mat.

Layout Application activity; four matched simulations. Sim 1 shows the motion; Sim 2 adds a list of initial conditions; Sim 3 adds the motion diagram; Sim 4 adds graphs and presents the full solution to the problem.

Pointers Like Activity 1.9, two motions meet at one point in time, so look for continuity at that point. In particular, the final speed under gravitational acceleration must be the initial speed of the pole-vaulter's deceleration by the mat. This is an *excellent* problem for developing sequencing skills.

1.11 Car Starts, Then Stops

Three different sets of equations of motion are needed to find the total time of travel for a car between two points.

Layout Application activity; four matched simulations; one audio clip. Sim 1 shows the motion; Sim 2 shows the motion diagram; Sim 3 adds kinematic graphs; Sim 4 presents the full solution to the problem.

Pointers This investigation is similar to Activity 1.10 but with three connected parts. The total distance and time is the sum of the three distances and times covered during the three sequential motions.

1.12 Solving Two-Vehicle Problems

Two cars, each with their own initial conditions and equations of motion, pass each other in opposite directions. The goal of the problem is to determine the time and position when they pass each other.

Layout Application activity; five matched simulations; one audio clip. Sim 1 shows the motion; Sim 2 adds kinematic quantities for each car and labels the unknowns. Sim 3, which shows the motion diagram, is located in the Advisor section. Sim 4 shows kinematic graphs for each vehicle (six plots in all), and Sim 5 presents the full solution to the problem.

Pointers This activity asks you to look for errors in the set-up, which is quite helpful for teaching you how to spot your own unintentional mistakes. As with previous problems that include two equations of motion applying to a single object, you must discover the relationships between the motions, such as a common velocity or two displacements that add together to a total displacement.

1.13 Car Catches Truck

The equations of motion for two vehicles, one accelerating and one moving with constant velocity, are solved simultaneously based on common kinematic quantities.

Layout Application activity; four matched simulations. Sim 1 shows the motion; Sim 2 shows the motion diagram; Sim 3 adds kinematic graphs; Sim 4 presents the full solution to the problem.

Pointers This investigation is similar to the example given in the Overview. Use the same techniques used in Activity 1.12.

1.14 Avoiding a Rear-End Collision

Set the initial velocity of a car and the accelerations of both a car and a truck to avoid a rear-end collision, given the initial separation of the two vehicles.

Layout Advanced activity; five matched simulations. Sim 1 shows the motion; Sim 2 shows the motion diagram; Sim 3 includes velocity and acceleration vectors; Sim 4 adds kinematic graphs; Sim 5 presents the full solution to the problem.

Pointers Appropriate initial kinematic values are set in this investigation to meet a particular condition, and more than one set of values will work. The key principle to recognize is that at a certain position the two speeds must be the same, with one decreasing (or constant) while the other is increasing (or constant). Use this activity to test your understanding of the concepts presented throughout this unit.

UNIT 2 FORCES AND MOTION

Kinematics is the study of *how* things move, and Unit 1 introduced four fundamental quantities that completely describe the motion of objects: position, velocity, acceleration, and time. On the other hand, the study of *why* things move is the study of dynamics.

The fundamental principles of dynamics are summarized by Isaac Newton's three laws of motion. The laws of motion are not easy to understand and they tend to contradict our human intuition. Consider, for example, these two classic questions:

1. A ball is tossed straight up in the air. At the highest point of the motion, the velocity is momentarily zero. What is the acceleration at that point?

2. A ball attached to a string is traveling in a circle on a flat tabletop. The string suddenly breaks. Does the ball now still move inward along a curved path, outward along a curved path, or along a straight line?

Education research has shown that all of us have developed a "science" to explain how the universe works; however, since it is not based on correct data most of our concepts and theories are just plain wrong. These "naive concepts" aren't a bad thing; in fact, they are necessary to help us make sense of the world, and they demonstrate our natural curiosity and intelligence. However, the same research has also shown that we are all very stubborn when it comes to our own theories, and even in the face of evidence to the contrary we really don't want to change our minds.

This means that the ability to solve mathematical word problems is not enough to succeed in physics. Technical efficiency cannot substitute for a true understanding of physics concepts, and false concepts lead to wrong equations and the search for forces, masses, or accelerations that simply do no exist. Force concepts can be difficult to grasp, and the problem-solving approach isn't any easier. On the other hand, if you can successfully complete the portion of the physics course on Newton's laws, then the rest of the course should be less trouble for you since you will have the tools to think through a problem and challenge your own preconceived notions.

With respect to the two example questions, you should recognize from Unit 1 that velocity and acceleration are different kinematic concepts. Since the velocity at the top of the motion is zero, most people assume that the acceleration must also be zero. However, the acceleration of gravity is constant, so the correct answer is 9.8 m/s^2. As for the second question, our naive concept concerning motion is that moving objects naturally slow down and come to rest. However, Newton's first law of motion states that the natural state of an object is to move with constant velocity; accelerations are caused by unbalanced forces. A force (tension in the string) causes the object to deviate from its natural motion and be accelerated in a circular path (see Unit 4). Therefore, once the force no longer acts, the ball will travel with a constant velocity, which means in a straight line with a constant speed.

GAME PLAN

This unit of *ActivPhysics*, like the previous one, focuses on important skill-building activities that are fundamental for success in the rest of the general physics course. The 14 investigations follow a progression based on the type of motion problem and the level of difficulty. Understanding the organization of the unit will help you use it to your greatest advantage.

The unit begins with Activity 2.1, *Qualitative Questions*. Five examples of motion are given, followed by a multiple-choice question. These questions will help you understand that forces cause *accelerations*; forces do not cause *velocities*. Answer these questions first. All five questions can be answered in less than half an hour and should be completed at one sitting in order to reinforce this basic principle.

The next three activities explore forces acting in one dimension. Activities 2.2 *Lifting a Crate* and 2.3 *Lowering a Crate* are a matched set that demonstrate once again how direction makes a difference for force vectors as well as velocity and acceleration vectors. Because unbalanced or net forces cause accelerations, both the net force vector and the acceleration vector must be pointing in the same direction. The first step is to determine the direction of the acceleration (up or down) and from that determine which of the two forces acting should have the larger magnitude.

Activity 2.4 *Rocket Blasts Off* is something new in *ActivPhysics* and is unique to physics simulations. Textbook examples and problems by their nature focus on finding a single answer to a set of conditions. The advantage of activities like this one is that initial conditions can be set with adjustable sliders; therefore, it is possible to explore many aspects of physics through a single investigation. This activity will help you see that the net force is the sum of all forces acting on a body; it will also give you more practice with kinematic equations.

Activities 2.5 *Truck Pulls Crate*, 2.6 *Pushing a Crate*, and 2.7 *Pushing a Crate Up a Wall* are a set of investigations that explore force vectors and motions acting in two dimensions. Newton's second law is applied to the motion of the object in both the x- and y-directions in order to solve the full problem. That is also true of the third set of activities, 2.8 *Skier Goes Down a Slope*, 2.9 *Skier and Tow Rope*, and 2.10 *Pushing a Crate Up an Incline*, except the net force acts along the surface of an inclined plane. For this set of problems, the x-y axes are tilted, so the vertical weight of the object is written as x- and y-components.

The last four activities deal with connected systems: 2.11 *Pole-Vaulter Vaults*, 2.12 *Truck Pulls Two Crates*, 2.13 *Bricklayer Lowers Bricks*, and 2.14 *Modified Atwood Machine*. Activity 2.11 is related to Activity 1.10 *Pole-Vaulter Lands* and is not all that difficult; of the remaining three, 2.12 *Truck Pulls Two Crates* is the most difficult. The key to any connected-system problem is to draw a force diagram for each part of the system and then determine which quantities they have in common. The two typical common variables, as shown in these activities, is a force (usually tension) and the overall acceleration of the connected objects acting under net forces.

And finally, almost all of these investigations require the construction of a force diagram by moving arrows pointing in different directions. Slight errors will lead to unacceptable answers, and unfortunately *ActivPhysics* does not provide a quick check of the right solution. Here are some things to check if problems arise: correct relative magnitudes of the force arrows; correct locations where the forces act; and correct directions of the force vectors.

Each of these activities teaches an important concept about forces and motion, or reveals a common student error. So, as for a game plan, it would be easy for me as an instructor to simply say, Do them all! Of course, that is not practical, since only the most devoted of physics students could find the time to complete 14 activities plus assigned text problems. Therefore, I recommend alternating between these investigations and traditional text problems. Address the unit in the four sections outlined above: one-dimensional problems, two-dimensional problems, inclined-plane problems, and connected systems. Find the text problems that match each of these standard problem types and complete them in sections.

By the time you have reached the inclined-plane problems, you should have a sense of what works best for you. You may find that the best approach is to start with *ActivPhysics* to learn the concepts, then apply the principles to text problems. Or you may prefer to work through text problems until you get stuck, then let the activities serve as tutorials. Or you may decide to complete the activities after the text problems are done to serve as a check on your understanding and to see the big picture for the problem-solving approach. Whichever method works best for you, you will probably discover that it is also your best general game plan for the remaining units of study.

THE DETAILS

2.1 Qualitative Questions

Five examples of both accelerated and unaccelerated motion are presented. All solutions are multiple choice with full explanations given under the Solutions section.

Layout Introductory activities. Activity 2.1.1 has two matched simulations; Activity 2.1.2 three matched simulations; Activity 2.1.3 one simulation; Activity 2.1.4 two matched simulations. Activity 2.1.5 has one simulation and three video clips with audio.

Videos: Racing Balls—1, Racing Balls—2, Racing Balls—3 The three video clips reproduce the experimental conditions in the laboratory that are demonstrated in the simulation.

Pointers Read the information in the workbook under the heading *Constructing Force-Body Diagrams* before beginning this activity. These problems will introduce you to a number of common forces found in any unit on dynamics, including friction, tension, normal force, and weight. Remember that the net force must act in the direction of the acceleration, and if there is no acceleration, then there is no net force and the forces are balanced (equal and opposite). Also, if the forces change, then the acceleration must change, and therefore the velocity of the object is not constant.

2.2 Lifting a Crate,
2.3 Lowering a Crate

The magnitudes of forces acting on a vertically moving crate are calculated from kinematic data. The crate is slowing down as it is moving *upward* in Activity 2.2 and *downward* in Activity 2.3.

Layout Application activities. Each activity has four matched simulations, one force diagram, and one audio clip. Sim 1 shows a vertically moving crate; Sim 2 adds kinematic values of acceleration, velocity, position, and time; Sim 3 shows the force acting and their magnitudes; and Sim 4 adds kinematic graphs and presents the full solution to the problem.

Pointers These two activities are classic examples of how to solve a mechanics word problem using Newton's laws. If an object is accelerating, there must be a net force. For any given situation, what forces are acting? What are their directions? Which forces are larger or smaller? This exercise also demonstrates how to link kinematic quantities to the forces causing the motion through Newton's second law, $F = ma$. I strongly recommend completing Activity 2.3 immediately after Activity 2.2. If you have trouble completing the second activity correctly (whether you needed extra assistance on Activity 2.2 or not), then get help immediately from an instructor, tutor, or another student.

Force diagram hint: You must get the *location*, *direction*, and *relative length* of the forces on the force diagram correct. If the simulation claims you are still incorrect, make sure that all three of these conditions are met for each force vector.

2.4 Rocket Blasts Off

Concepts of balanced and unbalanced forces, time of thrust, and the importance of the initial velocity on the position of a moving object are thoroughly explored through guided choices of initial parameters for a toy rocket blasting off. (Be sure to adjust the sliders to the recommended values before you begin each question.)

Layout Exploratory activity; one audio clip and one simulation with adjustable thrust, time of thrust, and initial velocity.

Pointers This is *not* a single-solution word problem. Physics is more than just calculating numbers, and this activity more than any other will show you what doing physics is all about. (It is also a good review of the kinematics equations of Unit 1.) This is just the first of a number of activities that encourage you to explore an application of physics principles to a particular problem by changing the initial conditions of the problem. This is also a good investigation to do with friends so that you can thoroughly discuss your predictions as well as the experimental results.

2.5 Truck Pulls Crate

Adjustable parameters in this investigation change the magnitudes of four force vectors as a truck pulls an accelerating crate.

Layout Introductory activity; one simulation, showing a truck pulling a crate by a rope at an angle.

Videos: Truck Pulls Crate—1, Truck Pulls Crate—2 The two video clips show investigations similar to the simulation, using a toy truck to first pull a block, then to pull a block with extra weight.

Pointers Forces are vectors, possessing both magnitude and direction. In the first four activities, forces were acting along the same direction; this is the first example of a two-dimensional investigation. If you are unfamiliar with vector components, review an appropriate section of your physics textbook and complete Activity 3.5 first.

This is a teaching activity in that all the correct answers are given in the simulation even before it is run. The idea is to help you *see* and *understand* the interrelationship between forces acting in many directions and the projection of kinematic equations onto the *x*- and *y*-axes. The mathematics of two-dimensional force problems is thoroughly explained in the Advisor sections. Carefully examine how weight, normal force, friction, and tension change (or don't change) as the mass, coefficient of friction, or net acceleration are varied. Do you understand why those effects occur?

2.6 Pushing a Crate,
2.7 Pushing a Crate Up a Wall

The magnitudes of four force vectors and the resulting acceleration are calculated for a hand pushing a crate. The crate moves *horizontally* in Activity 2.6 and *vertically* in Activity 2.7.

Layout Application activities; four matched simulations and one force diagram each. Sim 1 shows the motion; Sim 2 draws in the force vectors; Sim 3 adds force magnitudes; Sim 4 presents the full solution to the problem.

Pointers Do you really understand the concepts of Activity 2.5 *Truck Pulls Crate*? Direction makes a difference! Like a good tutorial, these activities once again take you through the whole step-by-step process of identifying forces and determining components, then adding them together correctly in each of two perpendicular directions. Compare the results after completing both activities. The types of forces and equations are the same, but how those forces or force components are combined differs. Because these activities are so well matched, your instructor or tutor should be able to diagnose your misunderstanding of the basic principles if you still find yourself confused after completing them.

Once again, be very careful when constructing the force diagrams. Magnitudes do not change, but all forces must be placed at their correct point of application or *ActivPhysics* will ask you to try again.

2.8 Skier Goes Down a Slope

Calculate the magnitudes of the forces acting on a skier traveling down a slope, then find her acceleration and speed at a certain distance.

Layout Application activity; five matched simulations, one force diagram, one audio clip, one video clip with audio. Sim 1 shows the motion; Sim 2 draws in the force vectors; Sim 3 adds force magnitudes; Sim 4 reports the acceleration only; Sim 5 presents the full solution to the problem.

Video: Truck Slips on Incline A toy truck holds its position while it attempts to climb an incline. Estimate the coefficient of kinetic friction between the wheels of a toy truck and a board from the angle of the incline. (Because the velocity up the plane is zero, all the forces must be balanced.)

Pointers Inclined-plane problems can appear to be the most intractable of any type of problem encountered by beginning physics students in the full year-long course. (About the only thing worse is a car traveling around a banked track, which includes an inclined plane.) This unit tried to make life somewhat easier for you by introducing Activities 2.5–2.7 first. At this point you should feel comfortable with using angles and force magnitudes to calculate components in perpendicular directions. As you solve this problem, read the Advisor sections carefully. The *x*-axis is not the horizontal, it's the flat surface of the slope. A component of the weight balances the normal force while the other component provides the acceleration (after subtracting the effect of friction). Finally, be very careful here if you expect the cosine of an angle to always correspond to the *x*-component and the sine to correspond to the *y*-component, because in many situations involving inclines they do not.

2.9 Skier and Tow Rope

Find the tension pulling a skier up an incline at constant speed.

Layout Application activity; four matched simulations, one force diagram. Sim 1 shows the motion; Sim 2 draws in the force vectors; Sim 3 adds force magnitudes; Sim 4 presents the full solution to the problem.

Pointers If you have diligently completed all the previous activities and have found yourself successful, this may be an appropriate point for you to strike out on your own and solve the problem without consulting the text bar. The key is constant speed! The activity concludes with a concept question that you should be able to answer correctly if you understand Newton's laws.

2.10 Pushing a Crate Up an Incline

The magnitudes of three force vectors and the resulting acceleration are calculated for a hand pushing a crate.

Layout Application activity; four matched simulations, one force diagram, one audio clip. Sim 1 shows the motion; Sim 2 draws in the force vectors; Sim 3 adds force magnitudes; Sim 4 presents the full solution to the problem.

Pointers The unbalanced force causing the acceleration in Activity 2.6 was the weight of the object; the external force causing the acceleration in Activity 2.7 was a rope *pulling* the object, and now the external force causing the acceleration in this activity is a hand *pushing* the object. As before, choose the plane of the incline for the *x*- and *y*-axes and calculate the components of the weight appropriately. The difference between this problem and the previous one is the horizontal force. So how should you deal with it?

Most instructors and textbook writers use related word problems to teach concepts, so learn how to use a progression of ideas such as this to your advantage. Instead of immediately forgetting about a problem after it is completed, look for connections between it and other problems.

2.11 Pole-Vaulter Vaults

Find the force acting on a pole-vaulter as he decelerates onto a mat.

Layout Application activity; four matched simulations, one force diagram, one audio clip. Sim 1 shows the motion; Sim 2 adds kinematic values; Sim 3 draws in the force vectors; Sim 4 adds force magnitudes and presents the full solution to the problem.

Pointers This investigation is very similar to Activity 1.10 *Pole-Vaulter Lands*, and it is a good review of kinematic equations. As in that investigation, two motions meet at the point where the vaulter touches the mat: The difference in this exercise is that the magnitudes of the forces are calculated. If you have completed other activities in this unit, then this one should not be too difficult.

2.12 Truck Pulls Two Crates

Force diagrams are constructed for three connected objects, showing how changing parameters for one object affects the forces acting on other objects in the system.

Layout Exploratory and application activity, two simulations, one audio clip. Sim 2 (= Sim 1) shows correct values for one of the application problems.

Pointers This is an advanced activity that engineering students in a calculus-based physics course should *examine* and try to solve. Unless you have strong physics skills, working with a partner would be a good idea. At the very least, after completing this investigation you should appreciate the possible complications and scientific nuances of Newton's three simple laws of motion.

2.13 Bricklayer Lowers Bricks

Unbalanced forces cause a bricklayer to rise into the air.

Layout   Application activity; four matched simulations, one audio clip. Sim 1 shows the motion; Sim 2 adds the force vector magnitudes for the bricks; Sim 3 adds the force vector magnitudes for the bricklayer; Sim 4 includes an adjuster for the initial velocity of the bricklayer.

Pointers   This activity presents a connected system of a type that is often encountered on an exam. Separate force diagrams need to be constructed for each object in the system. The equations resulting from each object are connected by a common force magnitude in the rope and the same net acceleration for both bricklayer and bricks.

2.14 Modified Atwood Machine

Find the overall acceleration of a connected system, first without and then with friction.

Pointers   Exploratory and application activity; four matched simulations showing various combinations of parameters for two connected blocks, one video clip with audio.

Video: Truck Slips While Lifting a Load   The toy truck from Activity 2.8 is back. Once again the truck isn't moving, so the forces are balanced. How then is it possible to determine the coefficient of friction?

Pointers   This is another classic physics problem concerning forces and motion, and it is quite likely that you may encounter one like it on an exam. As with Activity 2.4 *Rocket Blasts Off*, treat this investigation as a full learning experience. It is an excellent supplement (or replacement) for the standard textbook explanations of this same topic.

After completing it, make adjustments of your own. For example, how would the acceleration change if friction were present (= 0.3)? Or what would happen if a third mass hung from a pulley attached to the other side of the block on the table? Or suppose the tabletop wasn't flat, but was set as an incline plane?

UNIT 3   PROJECTILE MOTION

Unit 1 examined the kinematics of objects moving along a straight line. In this unit the basic equations of motion developed for one-dimensional motion are applied to objects moving in two dimensions that experience a constant acceleration in one direction only.

Physical quantities that have a direction as well as a magnitude are called vectors. The activities in Unit 1 demonstrated that the directions of the displacement, velocity, and acceleration vectors are very important in understanding motion. In that unit we were able to use positive and negative signs to represent the direction in the equations of motion; but equations involving vectors cannot, in general, be solved algebraically. However, it is possible to use trigonometry to describe the motion of a projectile as two connected parts, with each part acting along a different axis. If the two axes are at right angles to each other, then the equations of motion along each axis can be solved independently of each other using the techniques and methods developed for one-dimensional motion. The results along each axis can then be recombined as the full two-dimensional answer.

The method of resolving vectors into component form using trigonometry is a very important mathematical technique. A vector can be specified with a magnitude and an angle with respect to a fixed line, or as a pair of x- and y-components. The mathematical relationship between angle magnitude and vector components is given by the sine, cosine, and tangent of the angle and the Pythagorean theorem (see your text and Activity 3.5). Because most physical motions occur in more than one dimension, this unit will help you learn how to convert vectors into their components quickly and easily, as well as provide more practice in solving word problems with more than one unknown quantity.

GAME PLAN

The problem with learning about motion from a textbook is that the figures are static. It is possible to draw motion diagrams to help understand the motion, but it is still hard to visualize it evolving in time. With *ActivPhysics* simulations, you can *see* the motion. Furthermore, slide adjusters allow you to vary initial conditions and observe the effects on the resulting motion. In the same way, the stepper allows you to examine each point of the motion individually.

But the most important and most helpful feature of this unit is that it has been set up as a full lecture-style tutorial on projectile motion. Activities 3.1–3.4 carefully develop the main principles of projectile motion in a logical, sequential fashion, and Activities 3.6–3.9 are solid application problems with clearly written solutions. In many respects, these activities represent the best that any supplemental physics materials can offer: a personal electronic tutor that can carefully and clearly guide you through the fundamental principles and methods of physics.

I recommend reading about trigonometry and vector components in the appropriate section of your physics textbook and attempting some of its sample problems first before exploring Activity 3.5 *Initial Velocity Components*, which demonstrates how to resolve any vector into its horizontal and vertical components. The mouse arrow in the simulation turns into a hand that is able to stretch and rotate a vector while the magnitude, angle, and vector components are continually listed in a table in the upper corner during the transformations. In my experience as a physics instructor, I have never seen a better method for showing and teaching vectors and vector components.

After completing Activity 3.5, work through Activities 3.1–3.4 sequentially. These simulations in particular are excellent dynamic examples of static textbook figures, and they do a much better job of showing the principles of projectile motion. Therefore, I suggest completing these activities before you read the textbook on projectile motion and then returning to your text as needed to fill in any missing information.

Finally, be sure to complete all four of the application problems, Activities 3.6–3.9. In the ideal situation, homework problems don't just test a student's ability to do algebra but also teach concepts. These activities should help you comprehend the ideas presented in the first five investigations. And be sure not to miss Activity 3.8, *Gravitational Constant on Planet Zeus*: First, the investigation allows you to solve for a variable that is usually a constant in these problems; and second, it's just plain fun.

THE DETAILS

3.1 Solving Projectile-Motion Problems

The motions of three different balls are compared: The first ball moves only horizontally; the second ball moves only vertically; and the third ball moves in both dimensions.

Layout Introductory activity; three simulations. Sim 1 shows a blue ball moving horizontally while a green ball travels in a parabolic arc; Sim 2 shows a red ball moving vertically under a constant downward acceleration while the green ball travels in the same parabolic arc; and Sim 3 combines the motions of all three balls.

Pointers There are no written answers for this activity; instead, this investigation demonstrates how the full parabolic motion can be projected onto horizontal and vertical axes. The text bar explains how to calculate the components of the green ball's velocity vector in each direction and also develops the horizontal and vertical equations of motion for projectiles. The information presented in this activity is the heart and soul of *all* projectile motion problems, so make sure you understand it completely.

3.2 Two Balls Falling

Two balls separated by a horizontal distance of 3 *m* fall simultaneously from a height of 5 *m*. The horizontal velocities of both balls may be adjusted separately. You are asked, first, to determine which ball lands first when they have different horizontal velocities, then, second, to choose initial horizontal velocities for the two balls so that they strike each other just as they reach the ground.

Layout Introductory activity; one simulation showing two falling balls with adjustable horizontal velocities.

Pointers Time is found from the vertical equation of motion, which is then used to calculate the horizontal position of each ball when it lands. Because the vertical heights of the two balls are the same, the time of flight is the same. This simulation reinforces the concept that time of fall is independent of the horizontal speed and that vertical and horizontal motions are linked by a common time. The last question examines the concept of relative velocity.

3.3 Changing the x-Velocity

A white ball is launched from the origin with a *y*-velocity of 10 *m/s* and an *x*-velocity of 2 *m/s*. The height, range, and time of flight of the trajectory are recorded, then the *x*-velocity *only* is changed and you are asked to predict which of these three quantities will change.

Layout Introductory activity; one simulation showing a projectile traveling in a parabolic arc.

Pointers Activity 3.2 compared the horizontal motion of two different balls with the same vertical motion. This investigation is similar, but the mathematics is applied to a single ball only.

3.4 Projectile x- and y-Accelerations

A white ball travels in a parabolic path with the velocity vector and its *x*- and *y*-components plotted as it moves through its trajectory. Simulation data is used to determine the *x*-acceleration in Question 1 and the *y*-acceleration in Question 2. Question 3 asks you to predict the change in *y*-velocity for different time intervals.

Layout Introductory activity; one simulation that tracks a projectile and includes the velocity vector and its components at equal time intervals.

Pointers This activity serves two purposes: First, it reinforces the concepts that the vertical motion acts under constant acceleration and the horizontal motion has zero acceleration; and second, it requires you to calculate acceleration graphically from its definition as the change in velocity as a function of time. This investigation may be especially useful if you are still having trouble with one-dimensional kinematic concepts.

3.5 Initial Velocity Components

The *x*- and *y*-components of four different vectors are calculated and then checked by grabbing a vector and changing its length and direction with the mouse until it matches the length and angle described by the question.

Layout Introductory activity; one simulation showing an adjustable vector and its components.

Pointers This is one of the few simulations of *ActivPhysics* that isn't actually run. On the other hand, there is no better method for *showing* vector components, since the magnitude, angle, and components are given in the upper corner of the simulation. This activity can be used to check the components of *any* vector, not just velocity vectors and not just for this physics topic. It is very important to calculate the components of a vector quickly and easily, so if you still have difficulty with this technique after completing the first four activities, make up more vectors on your own and check their components using the simulation.

3.6 Target Practice I

Choose different combinations of initial velocity *x*- and *y*-components of a ball 5 *m* above the origin so that it will land on a target 8 *m* in front of it. In the first two cases, the *y*-velocity is set and the

x-velocity is calculated; in the last two cases, the x-velocity is set and the y-velocity is calculated.

Layout Application activity; one simulation showing a ball traveling as a projectile, with adjustable initial x- and y-velocities.

Pointers The time of flight should be first calculated from the equation of motion from the known velocity component and the defined distance of travel for that direction. Afterward, apply the time of flight to the other equation of motion to calculate the unknown initial velocity component.

3.7 Target Practice II

A toy airplane traveling horizontally with a speed of 6 m/s and 3 m above the ground must drop a payload so that it lands on a target 8 m from the origin. The goal of this activity is to determine when and where the plane should release its cargo.

Layout Application activity; one simulation of the motion of a toy airplane and the path of its cargo as it falls through the air.

Pointers The text bar does not make it perfectly clear that the toy airplane is traveling horizontally; therefore, both the plane and its payload have an initial y-velocity of zero. As in the previous activity, use the height to find the time of flight and from that information determine the horizontal position of the drop.

3.8 Gravitational Constant on Planet Zeus

Through trial and error, adjust the initial speed of a ball until an assistant sitting on a wall catches a ball on the planet Zeus, then use that data to calculate the gravitational constant.

Layout Application activity; one simulation, showing the path of a projectile with an adjustable initial velocity and an assistant sitting on a wall of known height a measured distance in front of the projectile.

Pointers This activity requires you to first apply trial and error to find the correct initial speed of the ball so that it reaches the assistant. The gravitational constant is not known, and it only appears in the vertical motion equation. Since time is also not known, you will need to solve the horizontal equation of motion first. These two equations will have only two unknowns after the initial velocity vector components are found.

3.9 Motorcycle Daredevil

From the initial velocity vector components and the height of the ramp at take-off, determine whether motorcyclist can clear an 8.0-meter water barrier.

Layout Application activity; one simulation showing the conditions of the problem; one video.

Video: Shot Put Initial Speed Estimate the initial speed of a shot put given its time of flight and horizontal distance traveled. Estimations include the height of the shot-putter and angle of the shot put at take-off.

Pointers You will probably encounter at least one variation of this problem in a textbook. The time of flight determines the horizontal distance traveled.

UNIT 4 CIRCULAR MOTION

The ultimate goal of dynamics is to be able to describe the motion of any object in space along any path. Unit 1 examined the special case of one-dimensional motion, and Unit 3 explored the paths of projectiles, which was a special case of two-dimensional motion. This unit on Circular Motion considers the special case of an object moving along a circular path. However, it turns out that the ideas explored in these activities, along with concepts introduced in the other two units, provide all the tools necessary to describe the general motion of objects in two dimensions.

Acceleration measures the rate of change of velocity, and since velocity is a vector, both its magnitude and direction may vary over time. If the magnitude of the vector is the only changing quantity, then the object moves along a straight line and the motion is described by the one-dimensional kinematics developed in Unit 1. On the other hand, if the magnitude of the velocity stays constant and only the direction of the vector changes, then the natural path of the object is along a circle. The acceleration vector in that case always points along the radius and toward the center of the circle, so it is said to be either a radial or centripetal ("center-pointing") acceleration.

An object moving along a circular path may also be changing its speed, such as the case of a swinging pendulum (see Activity 4.1). When speed as well as direction are changing on a circular path, then the acceleration vector will not always be center-pointing. However, it is still possible to calculate a component of the acceleration that is centripetal (causing a change in direction only) and another component that results in the change in speed only. The magnitude-changing component of the acceleration vector is always tangent to the circle because the velocity vector always acts tangent to the circular path; therefore, it is called the tangential acceleration. Since a tangent line is always perpendicular to the radius, these two accelerations must completely and uniquely describe the acceleration of the object, just as the two perpendicular components of a projectile completely describe its motion.

It is always possible to calculate tangential and radial components of an acceleration vector, even when the path is not perfectly circular. Calculus provides a technique for finding the tangent line to any curve, and once that line is defined, it is not difficult to define the line perpendicular to it. Therefore, using the concepts of "direction-changing" and "magnitude-changing" acceleration vectors and the equations presented in this unit, it is always possible to calculate these two components, and we now have a general method for understanding the dynamics of any object moving in two dimensions.

GAME PLAN

Most of the activities of Unit 4 may be grouped together into particular sets following a common theme. Since forces cause accelerations and the direction of the acceleration must be the same as the direction of the net force, the first two activities in this unit show how to calculate accelerations for objects moving along circular paths. The method for doing that is to estimate from the differences in velocity vectors at different times. Since both the directions and magnitudes of the velocities are changing in the two examples, the acceleration is neither always tangential nor always perpendicular to the tangent (or centripetal).

Activity 4.1 *Determining Acceleration Direction Graphically* shows the acceleration of a pendulum bob at different times, and Activity 4.4 *Circular Motion Problem Solving* continues the investigation of the pendulum by examining the forces acting on the bob (weight and tension) and how they cause the acceleration. Activity 4.6 *Ball Swings on a String* completes the study of the pendulum with a thorough analysis of the tension in a string at different locations of its path, much in the style of a textbook example.

Activity 4.2 *Acceleration Direction of a Car* considers a different case of an object speeding up and slowing down as it moves in a circle, and Activity 4.7 *Car Circles a Track* examines the particular forces that could cause this type of motion, which in this case is friction. Although both Activities 4.1 and 4.2 present the material well, it may be helpful to start with a simpler problem, Activity 4.3 *Magnitude of Centripetal Acceleration*. Since the object in that simulation is moving at a constant speed, the investigation clearly demonstrates how under those specific conditions the acceleration is always center-pointing. The purpose of the activity is to develop the equation relating centripetal acceleration to both the speed of the object and the radius of the curve's path.

The remaining three investigations of the unit examine other applications of circular motion. Activity 4.8 *Satellite's Orbit* applies centripetal force to the motion of satellites or planets, resulting in Kepler's laws. Demonstrating that Kepler's laws are only a special case of the laws of motion (plus the universal law of gravitation) was one of

Newton's most important accomplishments. Activity 4.9 *Bag Hits Bystander* is a relatively simple problem that combines concepts from both circular and projectile motion and is highly recommended. Activity 4.5 *Cart Goes over Circular Path* is somewhat more difficult than the other activities of this unit, and it may take some extra effort to understand the physics behind the motion.

THE DETAILS

4.1 Determining Acceleration Direction Graphically

The acceleration of a pendulum bob is estimated graphically by subtracting velocity vectors drawn at equal time intervals.

Layout Introductory activity; two matched simulations and three audio clips. Sim 1 shows a moving pendulum bob with velocity vectors tracked at different positions; Sim 2 adds acceleration vectors.

Pointers As the text bar states, the direction of the acceleration vector at different times may seem surprising. The key concept underlying this activity is to realize that an object moving on a curved surface does *not* always have an acceleration in the direction of motion. If you can accept this fact, it will be easier to accept the concept of a centripetal acceleration.

4.2 Acceleration Direction of a Car

The acceleration of a car moving in a circular path is estimated using velocity vector subtraction at equal time intervals.

Layout Introductory activity; three matched simulations. Sim 1 tracks a car speeding up and slowing down as it travels on a circular track; Sim 2 adds velocity vectors; and Sim 3 adds acceleration vectors at each point.

Pointers The observations made in this investigation are similar to those of Activity 4.1. Note that a component of the changing acceleration vector always points inward.

4.3 Magnitude of Centripetal Acceleration

A relationship between speed, radius of a circular path, and centripetal acceleration is developed by adjusting slider values for speed and radius and noting the effect on the acceleration.

Layout Introductory activity; two matched simulations and one video clip with audio. Sim 1 shows a ball moving in a horizontal circle with variable speed; Sim 2 shows a constant speed but varies the radius of the circular path.

Video: Cars Going Around a Track How do the speeds of the inner and outer toy cars racing around the curve of a race track compare?

Pointers The purpose of this simulation is to build the known equation for the magnitude of centripetal acceleration by observation, but the correct result is given in the summary (or in your text). However, this is a good opportunity to develop important scientific skills of observation and analysis, so avoid the temptation to peek.

4.4 Circular Motion Problem Solving

Calculate the tension in the rope of a pendulum bob at its lowest point as it travels in a circular arc.

Layout Introductory activity; four matched simulations and one video clip with audio. Sim 1 shows a moving pendulum bob of Activity 4.1; Sim 2 adds velocity and acceleration vectors; Sim 3 changes to force vectors; Sim 4 presents the full solution to the problem.

Video: Swinging a Bucket of Water Why doesn't water in a bucket swinging over your head pour out and splash you? The concepts outlined in this activity explain why.

Pointers When solving word problems, the forces causing centripetal acceleration must be handled differently from the methods learned in Unit 2. Centripetal force is not an independent force like weight or tension but is always the net force *resulting* from these real forces. This investigation will make more sense if Activity 4.1 is completed first.

4.5 Cart Goes Over Circular Path

The normal force of a cart at the summit of a hill is calculated.

Layout Application activity; five matched simulations and one force diagram. Sim 1 shows a cart traveling over a hill; Sim 2 adds velocity vectors; Sim 3 adds acceleration vectors; Sim 4 shows force vectors; Sim 5 adds numerical values for the normal force and speed of the cart.

Pointers Force vectors for objects moving along curved paths can never sum to zero because there is always the centripetal acceleration and therefore a net centripetal force. This investigation does more than just calculate the normal force, which would be quite possible to do without all the vectors and forces of the many matched simulations. However, good physics is not about getting a single numerical answer, but about understanding how the universe works, and this activity more than any other in the unit delves into the particular nature of centripetal force. For example, would you have predicted that the cart would leave the hill before reaching a vertical slope before viewing the simulation? Can you explain *why* the cart leaves the hill early? Can you correctly predict *where* the cart will lose contact with the hill?

4.6 Ball Swings on a String

The tension in a string at three different positions is calculated for a ball traveling in a circular path with a changing speed.

Layout Application activity; nine simulations (the first eight matched); and three force diagrams. Sim 1 shows a moving pendulum bob; Sim 2 adds velocity and acceleration vectors; Sim 3 changes to force vectors and adds position and velocity data; Sim 4 adds the value of the tension. All of these simulations pause at position I. Sim 5 and Sim 6 repeat the information of Sim 3 and Sim 4 but at position II; Sim 7 and Sim 8 do the same for position III. Sim 9 compares the motions of two bobs, with the string of one of them cut at the apex of the motion.

Pointers This investigation continues where Activity 4.4 left off. If you continue the player for the first four simulations and use the adjusted values instead of resetting the conditions, Sims 5–8 may be skipped. Question 4 and Sim 9 are qualitative but instructional. You can see that the net acceleration generally is not aligned with any real force vector because of the centripetal acceleration. Notice that the weight can (but doesn't always) contribute to the centripetal force, which is why the magnitude of the tension changes. Also notice in the bottom diagram of Sim 9, where the tension is both greatest and least.

4.7 Car Circles a Track

The maximum speed of a car on a circular track is calculated, given the coefficient of static friction and other parameters.

Layout Application activity; four matched simulations, a force diagram, and one video clip with audio. Sim 1 shows a car speeding up and slowing down as it travels on a circular track; Sim 2 adds velocity vectors, and Sim 3 adds acceleration vectors at each point; Sim 4 checks the maximum speed possible for the known static friction.

Video: Plane Flies at End of String From mass, length of string, and string tension, estimate the constant speed of a toy plane traveling in a circle. This is a two-dimensional problem; therefore, angle makes a difference. Weight balances only part of the tension, so the other component of the tension is the centripetal force.

Pointers If you need more practice with friction (and even if you don't), this is a good activity. Because centripetal force cannot exist by itself, it must have some external, real cause. Friction is the cause in this activity, just as string tension is the cause for a pendulum bob. Other types of external forces may also cause centripetal force.

4.8 Satellite's Orbit

A relationship is found for the orbital speed of a satellite and its distance from the main gravitational body.

Layout Application activity; two simulations. Sim 1 compares the orbits of three satellites circling a planet at different radii, each with an adjustable velocity. Sim 2 (also found under the Advisor) shows a single satellite with an adjustable velocity and a force vector orbiting a planet in order to show elliptical orbits.

Pointers Newton's laws of motion and the equation for centripetal force are used to determine orbital speed. This investigation is easily extended to develop Kepler's second law of motion: The cube of the radius of orbit is proportional to the square of the orbital period. Check this fact from the calculated orbital speeds. The derivation of Kepler's law from Newton's laws is found in most general physics textbooks.

4.9 Bag Hits Bystander

A sandbag moving in a circular path is suddenly released at the top of its path. At what position would a person have to be standing to be struck by the bag?

Layout Application activity; one simulation showing the path of a sandbag. The position of the bystander is adjustable. After the first reset, the tension in the rope and other physical quantities are listed.

Pointers This investigation combines circular motion and projectile motion. Centripetal force is used to find the horizontal speed of the bag when the rope is cut, which then becomes the initial velocity of the bag when it behaves as a projectile.

UNIT 5 WORK AND ENERGY

Newton's three laws of motion completely explain the causes of classical motion, including the special cases of projectile motion and circular motion. The force description of mechanics will be complete after exploring the concepts of torque and rotational dynamics in Unit 7, which is another special application of Newton's laws. But there are two other alternative descriptions of how objects move that are just as valid as the force description. It can be shown that these two approaches to understanding motion can be derived from the three laws of motion using calculus, and the three different perspectives therefore do not contradict each other but rather complement one another. The work-energy method is an alternative to Newton's laws explored in this unit.

Work is calculated from a force acting through a distance. Mechanical energy comes in two forms: kinetic energy, associated with an object whenever it has a nonzero speed; and potential energy, associated with an object by virtue of its position. Because work and energy are scalars instead of vectors, this approach to understanding mechanics is usually employed when particular information about directions isn't needed or is already known.

For example, suppose you want to calculate the speed of a child at the bottom of a curved slide. To solve this problem using forces and accelerations, you would have to calculate the net force and the radial and tangential accelerations of the child at each point of the path on the slide in order to calculate his velocity at the bottom of the slide. On the other hand, the speed of the child could also be calculated from just his vertical height above the base of the slide and his initial speed. The algebra of energy is much simpler than the mathematics needed for the force description, but what we gain in simplicity we lose in direction—we cannot know from the energy calculations alone what direction the child is moving at the bottom of the slide.

GAME PLAN

The 14 activities of this unit on Work and Energy are fun and easy. Each one should take around 20 minutes to complete. This unit introduces an extremely effective method for visualizing energy transfers, the work-energy bar chart, which shows exactly where the energy of the system is located at each instant of the motion. Therefore, it is possible to *see* how kinetic energy is converted into gravitational energy, or how spring energy is transferred into internal energy, or any other of the numerous possibilities of conversion of energy from one form into another. In fact, exploring any

(or all) of the activities in this unit should help convince you that energy and the principle of energy conservation is just a bookkeeping system. The only real issue in work-energy problems is the location of the energy at the start of the motion and when the motion is completed. If you can correctly identify those two points and equate the sum of all energies (which *is* the principle of conservation of energy), then you can generally solve these problems quickly and easily.

Begin with Activity 5.1 *Work Calculations*, which is a multiple choice problem. A creative student may want to jump into Activity 5.4 *Inventing Processes*; however, most students will prefer to work sequentially through Activities 5.2 *Ejector Pad* and 5.3 *Sliding on Snow and Grass* first to become more familiar with work-energy bar charts.

The remaining activities can be completed in any order. Different activities consider different types of energy conversions: spring potential energy to kinetic energy, kinetic energy to internal energy, spring potential energy to gravitational potential energy. Activities 5.10 *Skier Tow Rope* and 5.11 *Spring-Launched Ski Lift* are highly recommended because these investigations are solved by both the energy and force methods. The last three investigations, 5.12 *Modified Atwood Machine*, 5.13 *Bricklayer Perils*, and 5.14 *Cart Leaves Circular Hill*, all correspond to investigations covered in previous units and therefore may be of particular interest to students who have already solved those problems.

THE DETAILS

5.1 Work Calculations

The basic concepts of work as a force acting through a distance and the effect of vector angles on the amount of work done are presented through multiple-choice questions.

Layout Introductory activity; four simulations, showing objects being pushed by external forces acting in a variety of directions.

Pointers This activity is the obvious place to start, but watch out for trick questions and inconsistent thinking.

5.2 Ejector Pad,
5.3 Sliding on Snow and Grass

Energy changes are examined for two consecutive motions on the ejector pad: (uncoiling the spring and rising into the air) and while sliding (down a frictionless hill and horizontally across grass with friction).

Layout   Introductory activities; two matched simulations and two energy bar charts each, one video clip with audio for Activity 5.2.

Video: Grasshopper Spring Constant   The force constant for a toy grasshopper that behaves in a manner similar to the ejector pad is estimated.

Pointers   These problems are conceptual introductions to the various forms of energy—kinetic, spring potential, gravitational potential, and internal—and the transfer of energy between them. The video showing the height reached by a toy grasshopper is a good application of the ideas presented in Activity 5.2.

5.4 Inventing Processes

Real-world motions are 'invented' that correspond to five different examples of energy transfers represented by work-energy bar charts.

Layout   Exploration activity; ten simulations in five matched sets. In each case, the first simulation presents a work-energy bar chart and the second includes a simulation that could correspond to the chart.

Pointers   Instead of having to continually keep track of every force and acceleration throughout a motion, the energy bar chart shows the location of the energy associated with a force or motion at different points in time. However, in order to use the energy concept effectively, it is important to understand *which* energy is associated with different kinds of real-world motions and the method of energy transfer through work, which is the purpose of this investigation.

5.5 Upward-Moving Elevator Stops,
5.6 Stopping a Downward-Moving Elevator

The tension of a cable raising or lowering an elevator is calculated using the conservation of energy principle.

Layout   Application activities; three matched simulations and one work-energy bar chart each. Sim 1 shows the motion; Sim 2 adds work-energy bar charts; Sim 3 reports the numerical value of the tension.

Pointers   Because there is an external force acting throughout these motions, it is possible (and necessary) to calculate the work done by that external force, which is the tension in the rope. Compare the solutions using the work-energy approach to Activities 2.2 and 2.3. Note that some energies can be positive or negative.

5.7 Inverse Bungee Jumper

The force constant of a spring is adjusted so that a young woman on a trapeze just reaches the ceiling.

Layout   Application activity; two matched simulations and one work-energy bar chart. Sim 1 shows the motion; Sim 2 adds energy and work bar charts.

Pointers   If you are curious (or sadistic), watch what happens if the spring constant is too large.

5.8 Spring-Launched Bowler

Set the spring constant so that a young lady coasting on the horizontal ramp just reaches the glass of lemonade.

Layout   Application activity; two matched simulations and one energy bar chart, two video clips with audio. Sim 1 shows the motion; Sim 2 adds work-energy bar charts.

Videos: Force Constant of Hot Wheels Launcher—1; Force Constant of Hot Wheels Launcher—2   A toy car is launched off a table horizontally by a spring-loaded launcher, which then travels as a projectile. From the distance traveled and other parameters given in the text bar, estimate the speed of the car at take-off.

Pointers   This activity is similar to the previous one, but the motion is horizontal instead of vertical.

5.9 Skier Speed,
5.10 Skier Tow Rope

In the first investigation, determine the speed of a skier at the base of a frictional slope; in the second, find the tension in the tow rope.

Layout   Application activities; five matched simulations, a force diagram, and a work-energy bar chart for each. Sim 1 shows the motion; Sim 2 shows the force vectors; Sim 3 includes force magnitudes; Sim 4 adds work-energy bar charts; Sim 5 is the full solution including the speed. Activity 5.9 includes three video clips with audio.

Video: Hot Wheel Projectile—1, Hot Wheel Projectile—2; Tension in Swinging Cables   The first two video clips show a toy car accelerating down a ramp; the last one shows a person swinging on a swing. The first set of video clips is similar to those of Activity 5.8 but uses gravity instead of a spring to launch the car. The second video is related to the motion of a pendulum, first encountered in Unit 4 on circular motion.

Pointers   The motion of a skier is found using two of Newton's laws—force method and the conservation of energy principle. The comparison is useful in seeing how these two methods interrelate. These investigations demonstrate that the mathematics must be the same even though the equations are based on different concepts and principles. They are also examples of applied forces that do not act in the direction of travel.

5.11 Spring-Launched Ski Lift

The maximum height of a sled launched up an incline is calculated, both without and with friction.

Layout Application activity; two matched simulations and two work-energy bar charts. Sim 1 shows the motion; Sim 2 includes work-energy bar charts.

Pointers This investigation is similar to Activities 5.7 *Inverse Bungee Jumper* and 5.8 *Spring-Launched Bowler*, only now the motion is along an incline instead of strictly horizontal or vertical. The methods developed for other activities involving inclines are employed here.

5.12 Modified Atwood Machine

The modified Atwood machine of Activity 2.14 is revisited. Adjustable sliders for height, initial speed, mass of one block, and initial speed of another block allow for variations on the motion. In the first part of the investigation, the final speed of a block is found; in the second part, a maximum height is found.

Layout Exploration and application activity; three simulations, two work-energy bar charts. Sim 1 shows the motion; Sim 2 (= Sim 3) includes work-energy bar charts for the motion.

Pointers As with other adjustable-slider exploration/application activities, you can choose to

either solve the problems as presented or invent more variations of your own. This activity is a good capstone to the work-energy unit.

5.13 Bricklayer Perils

The bricklayer problem of Activity 2.13 is reexamined from an energy perspective. The purpose of this investigation is to determine the speed of the bricklayer at the height of the motion. In the third question, the mass of bricks is calculated to cause a predetermined final speed.

Layout Application activity; three matched simulations and two work-energy bar charts. Sim 1 shows the motion; Sim 2 adds work-energy bar charts; Sim 3 presents the full solution to the problem.

Pointers Unlike Newton's laws—force method, the solution to the problem, does not require a calculation of the acceleration of the system.

5.14 Cart Leaves Circular Hill

Activity 4.5 *Cart Goes Over Circular Path* is revisited from an energy perspective.

Layout Application activity; four matched simulations, one work-energy bar chart. Sim 1 shows the motion; Sim 2 adds work-energy bar charts; Sim 3 (= Sim 4) includes force vectors and position coordinates.

Pointers This activity can be a tough one. Unlike the other activities of this unit, it will take some concentration and careful analysis to appreciate the full solution, so make sure you are ready to put in the necessary time and effort.

UNIT 6 MOMENTUM

There are two alternative formulations of Newton's force laws. The first of these methods is the work-energy description explored in Unit 5; the second method is the impulse-momentum description explored in this unit.

When Newton formulated the laws of motion, he did not think of forces as causing accelerations; instead, he thought of forces as causing changes in momentum. Momentum is a vector defined as the mass of an object multiplied by its velocity. Newton's approach is actually superior to the standard definition of the second law because it allows the mass of an object to be changing in time, such as a rocket expelling exhaust gases as it blasts off.

Impulse is defined as the product of a force acting over a certain time. It can easily be shown mathematically that an impulse applied to an object will cause a change in its momentum. It can also be shown based on Newton's third law of motion that momentum, like energy, must be conserved. Therefore, for some physical investigations, knowledge of initial and final momentum conditions before and after an interaction may be sufficient for understanding the physics without knowing the particular behavior of the objects during the interaction.

A collision is defined as a short-time interaction between objects. The impulse-momentum method is useful when considering collisions because the forces acting usually aren't very well known and accelerations may only be approximated. Momentum is also a better approach than the work-energy description since direction definitely does make a difference on the physical consequences, and momentum will show the vector direction of an object in either one or two dimensions.

GAME PLAN

Students who have completed at least some of the previous five units of *ActivPhysics* should feel comfortable with the organization of this one. The first three activities introduce the major concepts and principles of momentum, impulse, and momentum conservation, and the fourth activity presents the basic method of solving momentum problems. The remaining six activities are all application problems.

The first activity, 6.1 *Momentum and Energy Change*, compares and contrasts the behavior of momentum and kinetic energy during an acceleration. Activity 6.2 *Collisions and Elasticity* demonstrates elasticity by example, and Activity 6.3

Momentum Conservation and Collisions formulates the equations of momentum conservation in two dimensions.

Also as in other units, Activities 6.5 *Car Collision: Two Dimensions*, 6.6 *Saving an Astronaut*, and 6.7 *Explosion Problems* are similar to certain textbook problems and may be considered standard or classic examples of momentum conservation. The last three activities, 6.9 *Skier and Cart*, 6.10 *Pendulum Bashes Box*, and 6.11 *Pendulum Person—Projectile Bowling*, include principles and concepts learned in previous units.

One advantage of computer simulations is that most of the application activities include the option of adjusting the elasticity. Even though only perfectly elastic and perfectly inelastic collisions can be solved easily, it is useful to explore the effects of more realistic elasticities on the resulting motion.

THE DETAILS

6.1 Momentum and Energy Change

Two pucks of different masses are pushed with the same constant force, and values of impulse and momentum are compared. Kinetic energy changes and work done at different locations or times are also examined.

Layout   Introductory activity; one simulation showing the motion of two objects with different masses.

Pointers   Work is defined as a force acting through a distance, $W = Fx$, and impulse is defined as force acting through a time, $I = Ft$. Focus on these two facts as you answer these multiple-choice questions.

6.2 Collisions and Elasticity

Momentum and impulse changes and energy transfers are examined for perfectly elastic and inelastic collisions, represented by pendula hitting stationary blocks.

Layout   Introductory activity; five matched simulations, three audio clips, two video clips. Sim 1 shows pendula hitting anchored blocks elastically and inelastically; Sim 2 (found under Question 2) shows the same collisions on unanchored blocks; Sim 3 adds impulse graphs. Sim 4 (= Sim 2) is found under the word *elastic* in Question 1, and Sim 5 (= Sim 3) is found under the word *inelastic* in Question 1.

Videos: Two Balls Dropped—1, Two Balls Dropped—2
The video clips demonstrate elastic and inelastic collisions on a table top.

Pointers Collision investigations go hand in hand with the study of impulse and momentum, and the concepts of elasticity and inelasticity are central to the study of collisions. This investigation is an excellent visualization of the same ideas presented in any standard physics textbook, and it goes into greater detail than most textbooks.

6.3 Momentum Conservation and Collisions

Conservation of momentum in two dimensions is explored through a series of simulations that track the momentum and kinetic energy of two objects before and after a collision.

Layout Introductory exploration activity; six matched simulations, an audio clip, a video clip with audio. Sim 1 shows two pucks colliding with variable relative masses, elasticity, and relative positions; Sim 2 adds a momentum bar chart; Sim 3 reports numerical values for the x-component of the momentum instead of showing a bar chart; Sim 4 reports numerical values for the x-component of the momentum; Sim 5 shows an energy bar chart instead of momentum; and Sim 6 reports numerical values of the energies instead of showing a bar chart.

Video: Collision of Metal Balls Different combinations of five metal balls hanging in a row from a bar are allowed to behave like a pendulum. The number of balls striking the stationary balls at the lowest point is always equal to the number of balls swinging upward after collision.

Pointers This exploration activity examines different initial conditions in order to deduce the physical principles governing the behavior of elastic and inelastic objects before and after a collision. As the Layout for this investigation suggests, the two key ideas explored are the relationships between momenta and also of kinetic energy before and after a collision. The principles of conservation of momentum and conservation of kinetic energy are developed from the bar charts and numerical data obtained from the different versions of the same simulation. (But watch out! Kinetic energy is *not* conserved under all conditions!) Be sure to test all three possible parameters for each case—relative mass, elasticity, and strike position—before coming to any conclusions.

6.4 Collision Problems

The principles of conservation of momentum are applied to simple elastic and inelastic collisions in one and two dimensions.

Layout Application activity; three matched simulations. Sim 1 shows an inelastic head-on collision of two pucks; Sim 2 shows an elastic head-on collision of two pucks; Sim 3 shows an angled elastic collision of two pucks.

Pointers Activity 6.3 developed the principles of conservation of momentum in two dimensions; this is the first application problem showing how those equations can be used to calculate unknown quantities. The three scenarios presented in this exercise are among the simplest possible: an inelastic head-on collision, an elastic head-on collision, and the calculation of a single final velocity vector from three other known velocity vectors. I recommend using the adjustable sliders for different parameters to create a few of your own problems to see whether you can correctly calculate the results using momentum conservation principles.

6.5 Car Collision: Two Dimensions

A collision between two cars is simulated.

Layout Application activity; one audio clip, one simulation representing a right-angled collision between two vehicles.

Pointers This is another simulation that allows you to create and explore other possible initial conditions after solving the three problems presented in the activity. For all three cases you will need to determine angles after collision from the dots that appear on the screen.

6.6 Saving an Astronaut

How long does it take the astronaut to reach her ship after casting off an oxygen tank?

Layout Application activity; two matched simulations. Sim 1 shows the motion; Sim 2 presents the full solution.

Pointers This is a relatively simple one-dimensional momentum problem that shouldn't be too difficult to solve. The equation for constant velocity is used to find the time of travel. Don't forget that the combined astronaut–oxygen tank *system* is initially moving at 2 *m/s*.

6.7 Explosion Problems

Determine the locations where two fragments of a projectile will land. The first three questions vary the relative masses of the two fragments, the fourth question changes the impulse, and the fifth question is a conceptual one.

Layout Application activity; one simulation, representing a projectile that breaks into two parts at the apex of its motion, with adjustable parameters.

Pointers This activity combines momentum principles and projectile motion. Since the explosion occurs at the apex of the motion, the key is to determine the x-velocity component for each fragment. (The y-components will be zero—why?) Determine the initial speed and impulse for the fragments and then solve for the landing points. Do any of the results surprise you?

6.8 Block Sliding Down an Incline

How fast are an incline and a block moving in opposite directions after the block slides down the plane? All surfaces are frictionless.

Layout Application activity; one simulation showing the block-plane system with on-off meters for the x- and y-accelerations of the block, normal forces, and x-velocities of the two objects.

Pointers This is one of the most interesting of the momentum problems and certainly not the easiest. The full solution involves the construction of a force diagram for the system. However, the activity does provide a step-by-step analysis from initial setup through final solution.

6.9 Skier and Cart

How much does a skier compress a spring after a collision?

Layout Application activity; four matched simulations. Sim 1 shows the motion; Sim 2 adds momentum and work-energy bar charts up to and at the point of collision; Sim 3 continues the motion (with bar charts) after the collision; Sim 4 presents the full solution of the problem, including bar charts.

Pointers Many momentum and collision problems, such as this activity and the next two, combine momentum changes and calculations at the point of collision with energy transfers either before or after the collision. The text bar for this investigation guides you through each step of the sequence.

6.10 Pendulum Bashes Box

How far does a box travel on a frictional surface after being struck by a pendulum?

Layout Application activity; five matched simulations. Sim 1 shows the motion; Sim 2 adds a work-energy bar chart for the pendulum; Sim 3 includes work-energy and momentum bar charts for both the pendulum and the block; Sim 4 shows the forces acting on the block after collision; Sim 5 presents the full solution to the problem, including momentum and work-energy bar charts for both objects.

Pointers This is one version of the classic bullet-and-block problem. There are three parts to the full solution: energy conversion as the pendulum falls; momentum conservation at the point of collision (notice the pendulum comes to rest); and deceleration caused by friction.

6.11 Pendulum Person—Projectile Bowling

A pendulum strikes a person on a chair at the edge of a cliff; the person flies through the air as a projectile; and the projectile lands in a cart and travels forward at a constant speed. Where should the cart be positioned to catch the chair? How fast will the cart be moving after it catches the person?

Layout Application activity; two matched simulations. Sim 1 shows the motion; Sim 2 presents the full solution.

Pointers From pendulum energy, to momentum conservation in a collision, to projectile motion, to another collision. Can you apply the right equations in the right places?

UNIT 7 ROTATIONAL MOTION AND STATICS

Rotational motion is the last major topic of mechanics. Even though new concepts and terminology are introduced, in many respects nothing new is added to our basic understanding of how the world works. Rotational dynamics complements linear dynamics just as radial acceleration along a circular path complements accelerations along a straight line.

Every physical quantity of linear motion has a counterpart in rotational motion. A comparison of linear kinematics and rotational kinematics shows that position is replaced by angle, velocity by angular velocity, and acceleration by angular acceleration. Each pair of quantities is related to the other by the radius of the circular path. To continue the analogy for dynamics, force is replaced by torque, momentum by angular momentum, and mass by moment of inertia. In addition, there is a new energy term, rotational kinetic energy. The relationships between these quantities also depend on a radius, which is the distance between the object and the "center of torque."

The mathematics that relates each linear quantity to its analogous rotational quantity is known as the vector product, because the result of multiplying two vectors together (such as a force vector and a displacement vector) is another vector (i.e., torque). One example of the vector product is given in Activity 7.1 when torque is first defined. Because rotational quantities are all derived in a similar fashion, the forms of the rotational equations match their linear analogs. For example, if by the second law $F = ma$, then for torque, $T = I\alpha$, where α is the angular acceleration and I is the moment of inertia.

The units of torque happen to be the same as those of work, and both quantities are defined as a force times a distance. However, work is not calculated from a vector product but by a different but complementary approach known as the scalar product. Work is a scalar and torque is a vector. Work is a measure of energy changes along the path of motion, whereas torque causes objects to spin about an axis. Work is caused by the component of the force acting in the direction of motion; torque is caused by the component of the force acting perpendicular to the direction of motion. So, just as the x- and y-components completely define the motion of a projectile or radial and tangential accelerations uniquely define the acceleration of an object in space, in the same way work and torque together completely define the effect of a force acting on an object, which is why this unit on rotational motion is fundamental for understanding how the universe behaves.

GAME PLAN

The 17 activities of this unit are divided into four sections, with each section considering a different aspect of this extensive topic. The first two investigations in the section Torques and Statics, Activities 7.1 *Calculating Torques* and 7.2 *A Tilted Beam: Torques and Equilibrium*, explain the concept of torque and the pertinent equations describing its behavior, providing a strong foundation for the rest of the activities in the unit. The key principle of static equilibrium (Activities 7.3–7.6) is that all the forces acting in the system and also all torques must be balanced, or sum to zero.

Under the section Rotational Kinematics and Dynamics, Activity 7.7 *Rotational Inertia* introduces a physical quantity that is very different from any other encountered thus far. Activity 7.8 *Rotational Kinematics* is also quite practical, presenting effective visualizations of angular velocity and angular acceleration. The four remaining activities in this section, 7.9–7.12, are all application problems.

The first of the three investigations in the section Rotational Energy, Activity 7.13 *Race Between a Block and a Disk*, uses observational evidence (in simulation form) to demonstrate the existence of rotational kinetic energy. Activities 7.14 and 7.15 are application problems that repeat rotational dynamics problems from the previous section, but from an energy perspective.

The last section, Angular Momentum Conservation, includes only two activities. The first investigation examines collisions involving rotating objects, and the second one illustrates the principle of scattering, which has a number of important applications in atomic physics.

THE DETAILS

Torques and Statics

7.1 Calculating Torques

The torques caused by different forces about a pivot point are calculated in an adjustable model system.

Layout Application activity; six matched simulations. Sim 1 shows a mass with an adjustable position and mass on a horizontal beam attached to a wall at a pivot point and held in place by a wire; Sim 2 shows all the forces acting on the system; Sims 3, 4, and 5 show the tension in the wire, normal force on the block, or the force at the pivot point (respectively) and the torque that force causes on the pivot point; Sim 6 lists all forces and torques acting on the pivot point.

Pointers The text bar does an excellent job of explaining how to calculate torques, through both words and figures. Don't miss the opportunity to move the block around or change its mass and see the effect on both forces and torques. Can you correctly predict the qualitative changes on all the forces and torques before adjusting a particular parameter?

7.2 A Tilted Beam: Torques and Equilibrium

All forces and torques are calculated for a system consisting of a brick hanging from a tilted beam attached to a wall at a pivot point and held in place by a horizontal wire.

Layout Application activity; two matched simulations. Sim 1 shows the system in place; Sim 2 presents the full solution to the problem.

Pointers This investigation is a good test of equilibrium concepts and correct use of the equations. Follow the guidance given in the text bar as needed and rely on the general solution format for this problem when you attempt similar textbook problems.

7.3 Arm Levers

Forces and torques acting in two equilibrium systems modeling the bicep muscle and the tricep muscle are calculated.

Layout Application activity; two sets of two matched simulations; one video with audio clip. Sim 1 is a model of the bicep muscle and Sim 2 presents its full solution; Sim 3 is a model of the tricep muscle and Sim 4 presents its full solution.

Video: Biceps Experiment An experimental model matching the first simulation is constructed in the laboratory using a meterstick, weight, and spring scale.

Pointers Students interested in the health sciences, especially physical therapy, should find these investigations quite instructive. The comparison of the bicep and tricep muscles show how the point of attachment and the direction of an applied force affect the calculation of the torques.

7.4 Two Painters on a Beam

Find the tension in two ropes supporting two painters on a horizontal beam.

Layout Application problem; two matched simulations. Sim 1 shows the system in static equilibrium; Sim 2 presents the full solution.

Pointers This activity is another classic problem in physics, and some version of it will certainly be found in most physics textbooks. Once again, I recommend that you take the time to adjust the masses or positions of the painters and predict the qualitative effects on the normal forces and torques after you complete the particular problem presented in the text bar.

7.5 The Back

The forces and torques acting in the human back are examined, demonstrating why it is important to lift from the legs.

Layout Application problem; one simulation modeling the mechanics of the back; one video clip with audio.

Video: Tension in the Arm Swinging Bucket Estimate the tension in the arm of a person swinging a bucket in a circle based on the body's tilt, the angle of the arm, and certain known masses.

Pointers Although the calculations made in this investigation are similar to the previous statics problems, the emphasis here is on seeing the connection between physics principles and body mechanics, in both the simulation and the video. However, for all of these application problems, the approach to the solution is the same: Determine all the forces, determine all the torques, and set the sums of all vector forces and torques to zero.

7.6 Lecturing from a Beam

Find the tension in a rope for a unique lecturing style.

Layout Application problem; two matched simulations. Sim 1 shows the static equilibrium; Sim 2 presents the full solution.

Pointers This last statics investigation is given a twist by connecting the two objects of the system (the professor and the beam) by a rope. Therefore, the professor's position enters the problem in two ways: First, as in other problems, the position will affect his applied torque; second, the tension in the rope now becomes a function of his position since they are connected. As a result, expect a set of coupled equations with his position as the common unknown.

Rotational Kinematics and Dynamics

7.7 Rotational Inertia

The role of mass in linear dynamics is compared to the role of moment of inertia in rotational dynamics, and the method of calculating moment of inertia for a system of point objects in one dimension is presented.

Layout Introductory activity; three simulations, two video clips with audio. Sim 1 shows the effect of mass on acceleration for the same constant force; Sim 2 shows the effect of moment of inertia on rotational acceleration for the same constant torque; Sim 3 shows four point-masses on a rod with adjustable positions and masses, and shows the calculation of the resulting moment of inertia about different points.

Videos: Windmill—1, Windmill—2 The significance of moment of inertia is demonstrated in the laboratory by comparing the angular accelerations of two spinning rods with the same applied torque, whose only difference is the placement of two large masses on the rod.

Pointers The first two simulations are included to show the similarity between mass and moment of inertia; there are no questions to be answered or calculations to be made. The third simulation is very important and worth examining carefully, especially the calculation of moment of inertia (I) for point masses is a course objective. The equation for calculating I is given in the simulation as well as its value for particular mass configurations and axes. Although the text bar questions are multiple choice, I recommend using the information in the figure to calculate the moment of inertia for each case in order to see how the equation is used and to verify that the answer given is correct.

7.8 Rotational Kinematics

The physical meanings of the three vector quantities—angle (θ), angular velocity (ω), and angular acceleration (α)—are visualized, and the directions of angular velocity and acceleration are assigned to six different rotational motions.

Layout Introductory activity; four simulations. Sim 1 shows two rotating disks, comparing angle measure in degrees and radians; Sim 2 shows three rotating disks with different constant angular velocities; Sim 3 shows two rotating disks with different constant angular accelerations; Sim 4 shows six rotating disks with different combinations of positive, negative, and zero constant angular accelerations and positive, negative, and zero initial angular velocities.

Pointers Position, velocity, and acceleration vectors are the three key concepts of linear kinematics, and the corresponding vector quantities in rotational kinematics are angle, angular velocity, and angular acceleration. The first three simulations are

particularly helpful in sorting out how angular velocity and acceleration are *not* the same thing, just as linear velocity and acceleration are different concepts in one-dimensional kinematics. And like their linear counterparts, direction makes a difference. The figures in the text bar show the standard method for assigning direction to vector quantities in rotational mechanics and stress how different combinations of up and down lead to different rotational motions, just like the linear analog. The last simulation asks you to assign directions to velocity and acceleration vectors for six particular cases. If the answers are hard to determine, this only shows that direction is important and should be considered carefully when completing these types of problems.

7.9 Car Peels Out

The effect of an applied torque on the normal and frictional forces of a moving vehicle are examined.

Layout Application activity; one simulation showing the normal and frictional forces acting on two wheels of a car with an adjustable applied torque; one video with audio clip.

Video: Truck Stops A truck rocks forward as it stops, in agreement with the concepts outlined in this activity.

Pointers Most application problems ask you to calculate a number for a particular quantity. This short application problem focuses on the qualitative effects of an applied torque on other forces acting on an object. For that reason, I recommend completing it before beginning any of the activities requiring numerical calculations. By now you should realize that understanding the physics of a situation is just as important as manipulating equations, and this activity may help you better understand torque and rotational dynamics and therefore do a better job of understanding and setting up rotational dynamics problems.

7.10 Rotoride—A Dynamics Approach

Calculate the force needed to produce an acceleration of 0.4 rad/s^2 in a particular rotating system.

Layout Application activity; two matched simulations. Sim 1 shows the motion; Sim 2 presents the full solution to the problem, including kinematic data and an energy bar chart.

Pointers This activity effectively demonstrates how to solve rotational dynamics problems. Compare the method for rotational dynamics to the method learned for linear dynamics in Unit 2.

A step-by-step solution to the problem is given in the text bar.

7.11 Falling Ladder

Calculate the angular acceleration of a falling ladder at a particular position given its mass and length.

Layout Application activity; two simulations. Sim 1 shows the motion; Sim 2 presents the full solution to the problem.

Pointers The text bar and Adviser sections present all the information needed to solve the word problem. Notice that the normal force decreases as the ladder falls and the forces *do not* sum to zero because the ladder is not in static equilibrium. In the same way, the angular acceleration is not constant because the torque is not constant.

7.12 Woman and Flywheel Elevator—Dynamics Approach

Calculate the speed of a person at a particular position who is falling while attached to a flywheel.

Layout Application activity; three matched simulations. Sim 1 shows the motion; Sim 2 adds forces vectors and accelerations; Sim 3 adds position, time, and velocity data.

Pointers This is the rotational version of the Atwood machine (see Activity 2.14), where the vertical (linear) acceleration (a_y) of the person is related to the angular acceleration of the flywheel (α) by the relation $a_y = \alpha r$, where r is the radius of the flywheel. A step-by-step solution is included in the text bar.

Rotational Energy

7.13 Race Between a Block and a Brick

A race between two objects of the same mass, with one rolling and the other sliding without friction, is used to introduce the concept of rotational kinetic energy.

Layout Introductory activity; one video and audio clip; two simulations; one work-energy bar chart. Sim 1 shows the race between a rolling disk and a sliding brick; Sim 2 adds work-energy bar charts for each object.

Video: Spinning Toy In a spinning toy, gravitational potential energy is converted into rotational kinetic energy and then back again in a manner analogous to a simple pendulum.

Pointers The two moving objects demonstrate the need for a rotational kinetic energy term, but the reason why such an energy should exist isn't given

in this investigation. One possible response could be that if other linear quantities like force and acceleration have rotational analogs, then kinetic energy ($KE = \frac{1}{2}mv^2$) should have one as well ($KE_{rot} = \frac{1}{2}I\omega^2$). A better answer is based on a discussion of the motion of point-masses in a rigid body. In any case, this activity is short and makes its point well, and no calculations are made.

7.14 Woman and Flywheel Elevator—Energy Approach

Calculate the speed of a person at a particular position who is falling while attached to a flywheel.

Layout Application activity; three matched simulations; one work-energy bar chart. Sim 1 shows the motion; Sim 2 adds the work-energy bar chart; Sim 3 presents the full solution to the problem.

Pointers Activity 7.12 is repeated using conservation of energy instead of torque and acceleration. Just as the linear acceleration of the person was related to the angular acceleration of the flywheel by the relation $a_y = \alpha r$ in that investigation, now the velocity of the person (v) is related to the angular velocity of the flywheel (ω) by the relation $v = \omega r$ where r is still the radius of the flywheel.

7.15 Rotoride—An Energy Approach

Calculate the time of the first revolution of a rotating system starting from rest acted on by a constant perpendicular force.

Layout Application activity; three matched simulations; one work-energy bar chart. Sim 1 shows the motion; Sim 2 adds a work-energy bar chart; Sim 3 presents the full solution to the problem.

Pointers Conservation of energy is used to calculate average angular velocity, and, from that, the time of one revolution. If work is force times distance, $W = Fx$, then by analogy it can also be calculated as torque times angle, $W = T\theta$.

Angular Momentum Conservation

7.16 Ball Hits Bat

The principle of conservation of angular momentum is illustrated by a ball moving with an initial constant velocity striking a rod rotating with an initial constant angular velocity. The vertical position of the ball and the elasticity of the collision are adjustable.

Layout Introductory activity; five matched simulations. All five simulations show the same animation of a ball striking a bat, but each one provides different numerical information concerning moments of inertia, angular momenta, or velocities of the ball, bat, or system.

Pointers If linear momentum is mass times velocity, $p = mv$, then angular momentum (L) is moment of inertia times angular velocity, $L = I\omega$. As with other rotational counterparts, $I = r \times p$, where r is the vector distance from the center of torque. If the vectors **r** and **p** are perpendicular to each other (as in this case when the ball strikes the bat), then the magnitude of the angular momentum of the object (the ball in this exercise) is $L = mvr$.

7.17 Scattering

The path of a moving object is altered by attractive forces of interaction with a second stationary object.

Layout Application activity; three matched simulations. Sim 1 shows the motion; Sim 2 adds x- and y-coordinates and x- and y-velocity components; Sim 3 shows the angular momentum of the scattered particle. The animation includes adjustable initial speed and vertical position (or impact parameter) of the scattered object.

Pointers The equation for calculating the angular momentum from position and velocity presented in this activity is derived from the matrix definition of the cross product. The most important question asked here is the last one: Why should angular momentum be conserved in this case?

UNIT 8 THERMODYNAMICS

The last three units of *ActivPhysics* depart from the foundations of mechanics—but they don't stray too far. The subject of Unit 8 is thermodynamics, which literally means "heat motion." Two key terms found in thermodynamics are *heat* and *temperature*. Thermodynamics is concerned with how energy flows between objects or "systems" consisting of large collections of particles obeying Newton's laws of motion and the effect of energy flow on the properties of the objects. The scientific term for a "large collection" is "macroscopic ensemble," and the study of the classical dynamics of large ensembles of microscopic particles is the closely related field of statistical mechanics.

Thermodynamics is one rare example in the sciences where experimental data preceded the theory explaining it. The link between thermodynamics and the theoretical subject of statistical mechanics came even later still, but one important result of that link is the kinetic theory of gases. However, to say that thermodynamics is "just" an application of classical dynamics would be like describing a building as "just" a collection of bricks held together by mortar. That definition may be literally correct, but there is much more to our concept of a building than bricks and mortar, and there is much more to the concepts of thermodynamics than matter in motion.

GAME PLAN

As a field of study, thermodynamics ranks with mechanics in terms of its complexity, depth, and interconnectedness. But whereas seven units of *ActivPhysics* were devoted to laying the foundations of mechanics, the subject of thermodynamics is covered in only one unit. This fact reflects the reality of our general physics courses: There simply isn't enough time to do the topic justice. Therefore, I recommend following the lead of your instructor as you decide which activities to explore more than any advice I may give here. If this is a calculus-based course, then there are many activities that present the mathematics in depth. (This is the only unit that presents any equations involving calculus.) On the other hand, if thermodynamics is presented in broad, qualitative terms, then ignore the calculations and focus on the animations, seeing how the principles of thermodynamics apply to different conditions of energy transfer.

There is no agreement among physics instructors on what format should be used to introduce thermodynamics. One approach builds the topic from the ground up by starting with classical dynamics applied to collisions between micro-

scopic particles and generalizing to a macroscopic ensemble. Another approach focuses on experimental variables such as pressure, volume, and temperature, and on practical applications based on thermodynamic processes. (A process is a change in one or more variables of a thermodynamic system caused by an energy transfer.) These two perspectives meet at the ideal gas law, which is a mathematical relationship between the pressure, volume, and temperature of a gas.

The first three activities tackle thermodynamics from a microscopic point of view. Of the three, Activity 8.1 *Characteristics of a Gas* is the easiest to understand, and Activity 8.3 *Maxwell-Boltzmann Distribution—Quantitative Analysis* may be skipped if the course doesn't delve too deeply into the mathematics.

The next three investigations lay the foundations of thermodynamics by introducing the two main players: the properties of a system and the methods of energy transfer. If the ideal gas law is unfamiliar to you, then Activity 8.4 *State Variables and the Ideal Gas Law* should help. This investigation is also central for defining the important variables of pressure, volume, and temperature encountered in the rest of these activities. It also explores the concept of a thermodynamic process in depth and illustrates three important types: constant temperature, or isothermal; constant pressure, or isobaric; and constant volume, or isochoric processes.

There are two primary methods of transferring energy in thermodynamics: work and heat. Activity 8.5 *Work Done by a Gas* explores the meaning of work from a thermodynamics point of view and Activity 8.6 *Heat, Internal Energy, and the First Law of Thermodynamics* examines the concept of heat. Heat is not the same thing as temperature, although the two ideas are related. Activity 8.7 *Heat Capacity* illustrates the relationship between the two by showing that the change in temperature for a given transfer of heat depends on the conditions of the system (heat capacity).

Activity 8.6 concludes with an examination of the three processes defined in Activity 8.4 and shows how each one conserves energy. An adiabatic process is also introduced in that investigation, which is one that doesn't allow for a transfer of heat into or out of the system. Activities 8.8-8.11 explore each of these four processes in greater depth by analyzing the energy transfers and their effect on the total energy of the system and by developing equations relating the state variables for each case.

The unit concludes by combining different processes to create cycles in Activities 8.12 *Cyclic Process—Strategies* and 8.13 *Cyclic Process—Problems*, and the culmination of all this groundwork and preparation is Activity 8.14 *Carnot Cycle*. The Carnot cycle has always been used in physics to explain the second law of thermodynamics—that it is impossible to convert all heat into useful work. The Carnot cycle can also be employed to define the concept of entropy, which is a natural result of the second law, but that is not done in this particular investigation.

THE DETAILS

8.1 Characteristics of a Gas

The path of a single particle in a model of an ideal gas is followed at different temperatures.

Layout　One simulation, showing a collection of point-particles colliding with each other elastically in a two-dimensional box.

Pointers　The fundamental assumption of kinetic-molecular theory is that an ideal gas behaves like a collection of point-particles undergoing perfectly elastic collisions. One result of that assumption is that the temperature of a gas is related to the average kinetic energy of all the particles, which should help you answer Question 5.

8.2 Maxwell–Boltzmann–Distribution Conceptual Analysis,
8.3 Maxwell–Boltzmann–Distribution Quantitative Analysis

The Maxwell-Boltzmann distribution curve is a plot of a statistical average speed (the root mean square speed, or v_{rms}) on the x-axis versus the number of particles in the system having that speed on the y-axis. The basic characteristics of the distribution are explained, and the effect of temperature on the shape of the curve is explored in these two investigations.

Layout　Introductory activities; the same simulation for both activities shows a collection of point-particles colliding with each other elastically in a two-dimensional box and includes a graph of the distribution of kinetic energies of the particles in the model.

Pointers　The Maxwell-Boltzmann distribution is the connection between classical mechanics and the laws and equations of thermodynamics. It is important to have a clear understanding of what the distribution is and how to correctly interpret it; however, it is not necessary to work through all of the mathematics. Students in an algebra-based course should follow the lead of the course instruc-

tor; physics majors and preengineering students in a calculus-based course should definitely study all of this material carefully.

8.4　State Variables and the Ideal Gas Law

The qualitative relationships between pressure, volume, and temperature of an ideal gas are displayed through appropriate animations before presenting the ideal gas equation. The graphical relationships between pairs of the state variables are deduced and the concept of a thermodynamic cycle is depicted.

Layout　Six simulations. Sim 1 shows a gas particle model; Sim 2 includes a movable wall. Sims 3, 4, and 5 show the behavior of gases with constant pressure, constant volume, or constant temperature, respectively, while the other two variables change; and Sim 6 shows the path of a cyclic process.

Pointers　This is a very long activity that presents a number of important concepts, and almost all of the remaining activities of this unit rely on the ideas illustrated in this investigation. The first half of the investigation develops the ideal gas law. Consider referring to a chemistry textbook for a further explanation of this important equation of state. The empirical gas laws that are the subject of the second half this investigation will also be discussed in the same chapter.

8.5　Work Done by a Gas

Positive and negative work are visualized by a movable piston.

Layout　Four simulations. Sims 1 and 2 show an ideal gas acted on by a movable piston; Sims 3 and 4 show pressure-vs.-volume diagrams for different processes.

Pointers　This activity explores the concept of work from a thermodynamics point of view. The first two simulations present the major concepts quite clearly; the last two simulations involve calculations of work done from graphs. The advice given under the Pointers for Activities 8.2 and 8.3 concerning the mathematics apply here as well.

8.6　Heat, Internal Energy, and the First Law of Thermodynamics

The relationships between the macroscopic concepts of heat and temperature are related to perfectly elastic collisions between the microscopic particles of an ideal gas. The principle of conservation of energy between any particular microscopic collision is generalized to the first law of thermodynamics.

Layout Introductory activity; one simulation.

Pointers This investigation begins by illustrating how the dynamics of elastic collisions on the microscopic scale are connected to the concept of heat flow and thermodynamic state variables, especially temperature. Three important principles are stressed in this activity. First, the average kinetic energy of the particles in a gas is proportional to the temperature of the gas. Second, energy may be transferred into or out of a system by one of two methods, either as work or heat. Third, because energy must be conserved, the sum of the work and heat must equal the change in the internal energy of the system, which for an ideal gas is the sum of all the kinetic energy of the gas particles. This last statement is the first law of thermodynamics.

8.7 Heat Capacity

Equations for the change in the temperature of a gas as heat is added to the gas (the heat capacity) under either constant-pressure or constant-temperature conditions is illustrated by appropriate animations.

Layout One simulation, showing heat, work, kinetic energy, and internal energy as a function of time as an ideal gas is heated under either constant-pressure or constant-volume conditions.

Pointers An algebra-based physics course rarely includes a discussion of heat capacity, and it may not even be mentioned in a calculus-based course. The most important conclusion of this activity is to realize that heat and temperature are not the same thing, but they are related through heat capacity. The fact that heat capacity depends on the conditions of heat transfer demonstrates that these two quantities cannot be measuring the same thing.

8.8 Isochoric Process,
8.9 Isobaric Process,
8.10 Isothermal Process,
8.11 Adiabatic Process

Changes in heat, work, and internal energy are visualized for constant volume (isochoric), constant-pressure (isobaric), and constant-temperature (isothermal) conditions, and for the case where no heat is transferred into or out of the system (adiabatic).

Layout One simulation with one bar chart each. The simulation visualizes an ideal gas under appropriate external conditions, with a graph showing the functional relationship between two of the three state variables and an energy bar chart showing changes in work, heat, and internal energy.

Pointers All four investigations follow the same format. Each activity repeats the qualitative results first shown in Activity 8.6, but in each one the mathematical equation for the change in internal energy for each process as a function of the state variables is also presented. Other mathematical relationships, such as the work done or the heat transferred (see Activity 8.7 on heat capacity), may also be included depending on the process. Each activity includes a number of calculations using the appropriate equations. All four of these activities are intended to lead into the last three activities on cyclic processes.

8.12 Cyclic Process—Strategies,
8.13 Cyclic Process—Problems

Work, heat, and changes in the internal energy are calculated for a thermodynamic system as it undergoes changes in pressure and volume. Activity 8.12 presents all the calculations for a series of changes represented by a rectangular path on a pressure-vs.-volume graph; Activity 8.13 requires similar calculations for three other triangular paths on the P vs. V diagram.

Layout Application activity, one simulation showing the path of a thermodynamic engine on a pressure-vs.-volume graph, and a bar chart showing the work, heat, and changes in internal energy as the system moves along the path.

Pointers A cyclic process (or engine) is one that takes a thermodynamic system through a series of energy transfers that change the properties of the system and yet return the system to its original properties when all energy transfers are completed. Although the processes in these activities are somewhat artificial, they are a prelude to a more realistic one in the last activity of the unit, *The Carnot Cycle*.

You should recognize two key concepts from these activities: First, all energy changes can be calculated from the properties of a system only; and second, the calculated values of heat, work, and internal energy confirm the first law. The pressure-vs.-volume graph is called a phase diagram in thermodynamics. Phase diagrams are useful because they help track energy transfers that are necessary for calculating thermodynamic efficiencies. It was the whole question of maximum efficiency of an engine that led to the development of the science of thermodynamics. That issue will be addressed in the last activity.

Videos: Engine—1, Engine—2, Engine—3 Each video shows an apparatus that produces mechanical work by heat transfer from a hot temperature source to a cool temperature source.

Pointers for the videos An engine converts heat energy into mechanical energy, but energy flow causes changes in state variables. If, for example, the desired result is to have a piston expand, then the piston must return to its initial state so it can expand again. If the piston simply returned to its initial state by contracting along the same path it took as it expanded, then by the first law any work gained by the expansion would have to be returned to the system by the compression.

That is the reason why cyclic processes are needed. A cycle returns a system to its initial conditions but by a different path. For example, an isothermal expansion may be followed by an adiabatic expansion. Both expansions would do work, but each would do a different amount of work. To get the system back to where it started from, these two processes may be followed first by an isothermal contraction and then by an adiabatic contraction. Because the expansion paths will be different from the contraction paths, the amount of work done by the gas will *not* be the same as the amount of work done on the gas. The overall result is that heat has been converted into work.

That is why cyclic processes are important: They are the heart and soul of thermodynamic applications in physics.

8.14 Carnot Cycle

Heat, work, and internal energy changes are calculated for each of the four processes of the Carnot cycle and the efficiency of the cycle is determined, which is found to be a function *only* of the two operating temperatures of the engine.

Layout Application activity; one simulation modeling the behavior of an ideal gas following the Carnot cycle, which is simultaneously traced out on a pressure-volume graph.

Pointers Cyclic processes allow for a conversion of heat into work, as demonstrated by the equations of Activities 8.8–8.11 applied to cyclic processes in Activities 8.12 and 8.13. The measure of the percentage of heat that may be converted into work is the efficiency of the cycle, and the Carnot cycle is the simplest and also the most efficient of any possible heat engine. One of the major discoveries of thermodynamics, which is clearly demonstrated by the Carnot cycle, is that it is physically impossible to have a 100% conversion of heat into work. This principle is now known as the second law of thermodynamics.

The discovery of this mathematical fact by Carnot dismayed contemporary scientists, who were trying to build better engines. It is hard to accept the fact that you can't always get what you want. On the other hand, the second law is also the reason why heat spontaneously flows from a hot body to a cold body, and without that basic principle no engine could ever be guaranteed to work as expected.

UNIT 9   VIBRATIONS

Vibrational motion is an extremely important application of Newton's laws. Imagine a pointlike object at rest and in equilibrium, so that the sum of all the forces acting on it is zero. Now suppose that whenever the object moves off its equilibrium position in any direction, a net "restoring force" acts opposite to the displacement, pushing it back toward the equilibrium point. If the object is pulled away from its equilibrium point and released, the net force will cause an acceleration toward the equilibrium point. Since the object will have a nonzero velocity as it reaches the equilibrium point, by Newton's first law it will continue moving. However, the restoring force will now act on it again in the opposite direction, causing it to accelerate back toward the equilibrium point, and the result is vibrational motion.

One of the simplest mathematical models of vibrational motion is to assume that the magnitude of restoring force is proportional to the displacement of the object, which is known as Hooke's law. It can be shown from calculus that an object following Hooke's law will trace out a sine or a cosine curve over time (see Activity 9.1). Another name for this type of vibrational motion is simple harmonic motion.

This unit of *ActivPhysics* explores the key concepts and equations of vibrational motion, including the kinematic equations describing simple harmonic motion, the concepts of period and frequency, and the vibrational motion of a pendulum. Because vibrational motion is another application of mechanics, many of the concepts developed in previous units are also used in these activities. Even so, vibrations are an important phenomenon found in many fields of physics.

GAME PLAN

Unit 9 on Vibrations combines many of the best features of previous units. Activity 9.1 *Position Graphs and Equations* animates simple harmonic motion and lets you manipulate the three parameters of vibrations in order to see the effects on the motion. I recommend viewing this investigation either before reading the text or immediately after the concept of vibrational motion is introduced. It is generally short, especially if you skip the section on velocity and acceleration.

Activity 9.2 *Describing Vibrational Motion* builds on the concepts presented in the first activity and focuses on the particular conditions of the turning points of the motion. The relationships between position, velocity, and acceleration for vibrational motion are examined in detail. Activity

9.3 *Vibrational Energy* uses the concepts of Unit 5 to explore energy exchanges in vibrational motion. Consider doing just the first three questions and completing the second half at a later time, as needed. All three of these investigations should increase your understanding of the fundamental behavior of vibrating systems.

Activities 9.4–9.9 are application problems that employ a combination of Hooke's law, equations from kinematics, and conservation of energy to solve for unknown quantities. Activities 9.5 *Ape Drops Tarzan*, 9.6 *Releasing a Vibrating Skier I*, and 9.7 *Releasing a Vibrating Skier II* are a great set of concept problems that consider how a sudden change in mass would affect the physics of vibrational motion. It may be worth while to complete all three consecutively. On the other hand, Activity 9.4 *Two Ways to Weigh Young Tarzan* is an excellent follow-up to 9.3 *Vibrational Energy*, which shows how both frequency and energy can be employed to find the same answer to a problem. Activity 9.9 *Vibro-Ride* is another solid application problem.

Activities 9.10–9.13 explore another vibrating system, the pendulum. These investigations should help you sort out the key concepts of vibrational motion and see both the similarities and differences between the pendulum and the motion of a mass on a spring. Activity 9.10 *Pendulum Frequency* develops the relationship between vibrational frequency and the variables present in a pendulum, and Activity 9.11 *Pendulum Timer* is a quick and simple application of the equation. Activity 9.12 *Risky Pendulum Walk* is another application problem based on the regular motion of the pendulum, and Activity 9.13 *Physical Pendulum* examines real pendulums in depth.

Activity 9.13 and the remaining investigations of this unit can all be considered supplementary. There is rarely time in a physics course to examine the physical pendulum or to explore the topic in Activity 9.8, *One- and Two-Spring Vibrating Systems*. (Another important physics topic, resonance, is shown in the video clip in Activity 9.10.) The final activity, 9.14 *The Sweet Spot*, is quite informative on a topic that should be of interest to tennis players, ball players, or golfers.

THE DETAILS

9.1 Position Graphs and Equations

The concepts of amplitude, frequency, and phase-shift angle are visualized by comparing the motion of vibrating blocks that change only one of these variables at a time. Equations of motion are deduced for two blocks based on simulation data. The activity concludes with a discussion of velocity and acceleration in vibrating systems.

Layout Introductory activity; five simulations, Sim 4 and Sim 5 matched. Sim 1 compares two blocks with different amplitudes; Sim 2 compares two blocks with different frequencies; Sim 3 compares three blocks with different phase-shift angles. Sim 4 shows two blocks with different equations of motion; Sim 5 includes velocities and accelerations for each. Sim 5 is found under the Question 6 Advisor.

Pointers This investigation is an excellent starting point for any study of vibrations. After completing it, you will have no doubt about the meaning of amplitude, frequency, and phase shift for vibrational motion. You may choose to skip Questions 5 and 6 on velocity and acceleration if they are not course learning objectives or if the course is not calculus-based.

9.2 Describing Vibrational Motion

The amplitude, period, and frequency of a vibrating block are determined from a simulation of its motion. Position-vs.-time, velocity-vs.-time, and acceleration-vs.-time graphs are constructed and compared.

Layout Application activity; seven matched simulations; one audio clip. Sim 1 shows a vibrating block; Sim 2 adds its position graph; Sim 3 (= Sim 4) adds a velocity graph; Sim 5 (= Sim 6) adds an acceleration graph. Sim 7 is found under the summary and is similar to Sim 5 without the force vector.

Pointers The derivative method for finding velocity and acceleration in a vibrating system is clearly explained. Even if graphing vibrational motion is not a course objective, it may be worthwhile to examine Sims 5 and 6 so that you can see the relationships between these quantities for a vibrating system. Knowing how these quantities relate to each other may help you solve some application problems in the text.

9.3 Vibrational Energy

The relationship between kinetic and potential energy in a vibrating system at different times is developed, and the conservation of energy equation for the motion is presented. An understanding of the equation is tested by solving for the amplitude, the force constant, or the speed of a block at a certain time in three different application problems.

Layout Introductory activity; 11 simulations, 3 matched sets; 3 energy bar charts. Sim 1 (= Sim 2) shows a vibrating block; Sim 3 adds energy bar charts; Sim 4 includes position and velocity data. Sim 5 begins with a similar block but with different parameters and includes position and velocity data; Sim 6 adds energy bar charts; Sim 7 reports the value of the force constant. Sim 8 shows a third block; Sim 9 adds energy bar charts; Sim 10 includes position and velocity data. Sim 11 shows damped motion, including a graph of the different energies as a function of time.

Pointers This is a long investigation (11 simulations!), but it can be completed in three parts. In the first part (Question 3), maximum amplitude is calculated; in the second part (Question 4), the force constant is found; in the third part (Question 5), the maximum speed of the block is deduced. The last simulation showing damped motion is another example of an *ActivPhysics* simulation exploring a topic more clearly and in greater depth than is possible in a standard textbook.

9.4 Two Ways to Weigh Young Tarzan

The mass of Tarzan Jr. is calculated by the frequency approach developed in Activities 9.1 and 9.2 and by the energy approach of Activity 9.3.

Layout Application activity; three matched simulations; one audio clip. Sim 1 shows Tarzan Jr. vibrating on a spring and provides some information; Sim 2 is the same as Sim 1 but with different information; Sim 3 presents the full answer to the problem.

Pointers This is an excellent yet simple word problem. Once you have completed it, you should have no doubt as to how to work these types of problems. Some of the data must be obtained from the simulation in order to obtain the solution, but try to solve it first without reading the hints and explanations written under the questions in the text bar.

9.5 Ape Drops Tarzan

How do the velocity and acceleration of a bouncing ape change after he drops Tarzan? How does a change in total mass affect these vibrational quantities?

Layout Application activity; three matched simulations. Sim 1 shows an ape and Tarzan vibrating on a spring; Sim 2 (= Sim 3) is located under the answers to the two questions and shows what happens after Tarzan is released.

Pointers This is a straightforward conceptual problem that tests your understanding of the physics of vibration. Although not asked for in the activity, can you explain why the position-vs.-time graph behaves the way it does?

9.6 Releasing a Vibrating Skier I,
9.7 Releasing a Vibrating Skier II

Predict how amplitude, frequency, and speed change when a skier releases from a spring at its maximum extension (9.6) or from its equilibrium position (9.7).

Layout Application activities; two matched simulations each. Sim 1 shows a vibrating skier who plans to release; Sim 2, located in the summary, shows what happens after release.

Pointers These are two similar conceptual problems. Compare these problems with Activity 9.5. Why are the results different? Can you also explain the speed of the skier when she releases in each case?

9.8 One- and Two-Spring Vibrating Systems

How does the motion of a block connected to two springs instead of just one (all having the same spring constant) affect the speed and frequency of the motion? The activity concludes with a video investigation comparing these two systems.

Layout Application activity; four simulations, two matched sets; two videos with audio clips. Sim 1 shows one vibrating block; Sim 2 adds numerical results. Sim 3 shows two vibrating blocks, one connected to a single spring and the other connected to two springs; Sim 3 adds velocity-vs.-time graphs to show how their motions compare.

Videos: Vibrating Cart on an Incline—1, Vibrating Cart on an Incline—2 The behavior of the blocks in the simulations is repeated for two carts connected to the same spring combinations presented in the activity.

Pointers Multiple-spring systems are an important and fascinating physical phenomenon that rarely get appropriate attention in an introductory physics course because of time limitations. Invest 5 minutes of your time to investigate this problem, especially if you liked Activity 9.5 *Ape Drops Tarzan* or Activities 9.6 and 9.7 *Releasing a Vibrating Skier I and II*. Those investigations explored the effect of changes in mass on vibrational motion, but what is the effect of a change in spring constant on the motion? (The results are related to the behavior of resistors in electrical circuits, of all things!)

9.9 Vibro-Ride

Find the amplitude and period of vibrating system after a skier attaches to a spring.

Layout Application activity; three matched simulations; one audio clip. Sim 1 shows the Vibro-ride; Sim 2, found under the answer to Question 2, adds bar charts; Sim 3 is the full solution.

Pointers This is one of only two word problems on simple harmonic motion in this unit (the other is Activity 9.4). The text bar provides a clear method of solution, but try to solve the problem without any help after viewing the simulation and reading the description of the problem.

9.10 Pendulum Frequency

Mass and spring constant determine the natural frequency of a spring system, but what factors determine the natural frequency of a pendulum?

Layout Introductory activity; one audio clip; six simulations in three matched sets; one video clip with audio. Sim 1 shows three pendula with different masses; Sim 2 adds force vectors to each pendulum. Sim 3 shows three pendula with different amplitudes; Sim 4 adds force vectors to each pendulum. Sim 5 shows three pendula with different string lengths, Sim 6 adds force vectors to each pendulum.

Video: Selective Pendulum Swinging The frequency of swinging of a rod causes some pendula to begin to swing but not others.

Pointers This is a very simple and straightforward activity that visualizes almost all the key aspects of pendulum motion. The concept of resonance is introduced in the video. After you run the simulations, I recommend that you get some washers and a piece of string and prove these results to yourself with a real experiment.

9.11 Pendulum Timer

The length of a pendulum on a planet with a different gravitational constant than Earth is calculated in order to create a pendulum with a period of exactly 3 s.

Layout Application activity; one simulation, showing a moving pendulum bob.

Pointers This problem is easy to solve if you have the equation relating the frequency of a pendulum to all pertinent physical variables. It is not given here, but it can be found in any textbook.

9.12 Risky Pendulum Walk

At what constant speed must the person in the simulation walk to avoid getting bopped by a swinging pendulum?

Layout Application activity; one simulation, showing a person and a moving pendulum bob.

Pointers The Advisor has all the information you need to complete this investigation. Observe what happens to the walker if you set the wrong speed!

9.13 Physical Pendulum

The mathematics behind real pendulums is examined.

Layout Supplementary activity; two matched simulations. Sim 1 shows two swinging pendulums (one is a rod); Sim 2 adds force vectors.

Pointers I especially recommend this activity for engineering students. As with Activity 9.10, the results can easily be verified by conducting the experiment.

9.14 The Sweet Spot

What is the sweet spot, and why should a golfer, tennis player, or baseball player care?

Layout Supplementary activity; one simulation, showing balls striking three bats at different locations.

Pointers A fun and simple real-life application that combines collisions, rotational motion, and center of mass. The hands in the simulation are *not* actually holding on to the bats.

UNIT 10 WAVES

The topic of waves is a close companion to the subject of vibrations. Unit 9 explored systems with a restoring force that caused vibrational motion. If a disturbance such as a vibration is able to propagate (or travel through) a medium, then a wave is formed. For that reason, many concepts from the previous study of vibrations such as frequency and amplitude are also present in this unit, but new concepts such as wavelength are added to the description.

A simple working definition of a medium is a material consisting of pointlike objects connected to each other by forces. The physical properties of a medium, including the strength of the restoring forces, determine how quickly waves move through it. On the other hand, it is also possible to show that the product of the frequency of a wave and its wavelength must also equal the speed of the wave in the medium; this relationship is known as the wave equation. Other important concepts covered in this unit include the principle of superposition, which explains what happens when two waves in the same medium meet; a special consequence of that concept, standing wave motion; and the Doppler effect.

GAME PLAN

There are a number of working models in this unit, including Activities 10.1–10.4, 10.7, and 10.10. Although not structured as a self-contained tutorial like Unit 3, the supplementary activities found here will clarify the concepts of wave motion through simple and accurate visualizations.

Definitely begin with Activity 10.1 *Properties of Mechanical Waves*. The three animated models pictured in the simulation will make written descriptions of waves much more understandable. Activities 10.2 *Speed of Waves on a String* and 10.3 *Speed of Sound in a Gas* will be of greater interest to engineering students and can be skipped without loss of continuity. Activity 10.4 *Standing Waves on a String*, however, is a fundamental one because standing wave motion is an extremely important concept in physics. The equations derived in Activity 10.2 are summarized in this activity or may be found in just about any general physics textbook.

The next two Activities, 10.5 *Tuning a Stringed Instrument: Standing Waves* and 10.6 *String Mass and Standing Waves*, are solid applications of standing wave motion and should be explored if this type of problem might be encountered on an exam. The same advice applies to Activities 10.8 and 10.9 on the *Doppler Effect*: It depends on the emphasis your instructor has placed on that material.

The remaining two activities, 10.7 *Beats and Beat Frequency* and 10.10 *Complex Waves: Fourier Analysis*, are supplementary investigations. As with other investigations of this type, they are interesting and important real-life applications of physics concepts, but completing them probably won't improve any exam score. Explore them based on your own time and interest.

THE DETAILS

10.1 Properties of Mechanical Waves

The concepts of transverse and longitudinal waves; the relationships between amplitude, frequency, and wave speed; and the wave equation are visualized for three different mediums: water waves, sound waves, and waves on strings.

Layout Introductory activity; one simulation. Sim 1 allows you to choose a string, air, or water as a medium and shows both a pulse and a continuous wave, both with adjustable frequency and amplitude.

Pointers This activity demonstrates and clarifies most of the important concepts of wave motion. Although we tend to think of periodic waves as wave motion, this investigation clearly shows that pulses also meet the definition of waves.

10.2 Speed of Waves on a String,
10.3 Speed of Sound in a Gas

The two factors that determine the speed of a wave through a material—one forcelike, the other masslike—are explored for waves in strings, metal rods, and air.

Layout Introductory activities, with one simulation common to both. Sim 1 allows you to choose a medium of string, a metal rod, or air and view the motion of a wave through the medium. Slide adjusters are used to change the physical properties of the medium.

Pointers The wave equation shows how frequency and wavelength are related to the speed of a wave, but it is the properties of the medium that determine what that speed must be. This investigation will make more sense to you if the physics course has included a chapter on the properties of materials (stress and strain, bulk modulus, and Young's modulus), but that knowledge is not necessary to understand the idea that every medium has a force or forcelike property and a mass or masslike property. It is the interplay of these two properties that determine the speed of the wave through the material.

Activity 10.2 explores waves on a string where the two properties are tension and mass per unit length; Activity 10.3 explores sound in a gas where the two properties are bulk modulus and density. A third medium, a solid rod (where the two properties are Young's modulus and density) is included but not discussed directly. After examining the other two materials, you will see the similarities between them and the metal rod.

10.4 Standing Waves on a String

Resonant standing wave patterns are created for a vibrating string, and the concept of a fundamental frequency and its harmonics is explored.

Layout Introductory activity; two videos; one simulation showing a vibrating string with adjustable tension, mass per unit length, and frequency.

Videos: Standing Wave Patterns—1, Standing Wave Patterns—2 The first video shows the production of standing waves on a coiled spring. The second video is an animation that shows the patterns and plays audio for the fundamental and the first two harmonics of a sound wave.

Pointers If a wave is able to reflect off the end of a medium, then it is possible to form a standing wave pattern. The necessary condition is that the wavelength divided by the length of the medium must be a certain whole-number ratio. The wavelength is determined by the frequency and speed of the medium. The speed, in turn, is fixed by the properties of the medium, which in this simulation are the tension in a string and the mass per unit length. In this activity, the properties of the medium and applied frequency may be adjusted to create standing wave patterns.

This is another example of an *ActivPhysics* investigation that can easily be reproduced as a laboratory experiment, as well as one that explains its topic in much greater depth than most textbooks. The second video in particular is very effective at showing standing wave patterns and their interrelationships.

10.5 Tuning a Stringed Instrument: Standing Waves, 10.6 String Mass and Standing Waves

Tension and mass per unit length are varied for the system shown in Activity 10.4 to explore how a string may be tuned to a particular frequency by varying these two quantities.

Layout Exploratory activities; one simulation, the same as in Activity 10.4. Activity 10.6 has an audio clip.

Pointers Activity 10.4 demonstrated the basic principles of standing waves; these two activities apply those ideas to the same system through the adjustment of frequency or mass per unit length to create a particular result. The investigations require you to link different equations through common terms or variables.

10.7 Beats and Beat Frequency

The principles of beats and beat frequency are visualized and explored, and the concept of a complex wave is introduced.

Layout Supplemental activity; one simulation, four video clips, one audio clip. Sim 1 shows two simple harmonic waves with adjustable frequencies and their sum.

Videos: Beats Near 256 Hz, Beats Near 440 Hz Video clips 1 and 2 produce a progression of beats as two sound waves approach a common frequency (256 Hz or 440 Hz). Video 3 is an introduction to complex waves and shows the waveforms produced by the vowel *o* and the vowel *e*. Video 4 is a laboratory investigation using two speakers with different frequencies and an oscilloscope to demonstrate the beat patterns seen in the simulation.

Pointers Few general physics texts devote more than a page to beat frequency, and this investigation is an effective visualization of how the superposition principle applied to two waves with close but not exact frequencies inevitably leads to a beat pattern. Moreover, the video clips allow you *hear* beats, which no textbook can do.

10.8 Doppler Effect: Conceptual Introduction, 10.9 Doppler Effect: Problems

The concept of the Doppler effect and the reasons for this property of waves in mediums are developed in the first activity, and the equations that describe the Doppler effect are applied to particular conditions in the second activity in order to calculate frequency shifts caused by moving sources and receivers.

Layout An introductory and an application activity; both activities employ the same simulation showing a moving source and listener. Both speeds and source frequency are adjustable. Activity 10.8 includes an audio clip.

Pointers Activity 10.8 explores different combinations of sound source and listener speeds to develop a qualitative rule concerning how the directions of motion may cause higher or lower frequency shifts. It may be helpful to begin with Questions 5 and 6 where either listener or source is at rest while the other moves. The workbook is very helpful for this exercise, which concludes with the full Doppler equation.

In Activity 10.9, frequency shifts are calculated for seven different source/listener speeds and source frequencies, and the results are checked by setting those conditions in the simulation. The last question includes the subject of beats.

10.10 Complex Waves: Fourier Analysis

The properties and formation of complex waves are explored by demonstrating how square, triangular, and other waveforms can be built from appropriate sets of a simple harmonic wave fundamental and its harmonics.

Layout Supplementary activity; one simulation, one video. Sim 1 shows how harmonic waves can add to different waveforms by adjusting amplitudes.

Video: Sawtooth Wave Changes in sound are identifiable as a sawtooth wave is built up in steps from a fundamental and its harmonics.

Pointers Engineering students in particular should explore this activity, especially those considering electrical engineering or acoustical engineering.

PART III

ActivPhysics 1 Workbook

ALAN VAN HEUVELEN

10. WAVES

DESCRIBING MOTION

A motion diagram uses a series of dots and arrows to represent the changing position, velocity, and acceleration of an object.

Advantages of Motion Diagrams:

* They help you develop mental images and intuition about the meaning of the kinematics quantities used to describe motion.

* They help you understand the signs of these quantities, especially when the quantities have negative signs.

* They are useful for checking the values of kinematics quantities when you are solving problems.

Examples of Motion Diagrams for Constant Acceleration (positive direction toward the right):

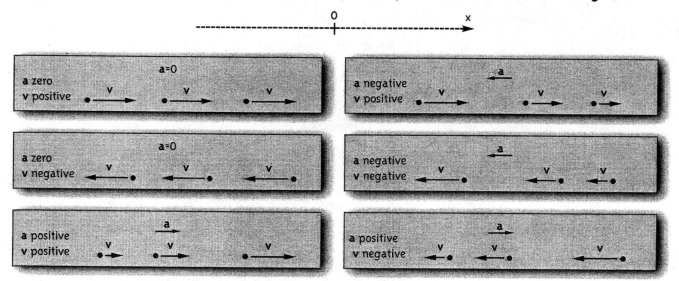

Rules for Constructing Motion Diagrams:

* The position dots indicate the location of the object at equal time intervals.

* The separation of adjacent position dots indicates roughly the average speed of the object in that time interval.

* $a = \Delta v / \Delta t$, and the direction of the acceleration arrow represents the change in the velocity Δv from one position to the next.

* The sign of the velocity or acceleration depends on the direction of the arrow relative to the coordinate axis (the positive direction is toward the right in these examples).

Question 1 — Meaning of x_0 : Set the initial velocity and acceleration sliders to zero and try different initial position settings. What is the meaning of x_0?

Question 2 — Meaning of v_0: Set the initial position and acceleration sliders to zero and try different initial velocity settings. What is the meaning of v_0 and v?

Question 3 — Meaning of a: Set the initial position to -48 m and the initial velocity to zero. Try different positive acceleration settings. How does the change in velocity each second relate to the acceleration?

Question 4 — Acceleration and Time: Set the initial position to -48 m and the initial velocity to + 12 m/s. Try different negative accelerations starting at - 1.0 m/s². Predict the time interval needed to stop the car.

Question 5 — Meaning of Negative a if v Is Negative: Set the initial position to +48 m and the initial velocity to zero. Try different negative accelerations. What does negative a imply about the motion if the object has a negative velocity? Start with a = -1.0 m/s².

Question 6 — Meaning of Positive a if v is Negative : Set the initial position to +48 m and the initial velocity to -12.0 m/s. Try different positive accelerations. Predict the time interval needed for the car to stop.

Question 7:

For each problem in Question 7, first run the simulation. Then adjust the initial position, the initial velocity, and the acceleration sliders so that the car has the same motion as the white dot. You should get the signs of the quantities correct on the first try but may need to experiment to get the exact values correct. After matching the motion, draw a motion diagram as a reminder of the motion that occurred.

Problem 1:

Initial slider-setting predictions:

$x_0 =$
$v_0 =$
$a =$

Slider settings that matched motion:

$x_0 =$
$v_0 =$
$a =$

Motion diagram that describes the motion:

Problem 2:

Initial slider-setting predictions:

$x_0 =$
$v_0 =$
$a =$

Slider settings that matched motion:

$x_0 =$
$v_0 =$
$a =$

Motion diagram that describes the motion:

Problem 3:

Initial slider-setting predictions:

$x_0 =$
$v_0 =$
$a =$

Slider settings that matched motion:

$x_0 =$
$v_0 =$
$a =$

Motion diagram that describes the motion:

Problem 4:

Initial slider-setting predictions:

$x_0 =$
$v_0 =$
$a =$

Slider settings that matched motion:

$x_0 =$
$v_0 =$
$a =$

Motion diagram that describes the motion:

The motion of a car is represented by motion diagrams and graphs. You can choose the motion by adjusting sliders for

- the initial position x_0
- the initial velocity v_0
- the acceleration

Answer the following questions and check your work by adjusting the sliders and running the simulation. The graphs that you are asked to draw are qualitative — don't worry about the detailed numbers.

Question 1— Initial Position: Describe in words the meaning of the quantity "initial position x_0."
Draw an x-vs-t graph for $x_0 = -8$ m, $v_0 = 0$, and $a = 0$.

Question 2 — Velocity and Changing Value of x: Draw x-vs-t and v-vs-t graphs for $x_0 = 0$, $v_0 = -4$ m/s and $a = 0$.
Predict the position x readings at $t = 0$ s, 1 s, 2 s, and 3 s.

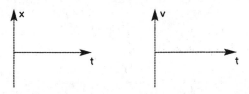

Velocity and Position-Versus-Time Graph: Draw the following x-vs-t and v-vs-t graphs.

(a) $x_0 = 0$, $v_0 = +2$ m/s, $a = 0$

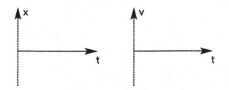

(b) $x_0 = 0$ m, $v_0 = +6$ m/s, $a = 0$

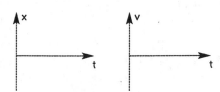

(c) $x_0 = 0$, $v_0 = -2$ m/s, $a = 0$

(d) $x_0 = 0$ m, $v_0 = -6$ m/s, $a = 0$

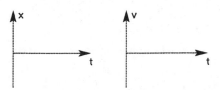

How is the slope of the x-versus-t graph related to the velocity?

Questions 3-4 — Velocity and Acceleration-Versus-Time Graphs: Draw the following graphs.

(a) $x_0 = -15$ m, $v_0 = 0$ m/s, $a = +3$ m/s^2

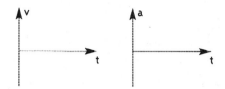

(b) $x_0 = +15$ m, $v_0 = 0$ m/s, $a = -3$ m/s^2

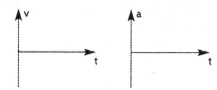

(c) $x_0 = -15$ m, $v_0 = +16$ m/s, $a = -2$ m/s^2

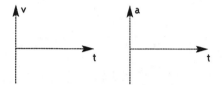

(d) $x_0 = +15$ m, $v_0 = -16$ m/s, $a = +4$ m/s^2

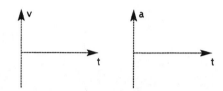

How is the slope of the velocity-versus-time graph related to the acceleration? Check to see if your rule is consistent with each pair of graphs above.

Question 5 — Position, Velocity and Acceleration-Versus-Time Graphs: Draw the following graphs.

(a) $x_0 = +15$ m, $v_0 = -12$ m/s, $a = +3$ m/s^2

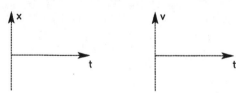

(b) $x_0 = -15$ m, $v_0 = +12$ m/s, $a = -3$ m/s^2

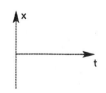

(c) $x_0 = +5$ m, $v_0 = -15$ m/s, $a = +5$ m/s^2

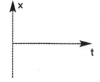

In each of the following five questions, you are first given a position-versus-time graph. From the graph, you are to construct a motion diagram that is qualitatively consistent with the graph. After making the motion diagram, add velocity-versus-time and acceleration-versus-time kinematics graph lines to the position-versus-time graph. (Don't worry about the numbers for the graphs—just the general shapes.) The acceleration is constant.

Question 1:

(a) Construct a qualitative motion diagram that is consistent with the x-vs-t graph.

(b) Construct v-vs-t and a-vs-t graphs that are consistent with the x-vs-t graph.

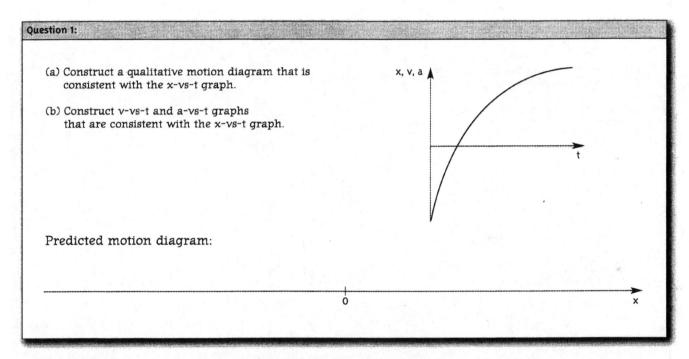

Predicted motion diagram:

Question 2:

(a) Construct a qualitative motion diagram that is consistent with the x-vs-t graph.

(b) Construct v-vs-t and a-vs-t graphs that are consistent with the x-vs-t graph.

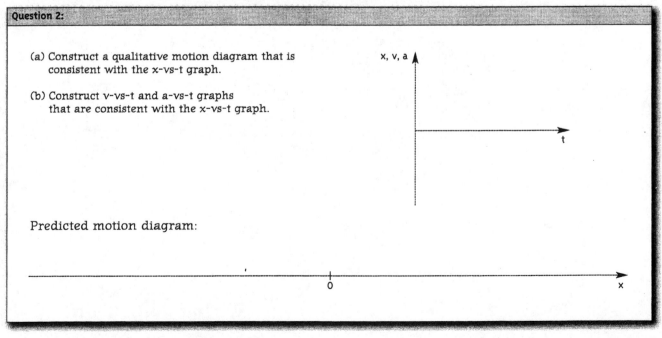

Predicted motion diagram:

Question 3:

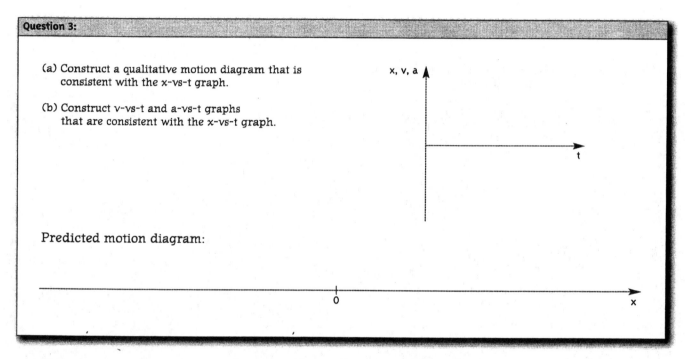

(a) Construct a qualitative motion diagram that is consistent with the x-vs-t graph.

(b) Construct v-vs-t and a-vs-t graphs that are consistent with the x-vs-t graph.

Predicted motion diagram:

Question 4:

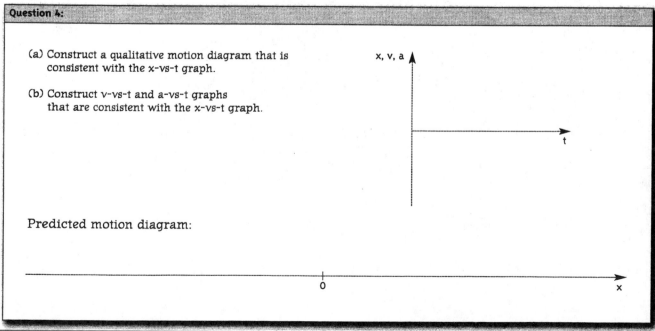

(a) Construct a qualitative motion diagram that is consistent with the x-vs-t graph.

(b) Construct v-vs-t and a-vs-t graphs that are consistent with the x-vs-t graph.

Predicted motion diagram:

Question 5:

(a) Construct a qualitative motion diagram that is consistent with the x-vs-t graph.

(b) Construct v-vs-t and a-vs-t graphs that are consistent with the x-vs-t graph. For your motion diagram, place the dots above the horizontal axis if the object is moving right and below if moving left.

x, v, a

t

Describe the motion:

Kinematics equations describe motion. The equation used in this activity

$$x = x_0 + v_0 t + (1/2) a t^2$$

describes the changing position of an object moving along a straight line with constant acceleration. The questions test your ability to identify the values of x_0, v_0, and a.

Question 1: Run the simulation. You see a car, an equation and a white dot whose motion is described by the equation. Adjust the sliders to make the car move with the same motion as the dot — on the first try.

$$x = +12.0 \text{ m} + (-12.0 \text{ m/s})t + 0.5 (+2.0 \text{ m/s}^2) t^2$$

Question 2: Run the simulation. You see an equation and a white dot whose motion is described by the equation. Adjust the sliders to make the car move with the same motion as the dot — on the first try.

Question 3: Run the simulation. You see an equation and a white dot whose motion is described by the equation. Adjust the sliders to make the car move with the same motion as the dot — on the first try.

Question 4: Run the simulation. You see an equation and a white dot whose motion is described by the equation. Adjust the sliders to make the car move with the same motion as the dot — on the first try.

A car initially travels west at 20 m/s (about 45 mph).
When the car reaches position 60 m, the brakes are
applied and the car's speed decreases at a constant rate
of 5.0 m/s² until the car stops. Describe the process using
a pictorial description, a motion diagram, kinematics
graphs, and kinematics position and velocity equations.
When you are finished, use these descriptions to
determine when and where the car stops.

Question 1 — Pictorial Description: Include a sketch, coordinate axis, symbols, and known values.

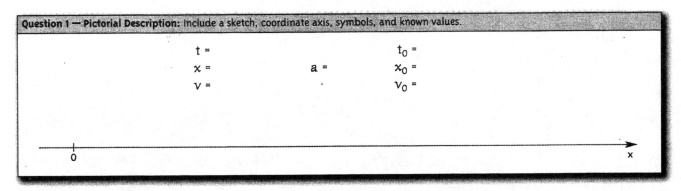

$t =$ $t_0 =$

$x =$ $a =$ $x_0 =$

$v =$ $v_0 =$

Question 2 — Motion Diagram: Draw a motion diagram. Compare arrow directions to the signs of quantities in your pictorial description.

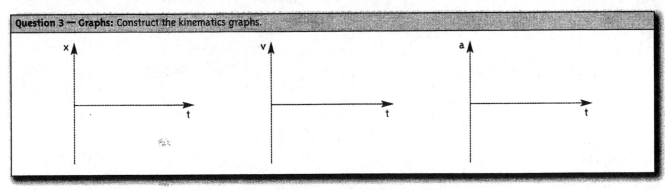

Question 3 — Graphs: Construct the kinematics graphs.

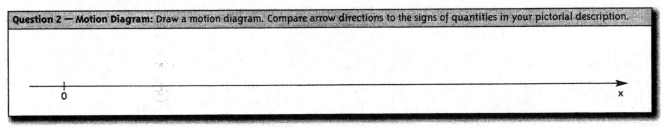

Question 4 — Equations: Use x and v equations to solve for the answer.

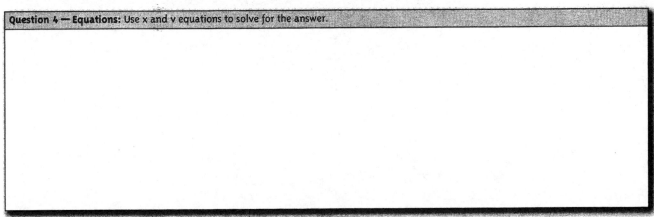

A skier travels 200 m to a finish line, a pole at the last tree. She starts at rest and her speed at the finish line is 31.7 m/s. Describe the process using a pictorial description, a motion diagram, kinematics graphs, and equations. Then determine the time interval needed for the trip and her constant acceleration. (Complete the descriptions below to answer Question 1.)

Question 1: Pictorial Description: Include a sketch, axis, symbols, and values.

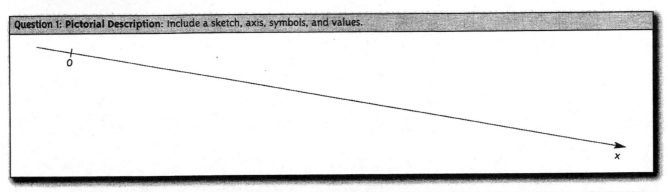

Motion Diagram: Compare directions of arrows to the signs of quantities in your pictorial description.

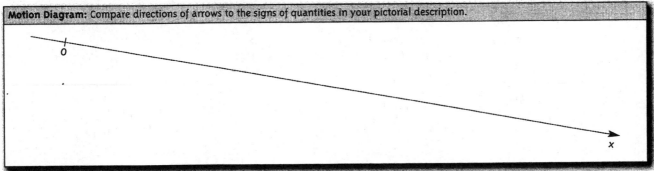

Graphs: Construct the graphs.

Equations: Solve for the answer.

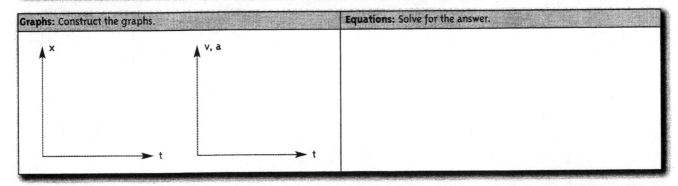

Question 2:

• Move the slider so that the time reads 10.1 s. Note the skier's speed at that time: _____. Also note the skier's acceleration: _____. Relying only on the meaning of acceleration and without using any equations, predict her speed at time 12.7 s.

• After moving the slider to 12.7 s, predict the skier's velocity at 3.0 s. Check your prediction by moving the slider back so the meter reads 3.0 s.

A balloonist ascending at a constant speed of 10 m/s accidentally releases a cup of lemonade when 15 m above the head of a crew member directly below the balloon. Determine the time interval that the crew member has to dodge the lemonade. Assume that the gravitational constant is 10 m/s².

Question 1 — Pictorial Description:

y

$t_0 =$

$y_0 =$

$v_0 =$

$a =$

$t =$

0

$y =$

$v =$

Question 4 — Motion Diagram:

y

0

Question 5 — Graphs:

x

t

v,a

t

Question 6 — Equations and Solution

Question 1: A truck traveling at 10 m/s (about 22 mph) runs into a very thick bush and stops uniformly in a distance of 1.0 m. Determine the average acceleration of the truck during the collision.

(a) Pictorial description:

(b) Motion diagram:

(C) Equations and solution:

Question 2: Repeat your calculation, but this time determine the acceleration if the initial speed is 20 m/s. After completing your work, adjust the speed slider in the simulation to 20 m/s and check your answer.

Question 3: You doubled the initial speed from 10 m/s to 20 m/s. Qualitatively, why did the acceleration quadruple instead of double, assuming the same stopping distance?

Question 4: Why wear seat belts? The crate on the flat bed of the truck simulates a person wearing no seat belt. Observe very carefully the acceleration of the crate when it hits the hard surface at the back of the truck's cab. Based on the maximum acceleration of the crate, estimate its stopping distance.

1.8 Estimation Video: Egg Hits Windshield

Based on your observations of the video at the end of this activity, estimate acceleration of the egg while stopping when (a) belted into it's seat and (b) when unbelted.

Concept(s) to be used:

Known or estimated quantities:

Unknown to be determined:

Calculations:

You are asked to help the state motor-vehicle department construct a table that gives the car-stopping distance for different initial car speeds. Suppose that a car's initial speed is 24 m/s (about 54 mph) and that the car's acceleration when the brakes are applied is -6.0 m/s^2. There is a 0.80-s reaction time from the instant the driver sees the need to stop until the brake is applied and acceleration starts. Your goal is to predict the car's stopping distance. Note: This is a two-part problem. (Complete the descriptions below to answer Questions 1–3.)

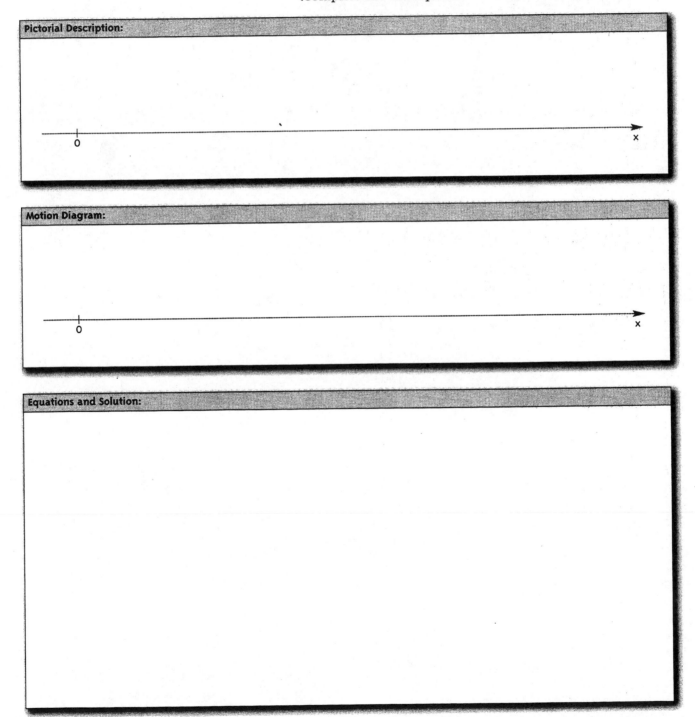

Pictorial Description:

0   x

Motion Diagram:

0   x

Equations and Solution:

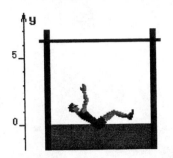

The problem starts with a pole-vaulter at the peak of his vault 6.1 m above the surface of a cushion. His fall stops after he sinks 0.40 m into the cushion. Determine the acceleration (assumed constant) that the vaulter experiences while he sinks into the cushion. Assume that the gravitational constant is 10 m/s^2. (Complete the descriptions below to answer Questions 1–5.)

Pictorial Description:

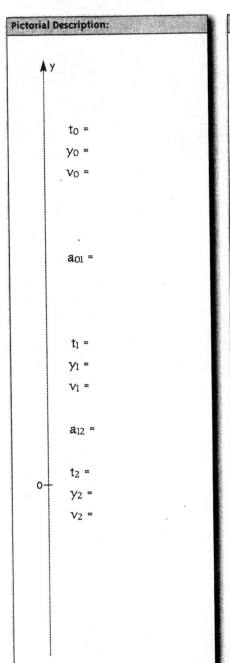

$t_0 =$

$y_0 =$

$v_0 =$

$a_{01} =$

$t_1 =$

$y_1 =$

$v_1 =$

$a_{12} =$

$t_2 =$

$y_2 =$

$v_2 =$

Motion Diagram:

Graphs:

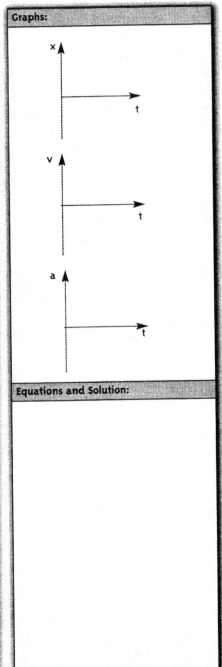

Equations and Solution:

A car starts at rest and accelerates at 4.0 m/s² until it reaches a speed of 20m/s. The car then travels for an unknown time interval at a constant speed of 20 m/s. Finally, the car decelerates at 4.0 m/s² until it stops. The car travels a total distance of 300 m. Determine the time interval needed for the entire trip. (Complete the questions below to answer Questions 1–5.)

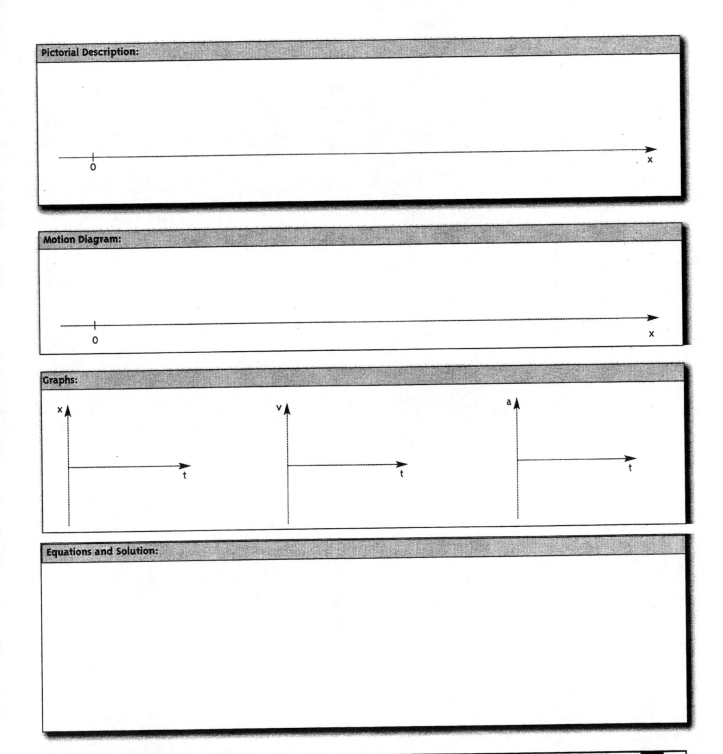

Pictorial Description:

0 ──────────────────────────► x

Motion Diagram:

0 ──────────────────────────► x

Graphs:

x | t   v | t   a | t

Equations and Solution:

The green car is traveling east at a constant 6.8 m/s speed. The front of the green car is initially at position zero. At the same instant, the front of the blue car is at position 12 m. The blue car is traveling west at 5.9 m/s. The blue car's speed decreases at a rate of (2.0 m/s)/s = 2.0 m/s². For each vehicle, construct a pictorial description, a motion diagram, kinematics graphs, and equations that describe the process. Then use these descriptions to determine the time when the fronts of the two vehicles meet, and the position where they meet.

Question 1 — Pictorial Description:

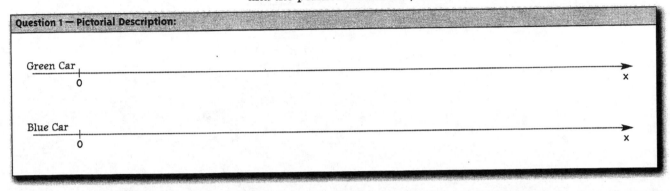

Question 2 — Motion Diagram:

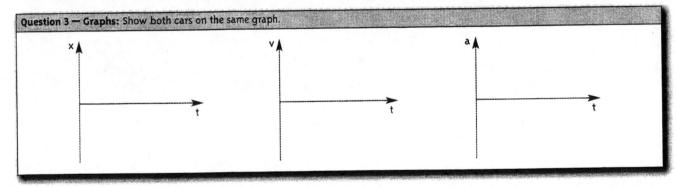

Question 3 — Graphs: Show both cars on the same graph.

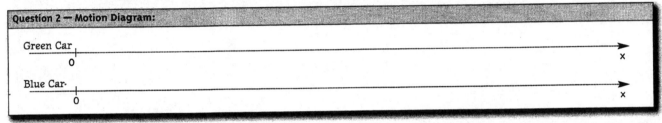

Questions 4-5 — Equations and Solution:

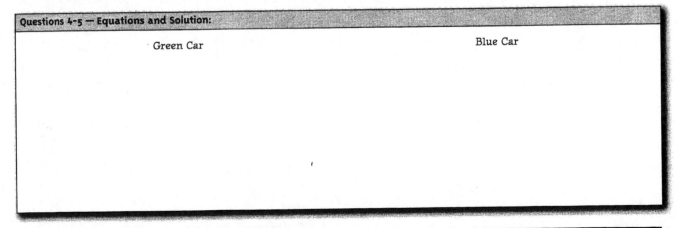

Green Car

Blue Car

A car at rest at a traffic light starts to move forward at the instant that a truck moving at a constant speed of 12.0 m/s passes. The car accelerates at 4.0 m/s². At what time and at what position does the car catch the truck? For each vehicle, construct a pictorial description, a motion diagram, kinematics graphs, and equations that describe the process. Then use these descriptions to solve the problem.

Question 1 — Pictorial Description:

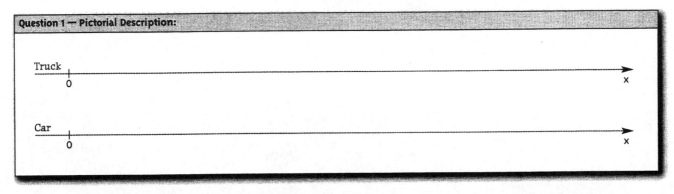

Question 2 — Motion Diagram:

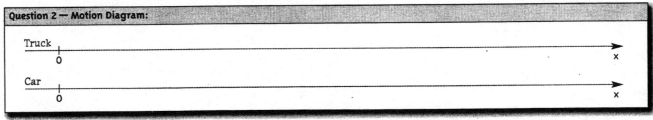

Question 3 — Graphs: Show the truck and car on the same graph.

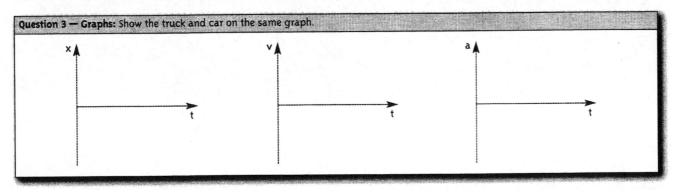

Questions 4-5 — Equations and Solution:

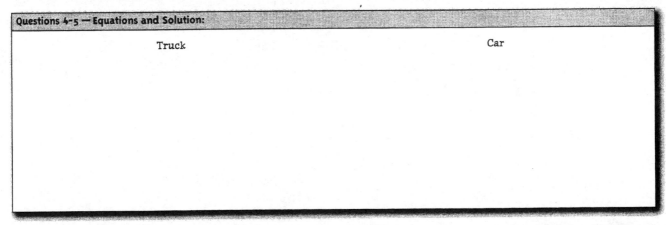

Truck   Car

You are hired by a movie studio to choose the parameters for a movie scene involving a car and a truck. At the start, the driver in the moving car hits the brakes. The truck starts at rest, and it's back end is initially 15.2 m ahead of the front of the car. The truck driver hits the accelerator. You are to decide the acceleration of the car and truck and the car's initial velocity so that farther down the road, the front of the car just barely misses the back of the truck. After finding slider values in Question 1 that just avoid the collision, develop the physics theory for the movie studio that supports your observations.

Note: More than one set of slider values will do the job.

Hint: Two conditions are necessary in order to avoid the collision.

Question 2 — Pictorial Description:

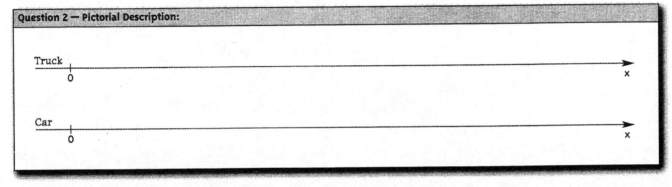

Question 3 — Motion Diagram:

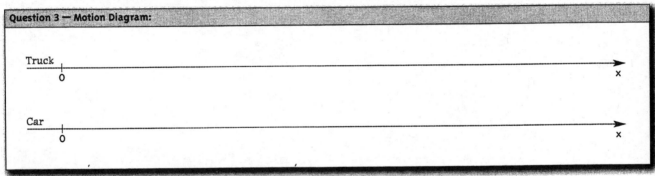

Question 5 — Equations and Solution:

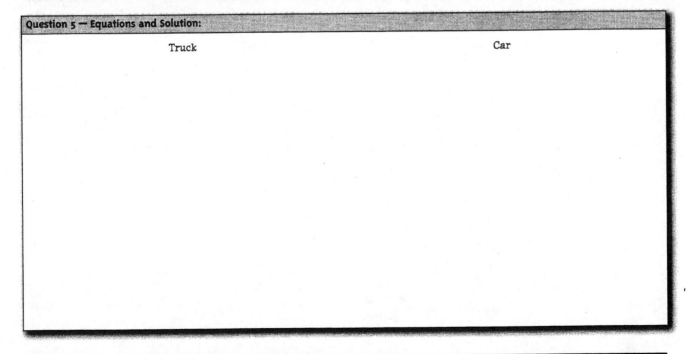

2

FORCES AND MOTION

Constructing Free-Body Diagrams

Draw a sketch of the situation described in the problem

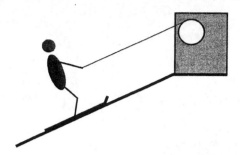

Use a line to encircle and identify the system, (the object(s) of interest)

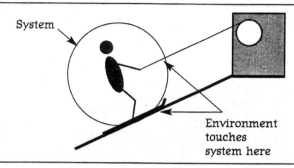

Look along the system boundary for objects in the environment that touch objects in the system. Choose symbols for the forces caused by these touching objects. Also, represent in symbol form any long-range forces exerted on the system. Describe in words the environmental object causing each force and the part of the system on which the force is exerted.

Short-range forces

Long-range force

N and F_k: Normal and kinetic friction forces caused by the snow on the skis.

T: Tension force caused by the rope on the skier.

W: Weight force caused by the gravitational pull of the earth on the person

Draw a separate sketch of the object(s) in the system. Then, draw arrows representing all forces exerted on the system. Label the arrows with the same symbols as used above. If possible, try to make the lengths of the arrows representative of the relative magnitudes of the forces.

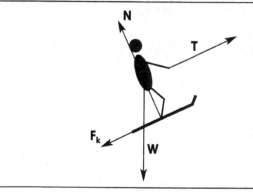

Pretend that the system has become a point particle and move the force arrows to the origin of a set of coordinate axes. Make one axis parallel to the direction of motion and the other axis perpendicular. The head of a coordinate axis arrow points in the positive direction. Do not use two-headed coordinate axis arrows!

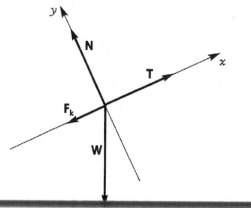

Comparing Force Magnitudes

A cable pulls the crate at constant velocity across a horizontal surface. Compare the magnitudes of the rope tension force T and the resistive kinetic friction force F_k.

(a) $T > F_k$ (b) $T = F_k$ (c) $T < F_k$

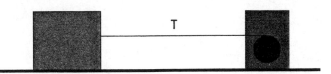

Question 1: Explain your choice.

Skydiver

The skydiver, after accelerating and falling for a short time, continues to fall at a constant terminal velocity. Compare the magnitudes of the downward weight force w and the resistive drag force of the air F_d.

(a) $w > F_d$ (b) $w = F_d$ (c) $w < F_d$

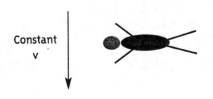

Constant
v

Question 1: Explain your choice.

Question 2: Construct qualitative graphs.

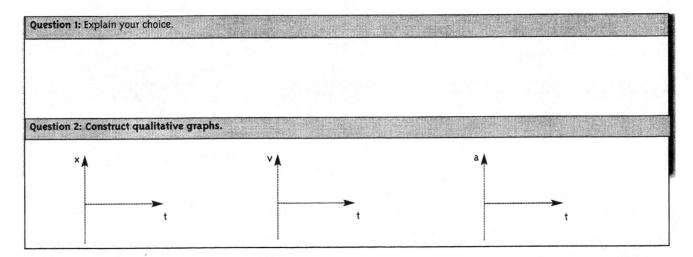

Tension Change

The crate is pulled across a horizontal frictionless surface by a cable with tension 2.50 N. Part way along the trip, the tension is quickly reduced to 1.25 N. Complete the qualitative velocity-versus-time and acceleration-versus-time graphs, starting from the instant the tension is reduced.

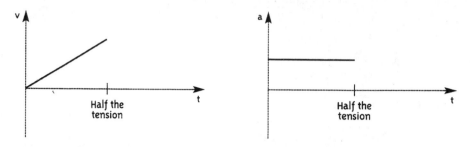

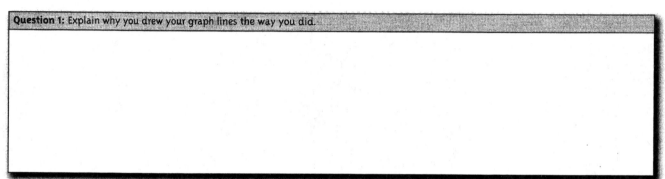

Question 1: Explain why you drew your graph lines the way you did.

Sliding on an Incline

The graphs show the velocity and the acceleration of a block that has been sliding upward along an incline. There is a small friction force exerted by the incline on the block. Complete the graph lines for the return trip back down the incline.

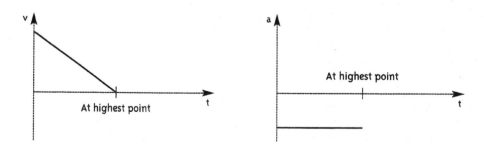

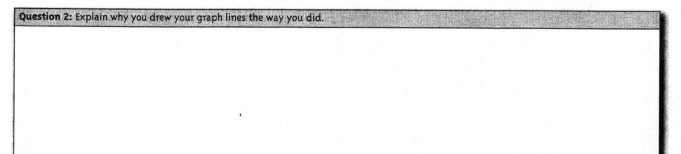

Question 2: Explain why you drew your graph lines the way you did.

Car Race

The two cars start with the same speed. The top car moves across a frictionless level surface. The bottom car moves down a frictionless incline and then back up again to the same level at which it started. Which car arrives at the finish line first, or do they tie?

(a) Car on level surface arrives first.   (b) Car on curved surface arrives first.   (c) It's a tie.

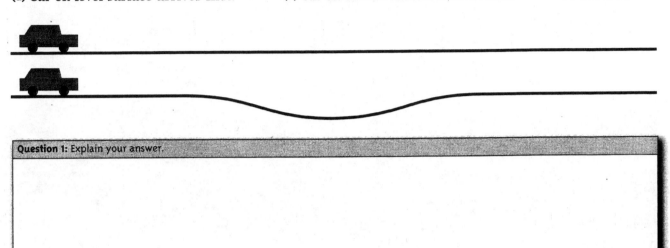

Question 1: Explain your answer.

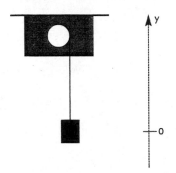

A 60-kg crate attached to a rope is initially moving upward at speed 4.0 m/s. The crate's speed decreases uniformly until it stops after traveling 4.0 m. Determine the tension in the rope while the crate's speed is decreasing. The gravitational constant is 10 N/kg.

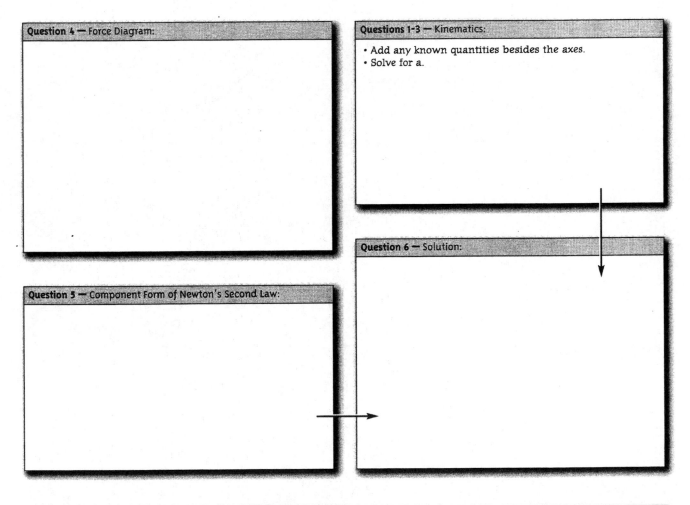

Question 4 — Force Diagram:

Questions 1-3 — Kinematics:

- Add any known quantities besides the axes.
- Solve for a.

Question 6 — Solution:

Question 5 — Component Form of Newton's Second Law:

Question 7 — Kinematic Graphs:

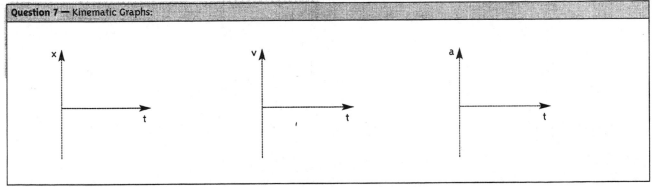

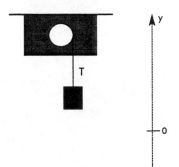

A 60-kg crate attached to a rope is initially moving downward at speed 4.0 m/s. The rope causes the crate's speed to decrease uniformly to a stop in 2.5 s. Determine the tension in the rope while the crate's speed is decreasing. The gravitational constant is 10 N/kg.

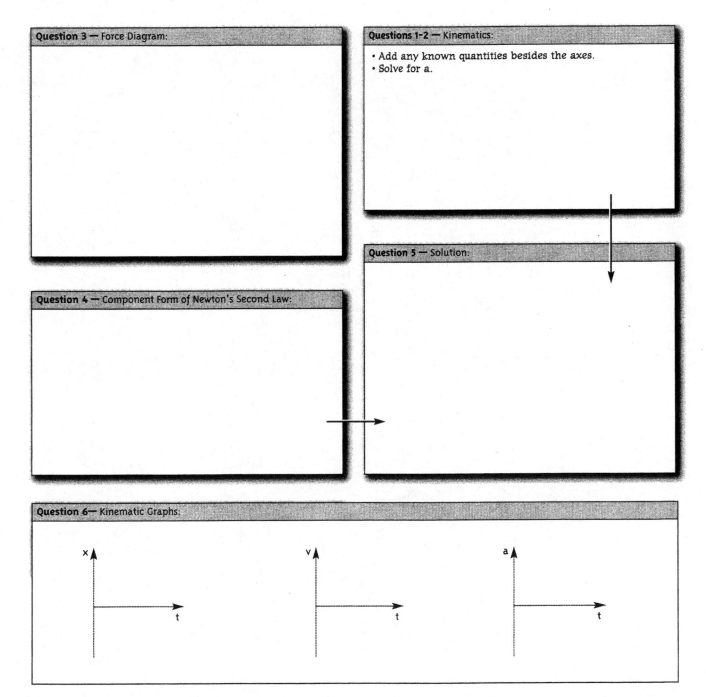

Question 3 — Force Diagram:

Questions 1-2 — Kinematics:

• Add any known quantities besides the axes.
• Solve for a.

Question 4 — Component Form of Newton's Second Law:

Question 5 — Solution:

Question 6— Kinematic Graphs:

The following two pages are used to analyze the vertical motion of a toy rocket. The rocket starts at rest. Fuel emitted from the engine produces an upward force on the engine and in turn on the rocket. This upward force is called the thrust force.

Sliders allow you to change
- the magnitude of this upward thrust force
- the time interval during which the thrust is exerted
- the rocket's initial upward speed

Meters indicate
- the position of the top of the rocket
- the velocity of the rocket
- the acceleration of the rocket
- the time (with $t_0=0$ being the time the thrust starts)

Question 1

A 5.0-N thrust is exerted on the 0.50-kg rocket for a time interval of 8.0 s. Determine the height of the rocket at the end of that time interval. The gravitational constant is 10 N/kg.

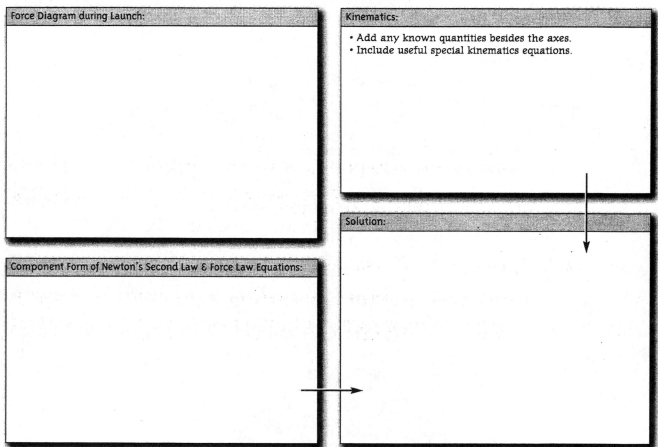

Force Diagram during Launch:

Kinematics:

- Add any known quantities besides the axes.
- Include useful special kinematics equations.

Component Form of Newton's Second Law & Force Law Equations:

Solution:

Question 2

This is the same situation in terms of thrust and rocket weight as in Question 1. Now, the rocket is initially moving up at 30 m/s. Describe (in words) what will happen to the rocket.

Questions 3-4

A 20.0-N thrust is exerted on the 0.50-kg rocket for a time interval of 8.0 s. The rocket then coasts upward more distance until its speed is reduced to zero. Determine the maximum height of the rocket. The gravitational constant is 10 N/kg.

Force Diagram during Launch:

Kinematics:

- List any known kinematics quantities.
- Apply any useful kinematics equations.

Speed and Height at End of Burn:

Component Form of Newton's Second Law & Force Law Equations:

After Burn:

Determine the time of flight after the burn and the additional distance traveled. Add this to the height at the end of the burn to find the total additional distance traveled.

A rope connecting a truck and a crate makes a 21.68° angle with the horizontal. The rope drags the crate along a horizontal surface. The gravitational constant is 10 N/kg. Adjust the sliders on the simulation as follows:

- crate mass = 50 kg
- coefficient of friction = 0.60
- acceleration (in the x-direction of the truck and the crate) = +3.0 m/s²

Determine if the meter readings are consistent with the y-component form of Newton's Second Law and with the kinematics equations of motion.

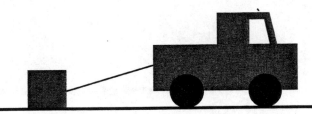

Crate Force Diagram:

y

x

Question 2 — x-Component Form of Newton's Second Law:

(Insert meter readings to see if they are consistent with the law.)

Question 1 — y-Component Form of Newton's Second Law:

(Insert meter readings to see if they are consistent with the law.)

Question 3 — Kinematics Equations:

(Are the meter readings consistent with the kinematics equations of motion?)

(a) Estimate the mass of the green block. The coefficient of kinetic friction between the block and the horizontal surface is 0.2.

(b) Why is the tension in the string so small in the second movie compared to the tension in the first movie?

Concept(s) to be used:

Unknown to be determined:

Known or estimated quantities:

Calculations:

You exert a constant 10-N force directed 37° below the horizontal while pushing a 1.0-kg crate along a level surface. The coefficient of friction between the surface and the crate is 0.20, and the gravitational constant is 10 N/kg. Determine the magnitudes of the crate's weight, the normal force, the kinetic friction force, and the acceleration of the crate.

Question 1 — Force Diagram:

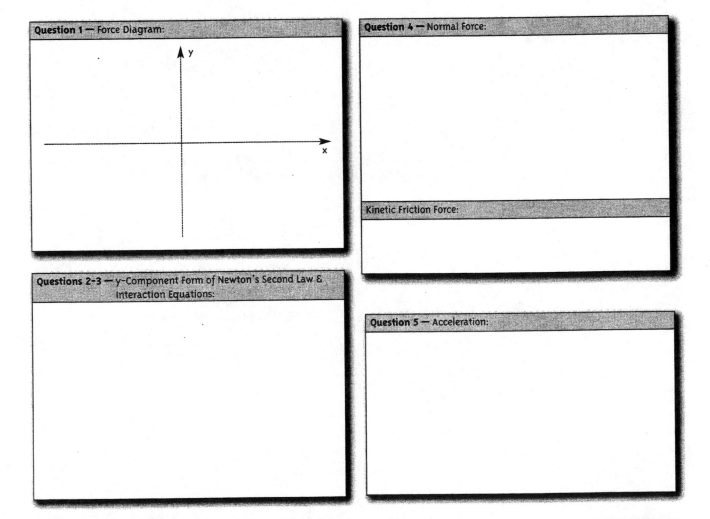

Questions 2-3 — y-Component Form of Newton's Second Law & Interaction Equations:

Question 4 — Normal Force:

Kinetic Friction Force:

Question 5 — Acceleration:

You exert a constant 20-N force directed 53° above the horizontal while pushing a 1.0-kg crate up a vertical wall. The coefficient of friction between the surface and the crate is 0.20, and the gravitational constant is 10 N/kg. Determine the magnitudes of the crate's weight, the normal force, the kinetic friction force, and the acceleration of the crate.

Question 1 — Force Diagram:

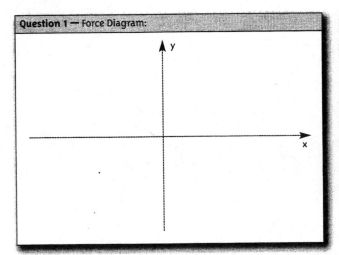

Questions 2 & 3 cont. — Solve for force magnitudes and acceleration:

Questions 2 & 3 — x and y Component Forms of Newton's Second Law & Interaction Equations:

Question 4 — Confirm that the simulation is consistent with the kinematic equations of motion:

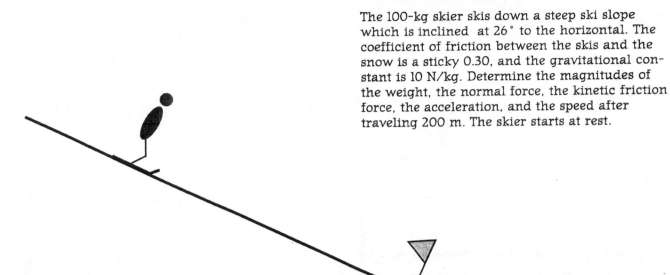

The 100-kg skier skis down a steep ski slope which is inclined at 26° to the horizontal. The coefficient of friction between the skis and the snow is a sticky 0.30, and the gravitational constant is 10 N/kg. Determine the magnitudes of the weight, the normal force, the kinetic friction force, the acceleration, and the speed after traveling 200 m. The skier starts at rest.

Question 1 — Force Diagram:

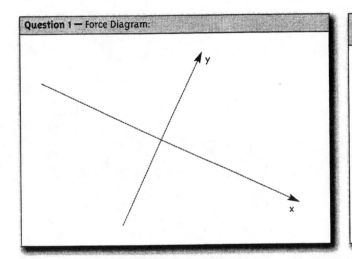

Question 4 — Use x component form of Newton's second law to solve for a:

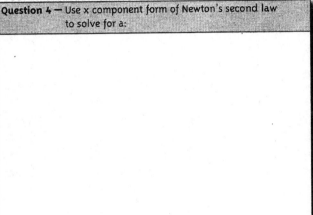

Questions 2 & 3 — Use y component form of Newton's second law and interaction equations to solve for w, N, and F_k:

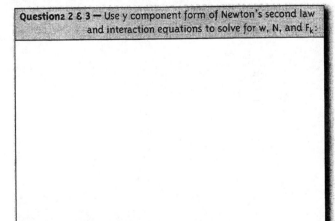

Question 5 — Determine the time interval needed to complete the 200-m trip:

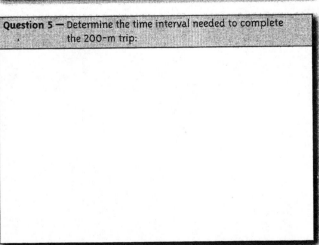

2.8 Estimation Video: Truck Slips on Incline

Estimate the coefficient of friction between the wheels of the truck and the inclined surface. Indicate if the friction is kinetic friction or static friction.

Concept(s) to be used:

Known or estimated quantities:

Unknown to be determined:

Calculations:

A rope pulls the 100-kg skier up a steep slope inclined at 38.5° to the horizontal. The coefficient of friction between the skis and snow is a sticky 0.20, and the gravitational constant is 10 N/kg. Determine the magnitude of the rope tension needed to pull the skier at a constant 1.0 m/s speed.

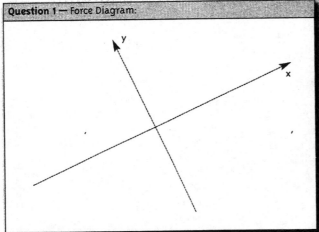

Question 1 — Force Diagram:

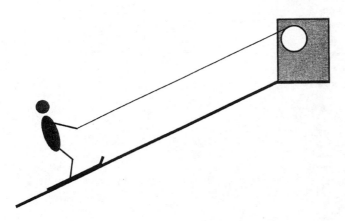

Questions 2 & 3 — Use y-component form of Newton's second law and interaction equations to solve for w, N, and F_k:

Questions 4 & 5 — Determine the acceleration and use the x- component form of Newton's second law to solve for the rope tension.

Question 6 — How does moving at twice the speed affect the previous calculations? Explain.

You exert a constant 30-N horizontal force while pushing a 2.0-kg crate up a steep 37° incline. (Note that the force is not parallel to the incline but horizontal.) The coefficient of friction between the surface and the crate is 0.143, and the gravitational constant is 10 N/kg. Determine the magnitudes of the crate's weight, the normal force, the kinetic friction force, and the acceleration of the crate.

Question 1 — Force Diagram:

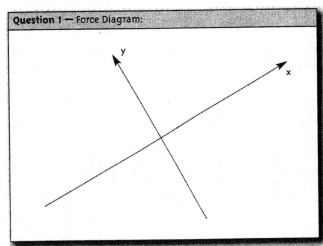

Questions 2 & 3 — Use y component form of Newton's second law and interaction equations to solve for w, N, and F_k:

Question 4 — Use x component form of Newton's second law to solve for a:

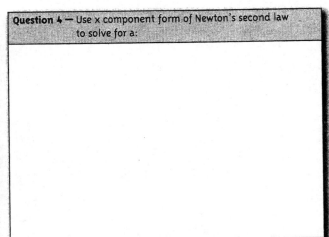

Question 5 — Confirm that the kinematic equations of motion are consistent with the motion of the crate:

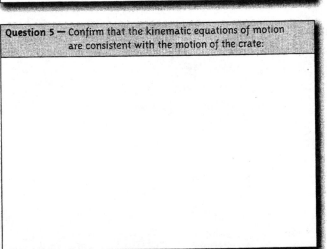

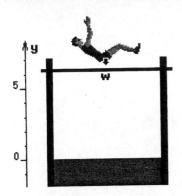

The 70-kg pole-vaulter at the top of his flight has zero speed and is 6.1 m above the cushion below. After he falls, he sinks 0.4 m into the cushion while stopping. Assuming uniform acceleration, determine the average force of the cushion on the vaulter while the cushion is stopping him. The gravitational constant is 10 N/kg. (Complete the information below to answer Questions 1–5.)

Plan a Solution.

Complete the solution.

Be sure to include a force diagram and apply Newton's Second Law. (Include ALL forces shown in the diagram.)

A 200-N force pushes forward on the 20-kg truck. The truck pulls two crates connected together by ropes, as shown. The gravitational constant is 10 N/kg. Determine the acceleration of the crates and truck and the tension in each rope for one of the following sets of conditions.

	Set 1 Question 1	Set 2 Question 4
Mass of Left Crate	20 kg	20 kg
Mass of Right Crate	20 kg	20 kg
Friction Coefficient	0.00	0.40

Left Crate	Right Crate	Truck
Force Diagram:	Force Diagram:	Force Diagram:
x-Component Form of Newton's Second Law:	x-Component Form of Newton's Second Law:	x-Component Form of Newton's Second Law:

Combine the above to solve for the unknowns.

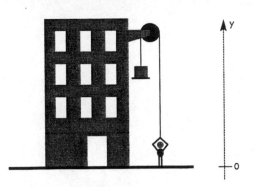

The 44-kg bricklayer plans to lower the barrel of bricks from the fourth floor of the building. Unfortunately, the mass of the bricks is 56 kg, and the bricklayer is pulled up in the air. Determine the speed of the bricklayer after traveling 7.0 m upward — the distance that the bricks fall. The gravitational constant is 10 N/kg.

Question 1 — Force Diagram for Descending Bricks:

Question 3 — Force Diagram for Ascending Bricklayer:

Question 2 — Component Form of Newton's Second Law:

Question 4 — Component Form of Newton's Second Law:

Write an equation to relate the accelerations of the two objects. Determine a and T.

Question 5 — Use one of the kinematics equations to solve for v.

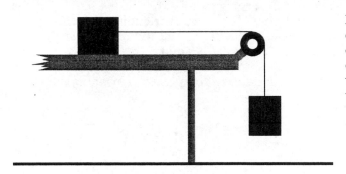

Determine the rope tension and the acceleration of the system with the hanging gray block's mass equal to 5.0 kg and the sliding red block's mass equal to 5.0 kg. Ignore friction and assume that the gravitational constant is 10 N/kg. (Complete the information below to answer Questions 1–6.)

Force Diagram for Block on Table:

Component Form of Newton's Second Law:

Force Diagram for Descending Block:

Component Form of Newton's Second Law:

Determine a and T.

Estimate the coefficient of friction between the wheels of the truck and the inclined surface. The truck's mass is 795 g and the hanging blocks' combined mass is 300 g. Be sure to justify your estimate based on physics reasoning.

Concept(s) to be used:

Known or estimated quantities:

Unknown to be determined:

Calculations:

©1997 Addison Wesley Interactive & Alan Van Heuvelen

3

PROJECTILE MOTION

If we ignore air resistance, the motion of a projectile can be considered as the combination of two independent types of motion, each described by its own set of equations.

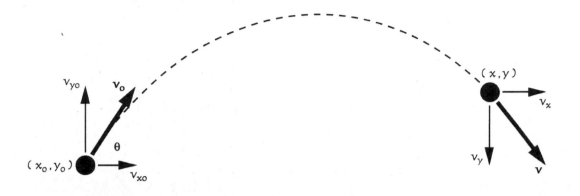

Horizontal motion in the x-direction

$$x - x_0 = v_{ox} t$$
$$v_x = v_{ox}$$

- Initial x-velocity component: $v_{ox} = \pm v_0 \cos \theta$

  where v_0 is the projectile's initial speed and θ is the angle that the projectile's initial velocity makes with respect to the x-axis. The initial x-velocity component is positive if in the positive x-direction and negative if in the negative x-direction.

- x-acceleration component: $a_x = 0$

Vertical motion in the y-direction

$$y - y_0 = v_{oy} t + (1/2) a_y t^2$$
$$v_y = v_{oy} + a_y t$$

- Initial y-velocity component: $v_{oy} = \pm v_0 \sin \theta$

  where v_0 is the projectile's initial speed and θ is the angle that the projectile's initial velocity makes with respect to the x-axis. The initial y-velocity component is positive if in the positive y-direction and negative if in the negative y-direction.

- y-acceleration component: $a_y = - g = - 9.8 \text{ m/s}^2 \approx - 10 \text{ m/s}^2$.

Question 1: Two balls start 5.0 m above a brick surface, each with a zero y-velocity component. Ball A's initial x-velocity component is zero, and Ball B's initial x-velocity component is 5.0 m/s. Which ball reaches the floor first, or do they tie? Explain your choice.

(a) Ball A   Explain your prediction:

(b) Ball B

(c) It's a tie.

Question 2: Try other initial x-velocity component settings for the two balls. Based on your observations, develop a rule for how the x-velocity component affects the time interval that a ball needs to fall to the floor.

Question 3: It takes 1.0 s for the balls to fall 5.0 m, assuming their initial y-velocity component is zero, that air resistance is negligible, and that the gravitational constant is 10 m/s². Choose three different pairs of initial x-velocity component settings for the two balls so that they touch just as they reach ground level, the floor.

Adjust the x-velocity component slider to 2.0 m/s. Watch the simulation very carefully and record

- the maximum height reached by the projectile _____
- the flight time _____
- the range of the projectile (the horizontal distance it travels) _____

Each division on the simulation is 1.0 m, and the gravitational constant is 10 m/s^2. Predict how each of these quantities will change when the horizontal x-velocity component is changed from 2.0 m/s to 10.0 m/s and the simulation is run again.

1. The maximum elevation:	(a) increases	(b) remains the same	(c) decreases

Explain your prediction:

2. The flight time:	(a) increases	(b) remains the same	(c) decreases

Explain your prediction:

3. The range of the projectile:	(a) increases	(b) remains the same	(c) decreases

Explain your prediction:

After completing your predictions and the reasons for the predictions, run the simulation to see how you did. Modify your reasoning if necessary.

Question 1: Determine the x-acceleration component of the ball by calculating the change in the x-velocity component during a time interval divided by that time interval.

Question 2: Determine the y-acceleration component of the ball by calculating the change in the y-velocity component during a time interval divided by that time interval. Do the calculation for the following time intervals:

0.0 s to 1.0 s:

1.0 s to 2.0 s:

2.0 s to 3.0 s:

3.0 s to 4.0 s:

What do you think the y-acceleration component is for the entire trip?

Question 3: By how much does the magnitude of the y-velocity component change during the following time intervals?

Δt = 1.0 s:

Δt = 2.0 s:

Δt = 0.10 s:

- The x-component of the initial velocity v_{xo} is

$$v_{xo} = \pm v_o \cos \theta$$

where the plus sign is used if the x component points in the positive x-direction, and the minus sign is used if the x-component points in the negative x-direction. The angle θ is the angle that v_o makes relative to the positive or negative x-axis.

- The y-component of the initial velocity v_{yo} is

$$v_{yo} = \pm v_o \sin \theta$$

where the plus sign is used if the y component points in the positive y-direction, and the minus sign is used if the y-component points in the negative y-direction. The angle θ is the angle that v_o makes relative to the positive or negative x-axis.

Question 1: Determine the x- and y-velocity components for a projectile whose initial velocity is 50 m/s at an angle of 53° above the positive x-axis.

Question 2: Determine the x- and y-velocity components for a projectile whose initial velocity is 80 m/s at an angle of 30° below the positive x-axis.

Question 3: Determine the x- and y-velocity components for a projectile whose initial velocity is 100 m/s at an angle of 37° above the negative x-axis.

Question 4: Determine the x- and y-velocity components for a projectile whose initial velocity is 100 m/s in the positive x-direction.

Question 1: $v_{oy} = 0$

Question 2: $v_{oy} = +4.0$ m/s

Question 3: $v_{ox} = +10$ m/s

Question 4: $v_{ox} = +11.0$ m/s

For each question, you adjust one initial velocity component and calculate the value of the other velocity component so that the ball lands on the target. Each division on the simulation is 1.0 m, and the gravitational constant is 10 m/s².

Make a sketch below to indicate all information known about the initial situation and the desired final situation:

Apply the x-component kinematics equations:

Apply the y-component kinematics equations:

Solve for the unknown:

Evaluate your solution in terms of magnitude, sign, and unit:

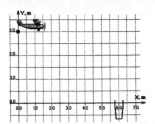

In a toy airplane contest, a small plane travels at a constant elevation and at a constant 6.0 m/s speed. You are to decide the position where the plane should release supplies so that they land in a target basket. The gravitational constant is 10 m/s².

Make a sketch below to indicate all information known about the initial situation and the desired final situation:

Apply the x-component kinematics equations:

Apply the y-component kinematics equations:

Solve for the unknown:

Evaluate your solution in terms of magnitude, sign, and unit:

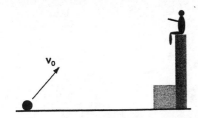

Adjust the ball's initial speed (in m/s) so that the scientist on the ledge can catch the ball. Each division on the screen is 1.0 m. The launch angle is 58.3°. Use any information provided here, distance measurements on the screen, and the projectile-motion concepts to determine the gravitational constant on this planet. HINT: For this question, you do not first use the y-axis equation to determine the projectile's flight time.

Make a sketch below to indicate all information known about the initial situation and the desired final situation:

Apply the x-component kinematics equations:

Apply the y-component kinematics equations:

Solve for the unknown:

Evaluate your solution in terms of magnitude, sign, and unit:

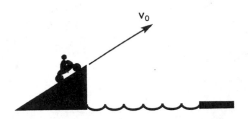

v_0

Five-foot two-inch, 109-pound Debbie Lawler, on March 31, 1973, sailed 76 feet over a line of parked cars to set the women's motorcycle distance-jumping record. Debbie's next dream is to jump her Suzuki motorcycle over two destroyers moored in the harbor. Suppose she came to ask you to be her consultant in planning the jump. To test your knowledge, she asks you if the cyclist in our simulation will make it to the opposite shore. The mass of the miniature cyclist is 20 kg. Each division on the simulation is 1.0 m, and the gravitational constant is 10 m/s². The x- and y-velocity components when the cyclist reaches the top of the ramp are 5.7 m/s and 4.2 m/s, respectively.

Make a sketch below to indicate all information known about the initial situation and the desired final situation:

Apply the x-component kinematics equations:

Apply the y-component kinematics equations:

Solve for the unknown:

Evaluate your solution in terms of magnitude, sign, and unit:

Estimate the initial speed of the shot put.
It travels 19.3 m and is in the air 1.65 s.

Concept(s) to be used:

Known or estimated quantities:

Unknown to be determined:

Calculations:

4

CIRCULAR MOTION

The direction of a moving object's acceleration when at some arbitrary position can be estimated if you know its velocity just before arriving at that position and just after. The procedure is illustrated below.

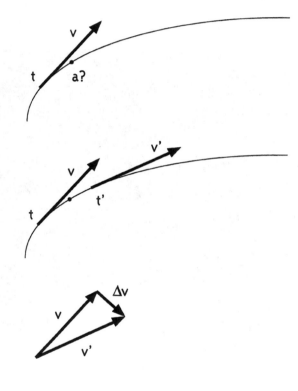

Original velocity:
Draw an arrow representing the velocity v of the object at time t just before arriving at the position of interest.

New velocity:
Draw another arrow representing the velocity v' of the object at time t' just after passing the point.

Velocity change:
To find the change in velocity Δv during the time interval $\Delta t = t' - t$, place the tails of v and v' together. The change in velocity Δv is a vector that points from the head of v to the head of v'. Notice in the figure at the right that $v + \Delta v = v'$, or by rearranging, $\Delta v = v' - v$ (that is, Δv is the change in velocity).

Acceleration:
The acceleration equals the velocity change Δv divided by the time interval Δt needed for that change: that is, $a = \Delta v / \Delta t$. If you do not know the time interval, you can at least estimate the direction of the acceleration because the acceleration arrow points in the same direction as Δv.

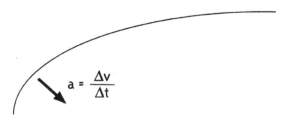

$$a = \frac{\Delta v}{\Delta t}$$

For each situation shown below, estimate the direction of the acceleration of the pendulum bob.

Question 1: Pendulum bob moving at bottom of swing

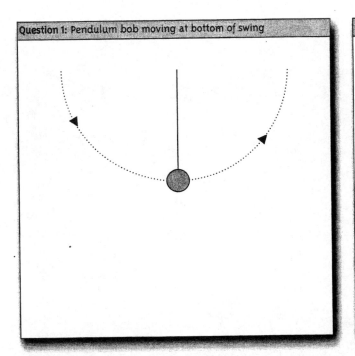

Question 2: Pendulum bob before it reaches bottom of swing

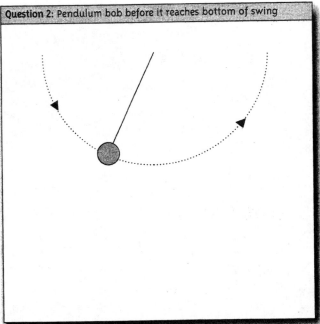

Question 3: Acceleration direction at another position

For Questions 1 and 2 below, estimate the direction of the acceleration of the car when the car is at the position shown in the diagram. (A top view is given.)

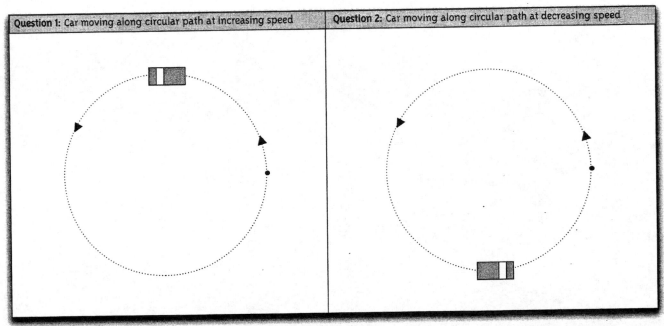

Question 1: Car moving along circular path at increasing speed

Question 2: Car moving along circular path at decreasing speed

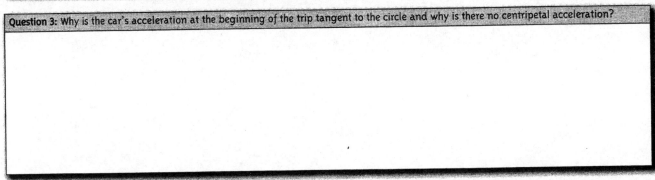

Question 3: Why is the car's acceleration at the beginning of the trip tangent to the circle and why is there no centripetal acceleration?

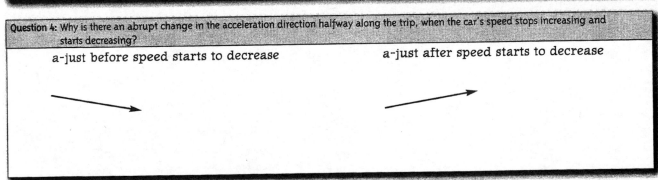

Question 4: Why is there an abrupt change in the acceleration direction halfway along the trip, when the car's speed stops increasing and starts decreasing?

a-just before speed starts to decrease

a-just after speed starts to decrease

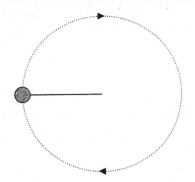

Record the meter readings for the magnitude of the centripetal acceleration as a function of speed and as a function of the radius of the circle. Then plot the data and decide how the magnitude of the acceleration depends on each quantity.

Question 1 - Dependence of Acceleration on Speed:

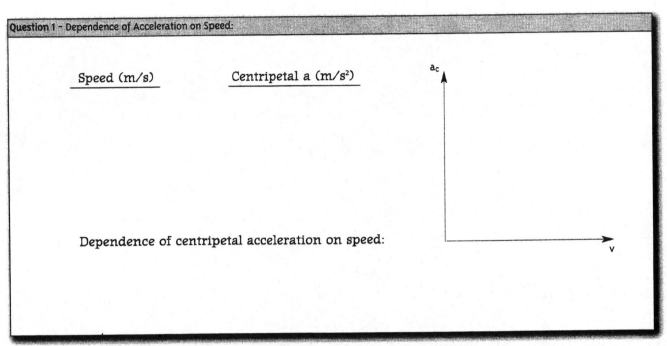

Speed (m/s)   Centripetal a (m/s²)

Dependence of centripetal acceleration on speed:

Question 2 - Dependence of Acceleration on Radius:

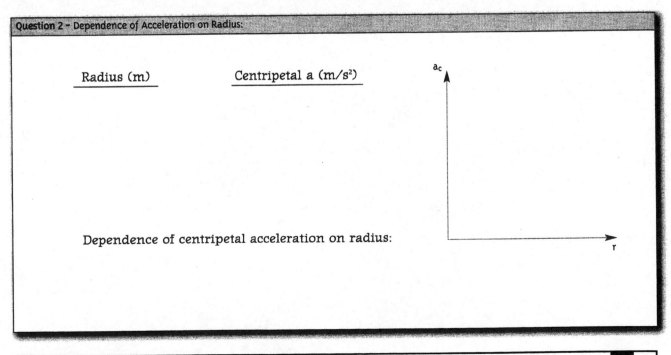

Radius (m)   Centripetal a (m/s²)

Dependence of centripetal acceleration on radius:

A 1.0-kg pendulum bob swings at the end of a 2.0-m-long string. Determine the tension in the string as the bob passes the lowest point in the swing. Its speed at this point is 6.3 m/s. Assume that the gravitational constant is 10 N/kg.

Question 3 - Force Diagram:

Question 2 - Acceleration (direction and magnitude):

Question 5 - Radial Component Form of Newton's Second Law:

Question 6 - Solution of Equation for Tension:

Evaluation:

• Units ok? _____   • Sign ok? _____

• Qualitatively, does the answer make sense?

4.4 Estimation Video: Swinging a Bucket of Water

Estimate the tension in the person's arm while swinging the plastic bucket that holds one gallon of water. Any other information you need will have to be estimated from the video.

Concept(s) to be used:

Known or estimated quantities:

Unknown to be determined:

Calculations:

A 10-kg cart coasts up and over a frictionless circular path of radius 2.08 m. As it passes the top of the path, its speed is 3.2 m/s. Determine the magnitude of the normal force of the hill on the cart when the cart is at the top of the hill. Assume that the gravitational constant is 10 N/kg.

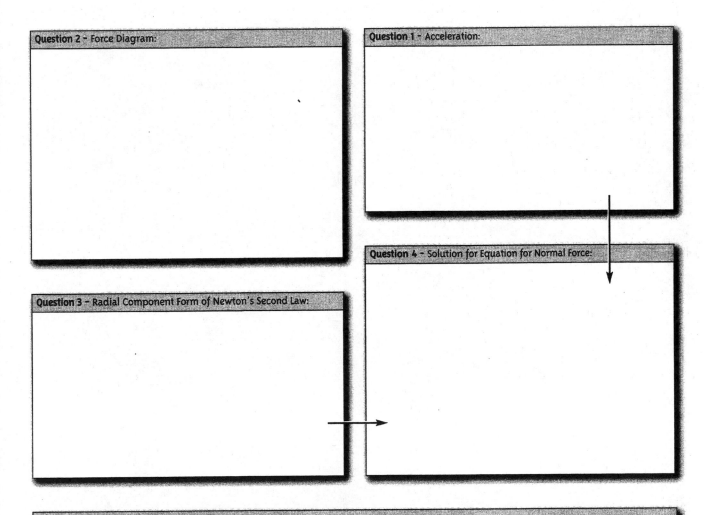

Question 2 - Force Diagram:

Question 1 - Acceleration:

Question 3 - Radial Component Form of Newton's Second Law:

Question 4 - Solution for Equation for Normal Force:

Evaluation:

• Units ok? _____

• Sign ok? _____

• Qualitatively, does the answer make sense?

A 1.0-kg ball swings in a vertical circle at the end of a 4.0-m-long string. You are to determine the tension in the string when the ball is at three different locations. The speed of the ball at each location is given below. Assume that the gravitational constant is 10 N/kg.

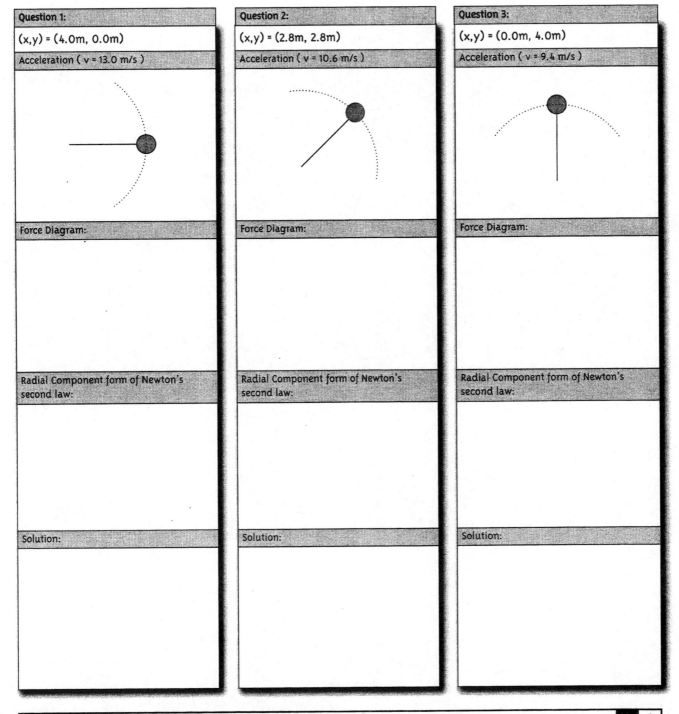

Question 1:	**Question 2:**	**Question 3:**
(x,y) = (4.0m, 0.0m)	(x,y) = (2.8m, 2.8m)	(x,y) = (0.0m, 4.0m)
Acceleration (v = 13.0 m/s)	Acceleration (v = 10.6 m/s)	Acceleration (v = 9.4 m/s)
Force Diagram:	Force Diagram:	Force Diagram:
Radial Component form of Newton's second law:	Radial Component form of Newton's second law:	Radial Component form of Newton's second law:
Solution:	Solution:	Solution:

A 1000-kg car moves at a maximum speed so that it does not skid off the 50-m radius level track. If the coefficient of static friction between the road and wheels is 0.80, what is the maximum speed? Assume that the gravitational constant is 10.0 N/kg = 10.0m/s.

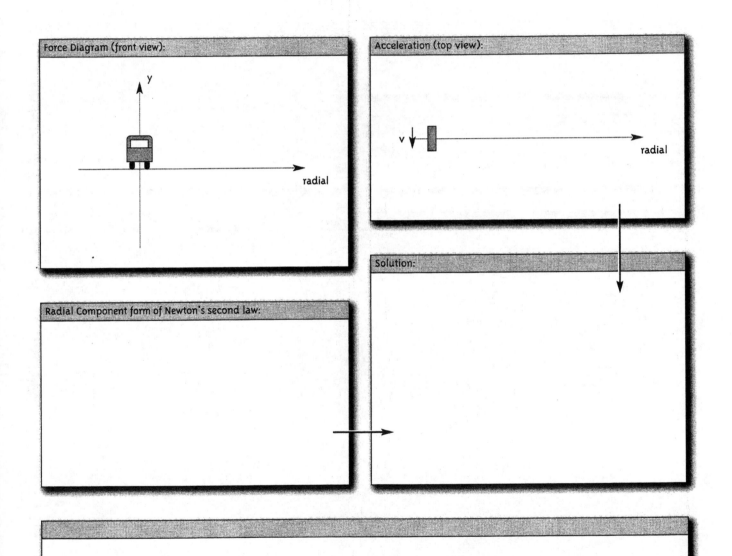

Force Diagram (front view):

Acceleration (top view):

Radial Component form of Newton's second law:

Solution:

• Unit ok? _____

• Sign ok? _____

• Qualitatively, does answer make sense?

4.7 Estimation Video: Plane Flies at End of String

Use circular dynamics (the circular form of Newton's second law) and circular kinematics to estimate the plane's speed while moving at the end of the string.

Concept(s) to be used:

Known or estimated quantities:

Unknown to be determined:

Calculations:

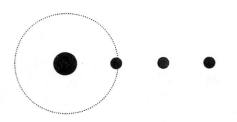

The satellite with orbital radius 1.0 unit moves in a circular orbit when its speed is 3.0 m/s. Determine the speed that the identical satellites with 2.0 and 3.0 unit radii must move to remain in circular orbits. With other speed settings, the satellites move in elliptical orbits. To solve the problem, develop a general Newton's second law theory for the satellite motion that relates speed and radius. Use the information about the 1.0 radius orbit to solve for other unknowns.

Force Diagram:

Acceleration:

Radial Component form of Newton's second law:

Satellite Equation:

Complete Problem Solution:

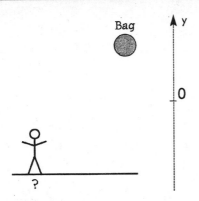

Bag

y

0

?

A 4.0-kg bag is attached to the end of a 4.0-m long rope. You swing the rope and bag in a vertical circle and release it when the bag is at the top of the swing. The tension in the rope at that point is 25.7 N. Where should a friend stand to catch the bag before it hits the ground. His head is 7.5 m below the release point of the bag. The gravitational constant is 10 N/kg.

Solution Plan:

Number of parts: _____

Indicate the conceptual knowledge used for each part and the unknown that you plan to determine for each part.

Part 1:

Force Diagram:	Radial Component form of Newton's second law:	Solve for Unknown:

Part 2:

5

WORK AND ENERGY

For each situation, determine the work done by one object on another, as specified in the question.

Question 1: Determine the work done by the cable with 12-N tension while pulling the 6.0-kg crate 4.0 m up the 37° incline.

Question 2: Determine the work done by the cable with 12-N tension while lowering the 6.0-kg crate 4.0 m down the 37° incline.

Question 3: The parachute of a skydiver weighing 50 N fails to open, and the diver lands in the snow. The snow exerts an average 300-N force on the diver while stopping her in a distance of 1.0 m. Determine the work done by the snow on the skydiver.

Question 4: The 1.0-kg pendulum bob swings down at the end of a 2.0-m-long string. Determine the work done by the string on the pendulum bob. The gravitational constant is 10 N/kg.

You are asked to help in the design of an ejector pad that will be used in a stunt. Your task for now is to analyze the energy transformations during the process.

At rest on the pad with the spring compressed

$U_{so} + U_{go} + K_o$

0

At the instant the person leaves contact with the pad

$U_s + U_g + K + U_{in}$

0

At the person's highest position

$U_s + U_g + K + U_{in}$

0

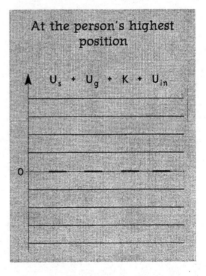

Question 3: Apply the generalized work-energy equation to the process (starting at the left and ending at the right)

5.2 Estimation Video: Grasshopper Force Constant

Estimate the effective force constant of the spring-like legs of the 5.4 g grasshopper.

Concept(s) to be used:

Known or estimated quantities:

Unknown to be determined:

Calculations:

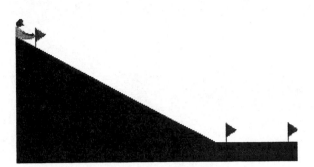

A person, initially at rest, slides down a slippery frictionless hill and then across a grassy field where friction stops the sled before it reaches a cliff on the other side.

Questions 1-2: Complete the work energy bar charts for the designated positions along the slide.

At rest on side of hill

$U_{go} + U_{so} + K_o + W$

0

Moving fast at bottom of hill

$U_g + U_s + K + U_{in}$

0

At rest after crossing field

$U_g + U_s + K + U_{in}$

0

For each bar chart, draw a picture of a process that is consistent with the bar chart. (There may be many processes described by the same chart.)

Initial Energy + Work = Final Energy   Picture of process:

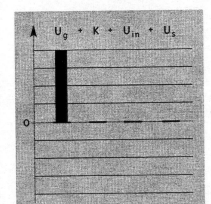

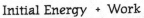

Initial Energy + Work = Final Energy   Picture of process:

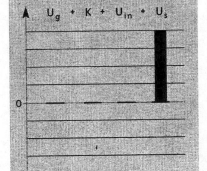

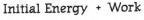

Question 3:

Initial Energy + Work = Final Energy

Picture of process:

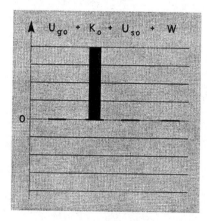
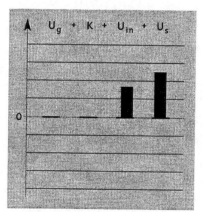

Question 4:

Initial Energy + Work = Final Energy

Picture of process:

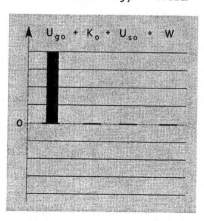
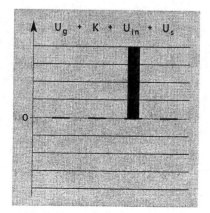

Question 5:

Initial Energy + Work = Final Energy   Picture of process:

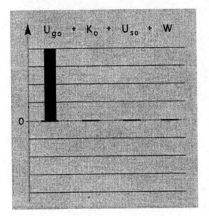

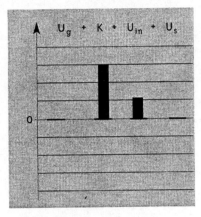

A 60-kg elevator initially moving up at 4.0 m/s slows to a stop in a distance of 4.0 m. Use the generalized work-energy equation to determine the tension in the elevator cable. Assume that the gravitational constant is 10 N/kg.

Question 1: Complete the work-energy bar charts.

Initial Energy + Work = Final Energy

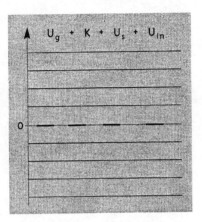

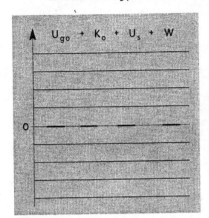

Question 2: Apply the generalized work-energy equation

Solve for the cable tension.

A 60-kg elevator initially moving down at 4.0 m/s slows to a stop in a distance of 5.0 m. Use the generalized work-energy equation to determine the tension in the elevator cable. Assume that the gravitational constant is 10 N/kg.

Question 1: Complete the work-energy bar charts.

Initial Energy + Work = Final Energy

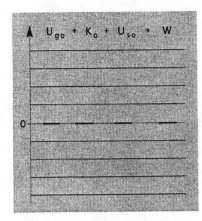

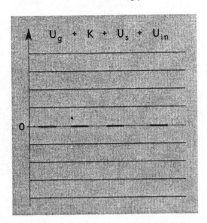

Question 2: Apply the generalized work-energy equation

Solve for the cable tension.

You are asked to help design an inverse bungee-jumping system. A 50-kg woman starts at rest with the top of her head 4.0 m below the support for the spring above. You are to choose the force constant for the spring so that after release she just makes it to but does not hit the support. The spring is initially stretched 3.5 m, and the gravitational constant is 10 N/kg.

Question 1: Complete the work-energy bar charts.

Initial Energy + Work = Final Energy

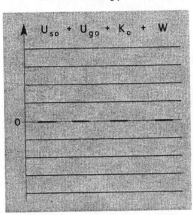
$U_{so} + U_{go} + K_o + W$

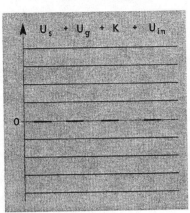
$U_s + U_g + K + U_{in}$

Question 2: Apply the generalized work-energy equation

Solve for the cable tension.

A 60-kg woman is sitting on a cushioned chair that is attached to a compressed spring and rests on a horizontal floor. The coefficient of kinetic friction between the chair and the floor is 0.10. When the spring is released, the woman is to slide 19.8 m to a glass of water. If she goes too far, she and the glass fall off the floor. If she stops too soon, she misses the glass. Determine the force constant for the spring that will cause her to stop at the glass. The spring is initially compressed 5.0 m, and the gravitational constant is 10N/kg.

Question 1: Complete the work-energy bar charts.

Initial Energy + Work = Final Energy

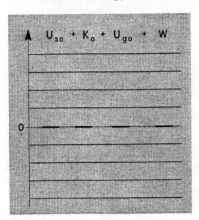

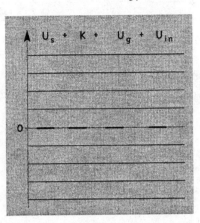

Question 2: Apply the generalized work-energy equation.

Solve for the magnitudes of the normal and friction forces.

Solve for the desired spring force constant.

Adjust the force constant of the spring to the predicted value and run the simulation to check your answer.

5.8 Estimation Video: Force Constant of Hot Wheels Launcher

Estimate the effective force constant of the spring that launches the 16.5 g hot wheels car. The spring is initially stretched to 15.5 cm. The car lands 6 m from the table. You will have to make estimates for any other quantities that are needed.

Concept(s) to be used:

Known or estimated quantities:

Unknown to be determined:

Calculations:

The 60-kg skier starts at rest on a hill inclined at an angle of 41.4° below the horizontal. The coefficient of kinetic friction between the skis and the snow is 0.20 (a sticky hill). Determine the speed after the skier travels 200 m down the hill. The gravitational constant is 10 N/kg. Start by determining the magnitudes of the normal and friction forces. Then construct initial and final qualitative energy bar charts for the motion. The origin of coordinates of the vertical axis is at the finish line.

Questions 1-2: Draw a force diagram and apply Newton's Second Law to determine the normal and friction forces.

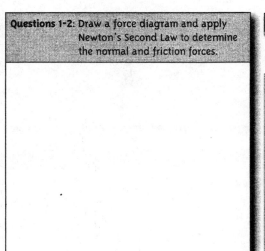

Question 3: Complete the work-energy bar charts.

Initial Energy + Work = Final Energy

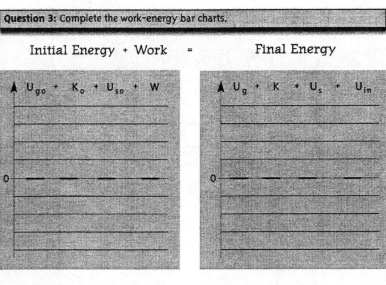

Apply the generalized work-energy equation and solve for the skier's speed.

5.9 Estimation Video: Hot Wheel Projectile

The Hot Wheels car starts 1 m above the tabletop. Is its landing place on the floor consistent with the principles of physics?

Concept(s) to be used:

Known or estimated quantities:

Unknown to be determined:

Calculations:

A young man starts at rest at the top of a ride on a swing. Based on your observations and the application of the principles of physics, estimate the tension in each cable of the swing as it passes through the lowest point in it's swing.

Concept(s) to be used:

Unknown to be determined:

Known or estimated quantities:

Calculations:

A 50-kg skier starts at rest and is traveling at 1.5 m/s after moving 500 m up a hill inclined at an angle of 37° above the horizontal. The coefficient of kinetic friction between the skis and the snow is 0.20 (a pretty sticky hill). Determine the tension in the ski rope. The gravitational constant is 10 N/kg. Will the skier be able to hold onto the rope?

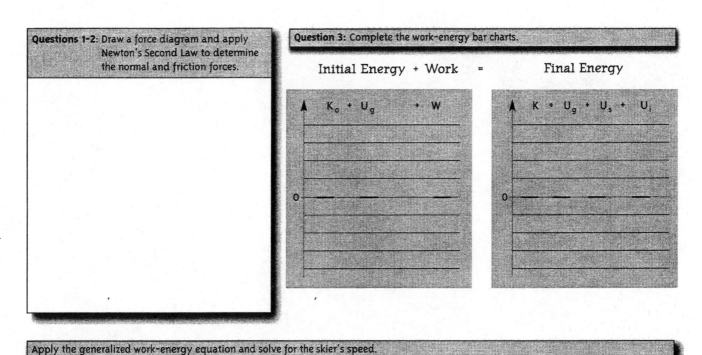

Questions 1-2: Draw a force diagram and apply Newton's Second Law to determine the normal and friction forces.

Question 3: Complete the work-energy bar charts.

Initial Energy + Work = Final Energy

$K_o + U_g + W$

$K + U_g + U_s + U_i$

Apply the generalized work-energy equation and solve for the skier's speed.

Compare your answer to the value on the simulation.

A 200-kg ski cart starts against a compressed spring. When the spring is released, it launches the cart up the 31° hill so that the cart stops about 50 m from its starting position. The spring is initially compressed 10 m. Determine the force constant of the spring needed to achieve this goal. Try the problem first for a frictionless hill and then for a hill that has a coefficient of kinetic friction between the hill and the skis equal to 0.20. The gravitational constant is 10 N/kg.

Draw a force diagram and apply Newton's Second Law to determine the normal and friction forces.

Question 1 and Question 3: Complete the work-energy bar charts.

Initial Energy + Work = Final Energy

U_{so} + U_{go} + K_o + W

U_s + U_g + K + U_{in}

0

0

Apply the generalized work-energy equation and solve for the force constant of the spring.

Adjust the force constant to your answer and run the simulation.

With the sliders set as described for Question 2, a 10-kg yellow block hangs at one end of a cord. The 5.0-kg red block is attached to the other end and slides on the horizontal surface with a coefficient of kinetic friction of 0.20. The blocks start at rest. Determine their speed after the yellow block falls 4.0 m. The gravitational constant is 10 N/kg.

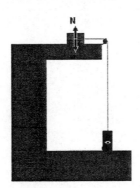

Question 2 and 4: Complete the work-energy bar charts.

Initial Energy + Work = Final Energy

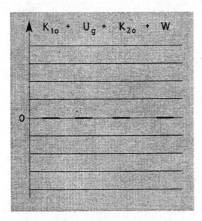

Question 1: Determine the magnitude of the friction force.

Question 3 and 5: Apply the generalized work-energy equation.

Solve the equation.

You can follow a similar process to solve Question 6.

Determine the speed of the 60-kg bricklayer after he rises 7.0 m. The 64-kg stack of bricks falls 7.0 m and is just ready to hit the ground. Assume that the gravitational constant is 10 N/kg. Ignore air resistance, friction in the pulley, and the pulley mass.

Question 1: Complete the work-energy bar charts.

Initial Energy + Work = Final Energy

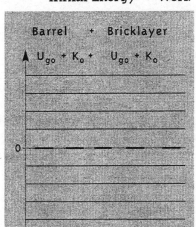

Barrel + Bricklayer

$$U_{go} + K_o + U_{go} + K_o$$

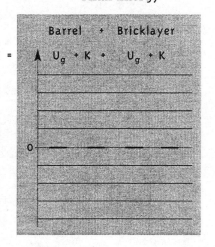

Barrel + Bricklayer

$$= U_g + K + U_g + K$$

0

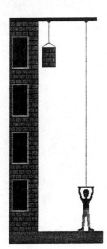

Question 2: Apply the generalized work-energy equation.

Solve the equation for the bricklayer's speed.

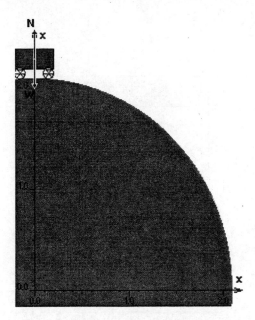

A 10-kg cart starts at rest at the top of a frictionless circular hill and coasts at increasing speed toward the right and down the hill. The radius of the circular path followed by the cart is 2.10 m. Determine the x- and y-coordinate positions when the cart leaves contact with the hill. The origin of the coordinates is at the center of the circle. Assume that the gravitational constant is 10 N/kg.

Question 1 — Solution Plan

• Describe the parts of the problem.
• Identify the best physics principle to apply for each part.
• Do you need any other concepts?

Question 2: Complete the work-energy bar charts.

Initial Energy + Work = Final Energy

U_{go} + K_o + U_{so} + W

0

U_g + K + U_s + U_{in}

0

Question 3: Force Diagram When Cart Leaves Surface

tangential

radial

Generalized Work-Energy Equation

Question 3: Radial Component Form of Newton's Second Law

Question 4: Geometry

Relate r and Θ to x and y.

Question 5: Solution

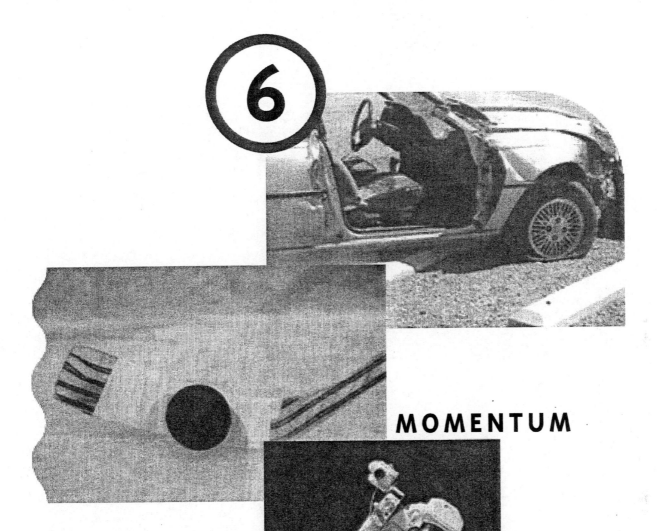

6

MOMENTUM

Finish
Line

Question 1: Two pucks initially at rest are pushed by identical 10-N forces caused by an object not shown. The blue puck has mass 1.0 kg, and the orange puck has mass 2.0 kg. Which puck reaches the finish line first?

Blue Puck   Orange Puck   It's a tie

Question 2: The pucks start again and travel until the blue puck reaches the finish line. At that time, which puck will have the greater change in momentum? Explain your choice.

Blue Puck   Orange Puck   They have equal changes.

Question 3: The pucks start again and travel until the blue puck reaches the finish line. At that time, which puck will have the greater change in kinetic energy? Explain your choice.

Blue Puck   Orange Puck   They have equal changes.

Question 4: Record the kinetic energy change when the blue puck reaches the finish line. When the orange puck reaches the finish line, will it have more, the same, or less kinetic energy change than the blue puck had when it reached the finish line? Explain your choice.

dK greater for Orange Puck   dK same for both pucks   dK greater for Blue Puck

Question 5: Record the momentum change when the blue puck reaches the finish line. When the orange puck reaches the finish line, will it have more, the same, or less momentum change than the blue puck had when it reached the finish line? Explain your choice.

dp greater for Orange Puck   dp same for both pucks   dp greater for Blue Puck

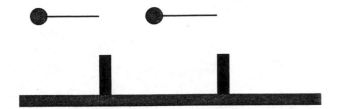

Question 1: Two identical balls swing down and hit equal mass bricks. The collision on the left is totally elastic and that on the right is totally inelastic. First observe the behavior of the balls when the bricks are anchored so that they cannot move.

Question 2: When the anchors holding the bricks are removed and the balls swing down to hit the bricks, which brick is most likely to be knocked over? Explain your choice.

Elastic collision   Inelastic collision   Equal chance

Question 3: Which collision causes the greater impulse on the brick? Explain your choice.

Elastic collision   Inelastic collision   Equal chance

Question 4: Which collision causes the greater change in momentum of the ball? Remember that momentum is a vector quantity.

Elastic collision   Inelastic collision   Equal chance

Are the answers to Questions 3 and 4 related in any way?

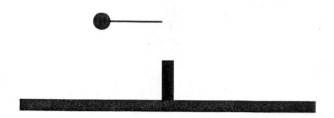

Question 5: For the simulation, adjust the elasticity slider for a perfectly elastic collision and run the simulation.

- Is the total energy, including internal energy, conserved?
- Is kinetic energy conserved?
- Is the net x-component of momentum conserved from just before the collision to just after it?
- How can the magnitude of the momentum of the box after the collision be greater than the magnitude of the momentum of the pendulum bob just before the collision?

Question 6: Adjust the elasticity slider for a perfectly inelastic collision and run the simulation.

- Is the total energy, including internal energy, conserved?
- Is kinetic energy conserved?
- Is momentum conserved from just before to just after the collision?
- Why is the momentum of the box after the collision less for the inelastic collision than for the elastic collision?

For the first simulation, adjust each slider, one at a time, to get a feel for its effect on the collision of the orange puck with the blue puck. Shortly, you will examine the readings on one or more meters and invent rules that apply to these collisions. The pucks slide on a frictionless surface.

Questions 1-2 — The x-Component of Momentum: This simulation indicates the x-component of momentum ($m\,v_x$) of each puck. Run the simulation several times and adjust the elasticity, mass ratio, and y-position before each run. Based on your observations, invent a rule that seems to describe for the x-component of momentum during these collisions.

Question 3 — The y-Component of Momentum: The next simulation indicates the y-component of momentum ($m\,v_y$) of each puck. Run the simulation several times and adjust the y-position, the elasticity, and the mass ratio before each run. Based on your observations for a variety of conditions, invent a rule that seems to describe the variation of the y-component of momentum during the collisions.

Questions 4-5 — Elasticity and Kinetic Energy During Collisions: The next simulation has energy bar charts that indicate by the lengths of bars the initial and final kinetic energy and internal energy of the two-puck system. Run the collisions under a variety of conditions by adjusting the sliders one at a time before each run. Then indicate

(a) under what conditions the total energy, including internal energy, is conserved

(b) under what condition(s) the total kinetic energy (the sum of the kinetic energy of the two pucks) is conserved during the collisions.

These collisions with conserved kinetic energy are called **elastic** collisions. If kinetic energy is not conserved, the collision is said to be partially or totally **inelastic.**

(a) Conditions for energy conservation (including internal energy) during collisions:

(b) Conditions for kinetic energy conservation during collisions:

SUMMARY

- If the net force in the x-direction exerted by other objects on a system of two or more colliding objects is zero, then the sum of the x-components of the momentum of the objects in the system is conserved or constant.

- If the net force in the y-direction exerted by other objects on a system of two or more colliding objects is zero, then the sum of the y-components of the momentum of the objects in the system is conserved or constant.

- If no external forces do work on the objects in the system (like the two pucks), then the total energy of the system is conserved. There may be considerable conversion of kinetic energy to internal energy.

- For so-called elastic collisions, the kinetic energy of the system is conserved.

Show that both energy and momentum cannot be conserved if the number of balls that swing down differs from the number that swing up after the collision. Now aren't they smart.

Concept(s) to be used:

Unknown to be determined:

Known or estimated quantities:

Calculations:

Question 1: A 1.0-kg green puck travels at 4.0 m/s in the positive x-direction and has a head-on collision with a 0.5-kg blue puck, initially at rest. The collision is totally inelastic — they stick together. Predict the velocity of the two pucks after the collision. How much internal energy is produced during the collision?

Question 2: A 1.0-kg green puck travels at 4.0 m/s in the positive x-direction and has a head-on totally elastic collision with a 0.5-kg blue puck, initially at rest. Predict the velocity of each puck after the collision. How much internal energy is produced during the collision?

Question 3: A 1.0-kg green puck traveling in the positive x-direction at 4.0 m/s has a glancing collision with a 1.0-kg blue puck. The collision is elastic. With the x and y-velocity components for the blue puck left off, run the simulation and observe the x- and y-velocity components of the green puck. Then predict the x- and y-components of velocity of the blue puck. After your calculations, click on the blue puck's velocity components and rerun the simulation to check your answers. Is kinetic energy conserved? Support your answer.

Question 1: A 2000-kg blue truck initially travels in the positive x-direction at 10 m/s, and a 1000-kg yellow car initially travels in the positive y-direction at 20 m/s. The collision is totally inelastic (elasticity 0.0). Determine all the final velocity components for the two vehicles. How much internal energy is produced during the collision?

Question 2: A 2000-kg blue truck travels in the positive x-direction at 10 m/s, and a 1000-kg yellow car travels in the positive y-direction at 20 m/s. The collision is totally elastic. Turn on the x-component velocity for the truck and the y-component velocity for the car. Run the simulation and use momentum conservation principles to determine all the final velocity components for the vehicles. How much internal energy is produced during the collision? Is this possible for real car collisions?

Question 3: A 2000-kg blue truck travels in the positive x-direction at 24 m/s, and a 1000-kg yellow car initially travels in the positive y-direction at 12m/s. They have a totally inelastic collision. Turn off all the velocity components. Determine all of the final velocity components for the two vehicles. How much internal energy is produced during the collision?

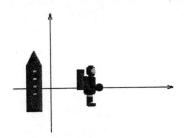

Question 1: A 60-kg astronaut drifts away from a spaceship at speed 2.0 m/s. She has no jets to help her return. When she is 20 m from the ship, she flings her 30-kg auxiliary oxygen supply into space. The oxygen supply now moves at 10 m/s relative to the spaceship. Does she have a reasonable chance of returning to the ship alive?

Determine her velocity just after flinging the oxygen supply.

Will she make it back to the ship in a reasonable time? Justify your answer.

Question 1: A 3.0-kg projectile traveling horizontally through the air at 3.0 m/s explodes into a 2.0-kg blue part and a 1.0-kg orange part. Each part experiences a 3.0 kg m/s impulse (positive on the blue part and negative on the orange). After the explosion, they take 1.0 s to reach the ground. If they are at position x = 0.0 m at the time of the explosion, where will the two parts land?

Question 2: A 3.0-kg projectile traveling horizontally through the air at 3.0 m/s explodes into a 1.0-kg blue part and a 2.0-kg orange part. Each part experiences a 3.0 kg m/s impulse (positive on the blue part and negative on the orange). After the explosion, they take 1.0 s to reach the ground. If they are at position x = 0.0 m at the time of the explosion, where will the two parts land?

Question 3: A 1.0-kg projectile traveling horizontally through the air at 3.0 m/s explodes into a 0.5-kg blue part and a 0.5-kg orange part. Each part experiences a 3.0 kg m/s impulse (positive on the blue part and negative on the orange). After the explosion, they take 1.0 s to reach the ground. If they are at position x = 0.0 m at the time of the explosion, where will the two parts land?

Question 4: A 1.0-kg projectile traveling horizontally through the air at 3.0 m/s explodes into a 0.5-kg blue part and a 0.5-kg orange part. Each part experiences a 2.0 kg m/s impulse (positive on the blue part and negative on the orange). After the explosion, they take 1.0 s to reach the ground. If they are at position x = 0.0 m at the time of the explosion, where will the two parts land?

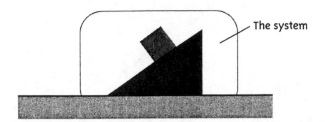

The system

Answer the following questions concerning the block and incline. All surfaces have negligible friction.
Assume that the gravitational constant is 10 N/kg = 10 m/s².

Question 1 — The System: Consider the block and incline as the system. Are there any external forces exerted on the system that have non-zero x-components? If so, describe these forces.

Question 2 — Mass of Incline: Run the simulation with the x-components of velocity turned on. Based on the meter readings after the 10-kg block leaves the incline and using the conservation of momentum principle, determine the mass of the incline.

Question 3 — Another Momentum Problem: Reset the simulation and change the block's mass to 2.00 kg. Turn off the block's x-component of velocity and run the simulation. Based on your observations, predict the x-component of velocity of the block after it leaves contact with the incline. Run the simulation again with block x on to check your work.

Question 4 — Force Diagram for Block and Incline: Construct a force diagram for the block and incline together during the time interval that the block and incline are moving and the block is about halfway down the incline. Use vertical and horizontal axes.

y

x

Question 4 — Apply Newton's Second Law: Apply the y-component form of Newton's Second Law ($\Sigma F_y = ma_y$) to the force diagram you drew. Show that the meter readings for the forces in the simulation are consistent with this law. Assume that the gravitational constant is 10 N/kg = 10 m/s².

Question 5 — Force Diagram for Block: Construct a force diagram for the block when it is moving, and it is about halfway down the incline. Use vertical and horizontal axes. Then apply the x- and y-component forms of Newton's Second Law to the force diagram. Use the meter readings and the Second Law equations to determine the angle of the incline. Each equation should produce the same answer. Assume that the gravitational constant is 10 N/kg = 10 m/s².

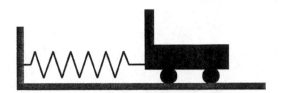

After coming down a ski slope, a 50-kg skier traveling at 12 m/s, runs into a 25-kg padded cart. Velcro fasteners cause the skier and cart to join together. After joining together, the cart and skier compress a 400-N/m spring that is initially relaxed. The skier gets a nice vibro-ride at the end of the ski run. Your task is to determine the maximum distance that the spring will compress before stopping the cart and skier. The surface is frictionless.

Before starting your work, construct qualitative energy bar charts for the following times:

Just before collision

$K_{so} + K_{co} + U_{so} + U_{in}$

0

Just after collision before compression

$K_s + K_c + U_s + U_{in}$

0

At maximum compression of spring

$K_s + K_c + U_s + U_{in}$

0

Concepts for the Parts: Break the big problem into parts, indicate the unknown to be determined for each part, and identify the concept that will be most useful for analyzing each part.

Question 1: Part I — The Collision: You might be tempted to use energy conservation for the whole problem. This does not work well for the collision because of the production of an unknown amount of internal energy during the collision — the skier might even break a bone or get some black and blue marks if the padding is not sufficient. However, if there are no external forces in the horizontal direction on the skier-cart system, then the x-component of momentum is conserved. Use that principle to determine the speed of the cart and skier together at the instant just after the collision.

Question 2: Part II — Compressing the Spring: You found that the cart and skier's speed together at the instant after the collision was 8.0 m/s. Now use another important conservation principle to determine the maximum distance that the 400-N/m spring gets compressed before stopping the skier and cart.

Question 3: After the collision, at what position does the skier feel the greatest force from the padded cart?
(a) just after the collision when moving fastest
(b) at the instant the cart stops when the spring is compressed the most
(c) when the spring is about half compressed
Justify your answer.

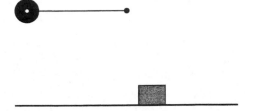

A pendulum bob swings down and hits a box. The box slides on a surface and comes to a stop at some unknown distance from its starting point. You are to determine that unknown distance given the following information:

- mass of pendulum bob is 0.50 kg
- mass of box is 1.0 kg
- length of pendulum string is 3.0 m
- coefficient of kinetic friction between the box and surface is 0.10

Construct qualitative work-energy bar charts for the following times.
The system includes the pendulum, the box, the surface, and the mass of the earth.

At start of process

Pend. Bob   Box

$K_o + U_{go} +$ K_o

0

Just before the collision

Pend. Bob   Box

$K + U_g$ + $K + U_{int}$

0

Just after the collision

Pend. Bob   Box

$K + U_g$ + $K + U_{int}$

0

Question 1: Determine the speed of the pendulum bob just before it hits the box.

When box has stopped at end

Pend. Bob   Box

$K + U_g$ + $K + U_{int}$

0

Question 2: Determine the speed of the box immediately after the pendulum bob hits it. (Why is energy conservation not appropriate for this calculation?)

Question 3: Determine the distance that the box travels after the collision.

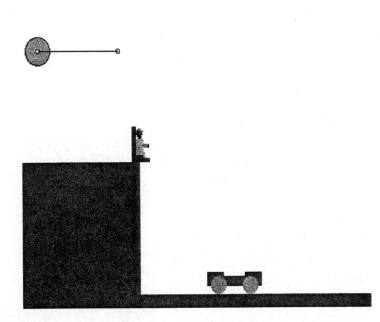

Question 1: A 3.0-m-long rope with a 40-kg medicine ball on the end swings down and hits an 80-kg person sitting on a ledge. The ball stops, and the person flies off and lands in a cart 3.6 m below (if the cart is located at the correct position). The person and cart then slide happily across a frictionless surface. The gravitational constant is 10 N/kg.

(a) Decide where the cart should be located so that the person lands in it.

(b) Decide how fast the cart moves after the person has settled into it.

RECOMMENDED STRATEGY:

- Identify the parts of the problem.
- Identify the unknown to be determined for each part.
- Identify the main principle to be used to determine that unknown for each part.
- Solve the parts and reassemble to answer the big problem.

7

ROTATIONAL MOTION AND STATICS

A rope slanted at 36.87° above the horizontal supports the right end of a 10-kg, 4.0-m-long horizontal beam. A pin through the beam supports its left end. If a 20-kg brick sits on the beam 3.0 m from the left end, the rope tension is 333.3 N. The gravitational constant is 10 N/kg.

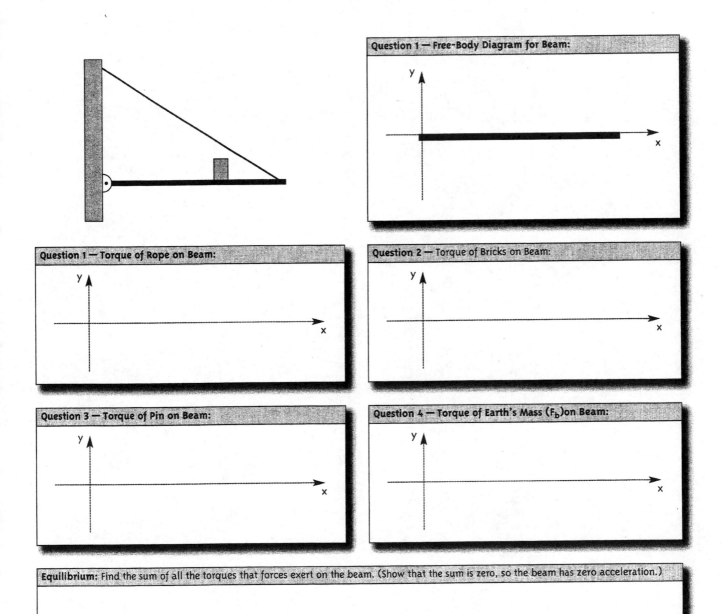

Question 1 — Free-Body Diagram for Beam:

Question 1 — Torque of Rope on Beam:

Question 2 — Torque of Bricks on Beam:

Question 3 — Torque of Pin on Beam:

Question 4 — Torque of Earth's Mass (F_b)on Beam:

Equilibrium: Find the sum of all the torques that forces exert on the beam. (Show that the sum is zero, so the beam has zero acceleration.)

A horizontal rope with tension 237 N supports the right end of a 4.0-m-long beam that is slanted 30° above the horizontal. A pin through the beam supports its left end. A 10-kg brick hangs from the beam 3.46 m from the pin supporting the beam's left side. The gravitational constant is 10 N/kg.

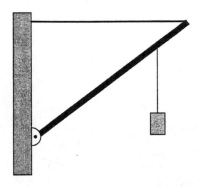

Free-Body Diagram for Beam:

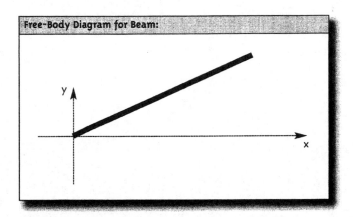

Question 1

Torque of Horizontal Rope on Beam:

Torque of Vertical Rope on Beam:

Torque of Weight on Beam:

Torque of Pin on Beam:

Question 2 — Sum of all Torques:

Question 3 — add the x-components of all forces (to equal zero).

Question 4 — add the y-components of all forces (to equal zero).

Biceps

Triceps

The simulations in the activity provide models for how the biceps and triceps work. The horizontal beam represents the lower arm, and the vertical beam represents the upper arm. The lower arm has a mass of 10 kg. Each division on the screen is 0.20 m. The block's mass is 10 kg. Determine the muscle tension and forces exerted on the lower arm.

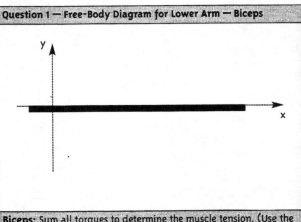

0.00 0.10   0.32   0.70 (m)

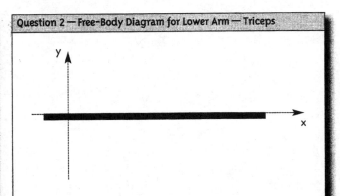

-0.10 0.00   0.32   0.70 (m)

Question 1 — Free-Body Diagram for Lower Arm — Biceps

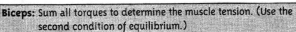

y

x

Biceps: Sum all torques to determine the muscle tension. (Use the second condition of equilibrium.)

Biceps: Find the sum of the y-components of forces to determine elbow force.

Question 2 — Free-Body Diagram for Lower Arm — Triceps

y

x

Triceps: Sum all torques to determine the force of the hand on the table caused by a 300-N triceps tension. (Use the second condition of equilibrium.)

Triceps: Find the sum of the y-components of forces to determine elbow force.

Two painters stand on a 10-kg, 4.0-m-long uniform beam that is supported by ropes on each end. The gravitational constant is 10 N/kg. Determine the tension in each rope. (Complete the information below to answer Question 1.)

Description of Situation:

• The mass of the painter on the left is
_____ kg, and he stands _____ m from the left rope.

• The mass of the painter on the right is
_____ kg, and she stands _____ m from the right rope.

Free-Body Diagram for Beam (draw axes):

First Condition of Equilibrium (y-components):

Second Condition of Equilibrium:

Complete Solution:

A 1.00-m-long beam represents the backbone. A 20-kg load hangs from the end. The beam has a 30-kg uniform mass. The back muscle connects to the beam 0.77 m from the pivot point at the lower left of the beam. The back muscle makes a 9.75° angle with respect to the beam. The gravitational constant is 10 N/kg.

Free-Body Diagram for Backbone (Beam)

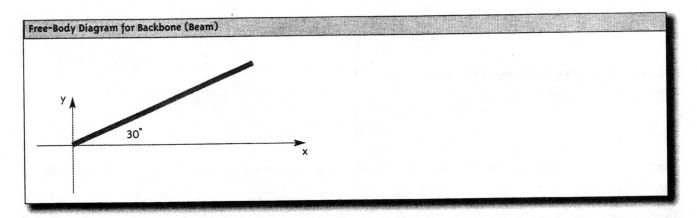

Find the sum of all the torques that forces exert on the backbone (beam).

Find the sum of the x-components of the forces exerted on the backbone (beam).

Find the sum of the y-components of the forces exerted on the backbone (beam).

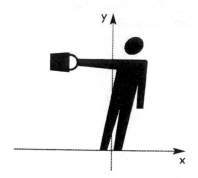

Estimate the tension in the arm of the 170-lb person swinging the bucket of water. Stop the movie about two-thirds of the way through when the person is facing you and use statics for your estimate.

Concept(s) to be used:

Unknown to be determined:

Known or estimated quantities:

Calculations:

©1997 Addison Wesley Interactive & Alan Van Heuvelen

A professor sits 2.0 m from the left fulcrum of a 5.0-m-long, 20-kg uniform beam. A rope connected to the other end of the beam passes up over a pulley and down to a harness worn by the professor. The rope makes a 45° angle with the beam. The gravitational constant is 10 N/kg. Determine the rope tension and the normal force of the beam on the professor. (Complete the following information to answer Question 1.)

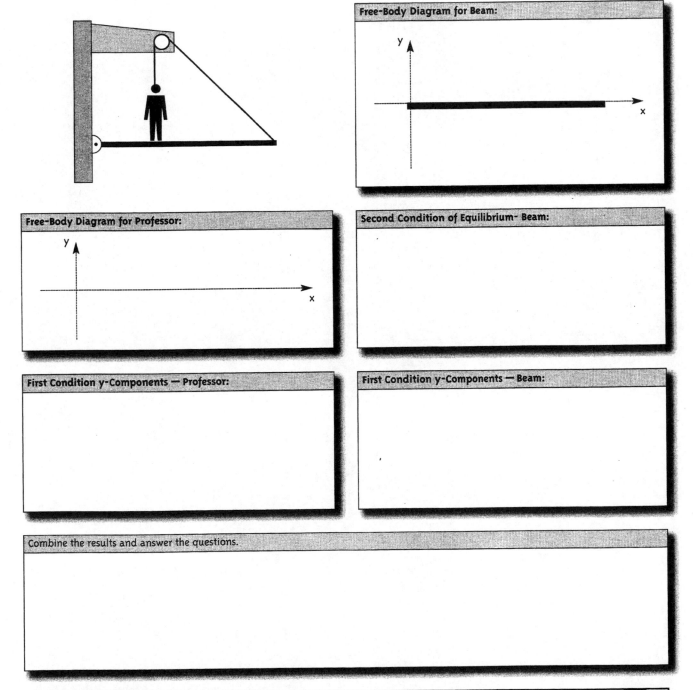

Free-Body Diagram for Beam:

Free-Body Diagram for Professor:

Second Condition of Equilibrium- Beam:

First Condition y-Components — Professor:

First Condition y-Components — Beam:

Combine the results and answer the questions.

Determine the rotational inertia of each beam
of four balls shown below. The balls rotate about
an axis perpendicular to and through
(a) the right end of the beam and
(b) the center of the beam. Each ball has a mass
of 1.0 kg, and the beam connecting the balls has
no mass.

Question 1 (a):

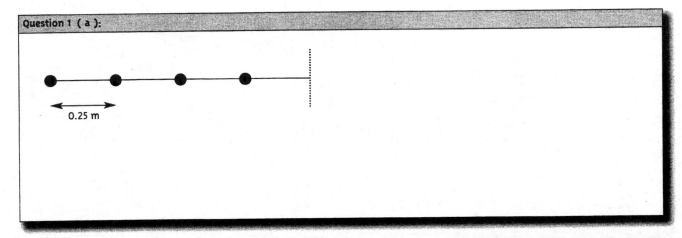

Question 1 (b):

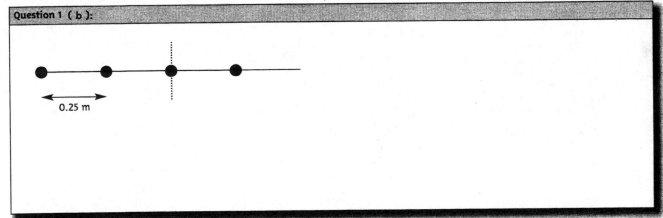

Challenge: Compare the magnitudes of the rotational inertia of a solid sphere and a hollow sphere that have the same radius and mass. Explain your answer choice.

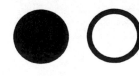

$I_{solid} > I_{hollow}$ $I_{solid} = I_{hollow}$ $I_{solid} < I_{hollow}$

Each disk below rotates about an axis through the center of the disk. The word *faster* means that the disk is turning faster and faster and does not imply anything about how fast it is turning. Similarly, the word *slower* means that the disc is turning slower and slower (its angular speed is decreasing). Add vectors to show the direction of the angular velocity ω and the angular acceleration α for the different types of motion.

Spinning Faster

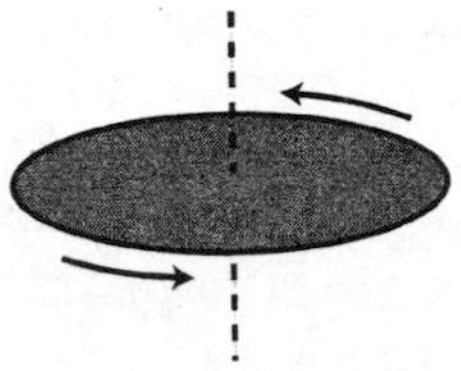

Sign ω: _____
Sign α: _____

Spinning Slower

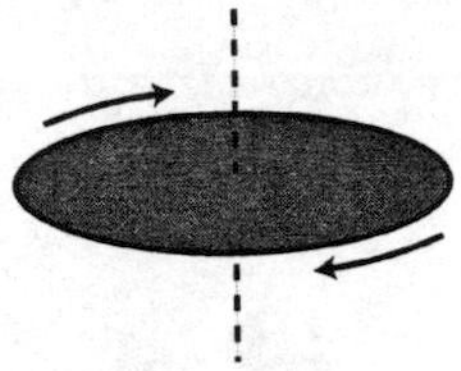

Sign ω: _____
Sign α: _____

Spinning Faster

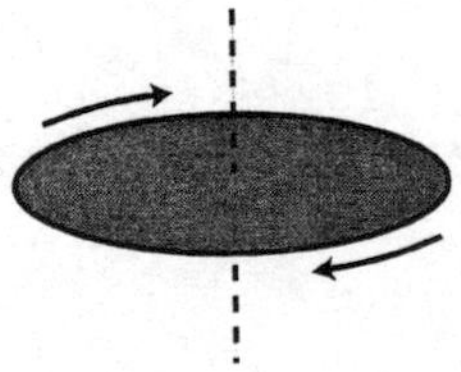

Sign ω: _____
Sign α: _____

Spinning Slower

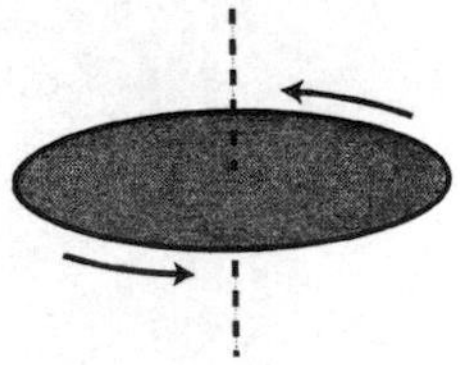

Sign ω: _____
Sign α: _____

Constant Spinning Rates

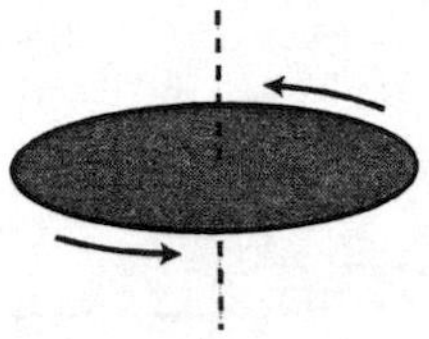

Sign ω: _____
Sign α: _____

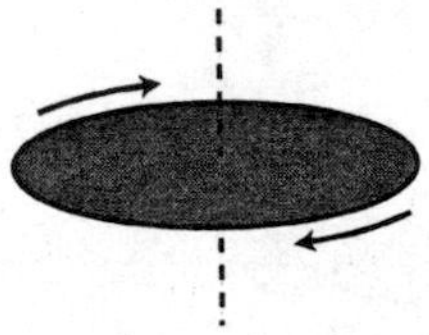

Sign ω: _____
Sign α: _____

A top view of the six disks from Question 1 is shown below. Each disk rotates about an axis through its center and perpendicular to the page. You are to run the simulation and determine the sign of the angular velocity ω and of the angular acceleration α for each disk. The choices are +, −, or 0. Note that for angular velocity ω:

• counterclockwise is positive (+)
• clockwise is negative (−)
• zero (0)

Yellow Disk (1st)

Angular Velocity ω: _____

Angular Acceleration α: _____

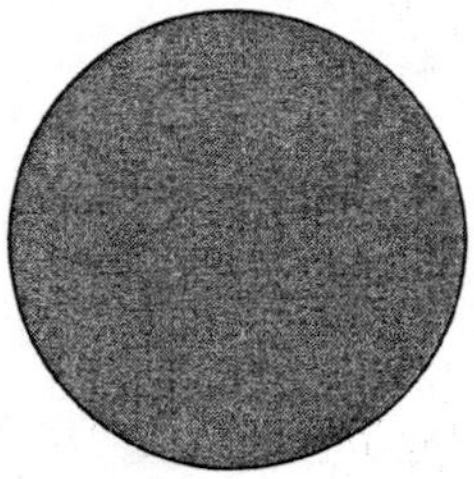

Turquoise Disk (2nd)

Angular Velocity ω: _____

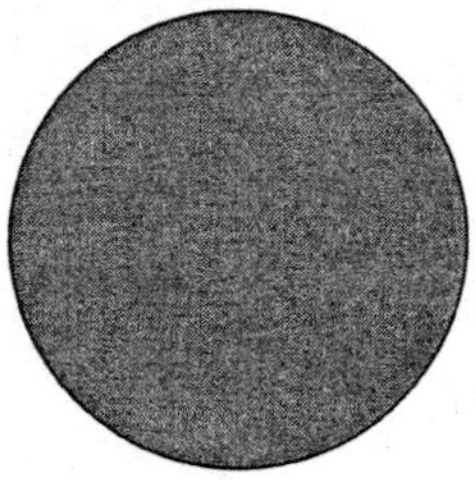

Green Disk (3rd)

Angular Velocity ω: _____

Angular Acceleration α: _____

Blue Disk (4th)

Angular Velocity ω: _____

Angular Acceleration α: _____

Gray Disk (5th)

Angular Velocity ω: _____

Angular Acceleration α: _____

Red Disk (6th)

Angular Velocity ω: _____

Angular Acceleration α: _____

The simulation shows the side view of a rear-wheel-drive car. The right wheel on the simulation represents the rear wheels, and the left wheel on the simulation represents the front wheels.

Question 1: The motor exerts a -400 N·m clockwise torque on the rear wheels (the right wheels) of the 100-kg car. Indicate the direction of the friction force of the road on the rear wheels and the direction that the car accelerates.

Question 2: The motor exerts a +400 N·m counterclockwise torque on the right rear wheels of the 100-kg car. Indicate the direction of the friction force of the road on the rear wheels and the direction that the car accelerates.

Question 3: When the car was accelerating forward (toward the left on the simulation), the normal force of the road was greater on the right rear wheels than on the left front wheels. Explain. Think about the torque of the motor on the wheels and the oppositely-directed torque of the wheels on the motor (and car).

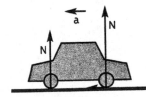

You are asked to determine the magnitude of the force (represented by the arrow) that a parent must apply continously on one pod of the rotoride so that the pod's angular acceleration is 0.40 rad/s². The 80-kg pod on each end, which includes the mass of the passenger, is connected by a uniform rod of rotational inertia 8.13 kg•m². This does not include the rotational inertia of the pods, which are located at each end 1.0 m from the center of the beam.

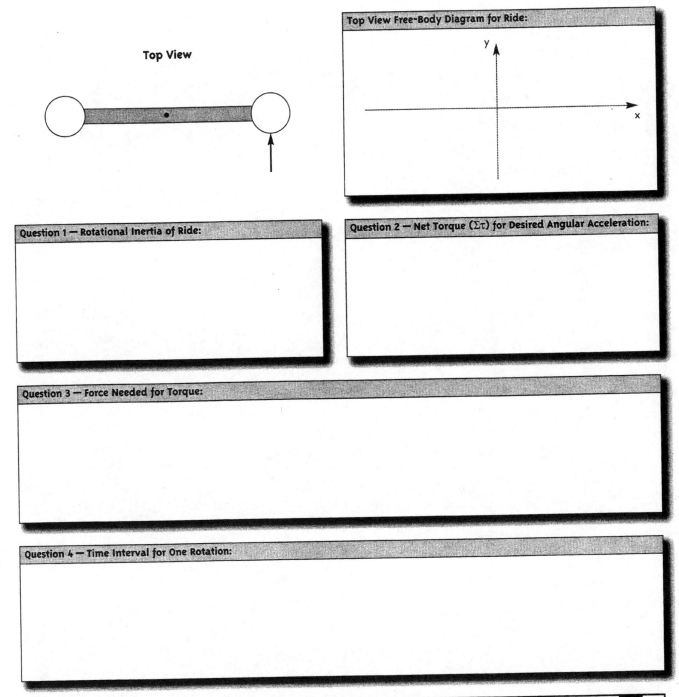

Top View

Top View Free-Body Diagram for Ride:

Question 1 — Rotational Inertia of Ride:

Question 2 — Net Torque ($\Sigma\tau$) for Desired Angular Acceleration:

Question 3 — Force Needed for Torque:

Question 4 — Time Interval for One Rotation:

A 5.0-kg, 4.0-m-long ladder falls. Determine the angular acceleration of the ladder at the instant it is tilted 1.0 radian above the horizontal. The ladder has a uniform mass distribution, and the gravitational constant is 10.0 N/kg.

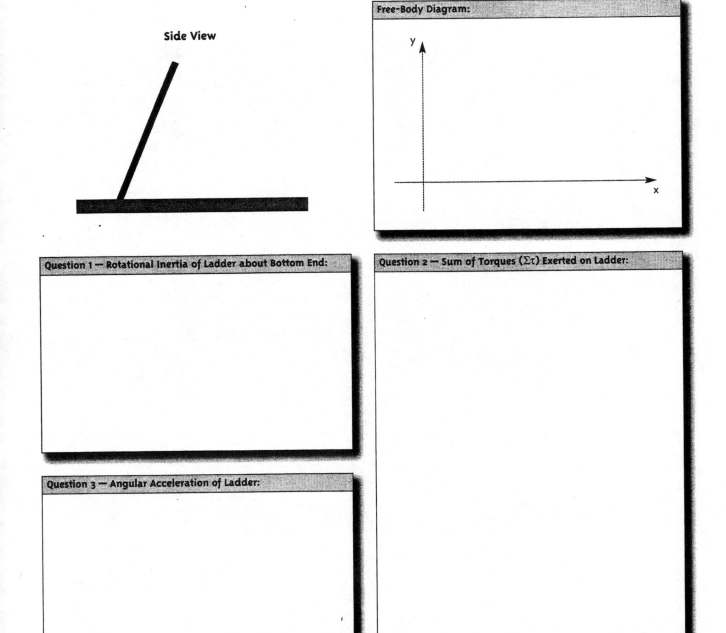

Side View

Free-Body Diagram:

y

x

Question 1 — Rotational Inertia of Ladder about Bottom End:

Question 2 — Sum of Torques ($\Sigma\tau$) Exerted on Ladder:

Question 3 — Angular Acceleration of Ladder:

A 60-kg student hangs from a trapeze held by a rope wrapped around a 1.0-m-radius flywheel with a rotational inertia of 180 kg•m². She starts at rest. Determine her speed after falling 5.0 m towards the ground. The gravitational constant is 10 N/kg.

Question 1 — Free-Body Diagram for Flywheel:

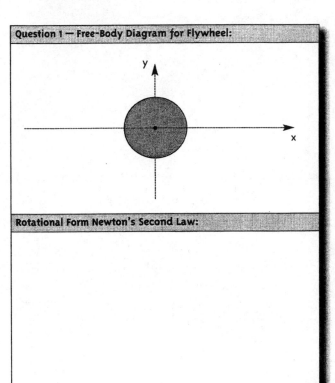

Rotational Form Newton's Second Law:

Question 2 — Free-Body Diagram for Student:

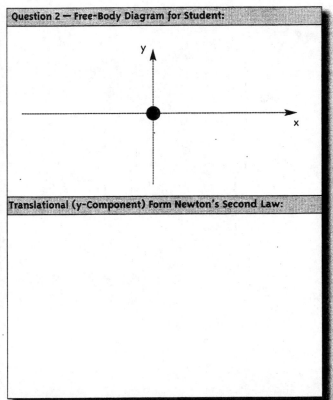

Translational (y-Component) Form Newton's Second Law:

Question 3 — Write an equation relating the acceleration of the woman and the angular acceleration of the flywheel. Solve the three equations you now have for the three unknowns.

Question 4 — Combine the results of Question 1-3 and use kinematics to find her speed.

A solid block slides down a frictionless incline. A solid disk of the same mass rolls down an identical incline. Decide which object reaches the bottom of the incline first or if they tie. Provide your reason. Next, complete the work-energy bar charts for the block system and for the disk system, starting with the objects at the top of the incline and ending when one or both reach the bottom. The kinetic energy can be in the form of translational kinetic energy (Kt) and/or rotational kinetic energy (Kr). Can you now understand why the race ends as it does?

Question 1: Your Choice of Winner and Reason:

Question 2: Predicted Energy Changes
Block System:

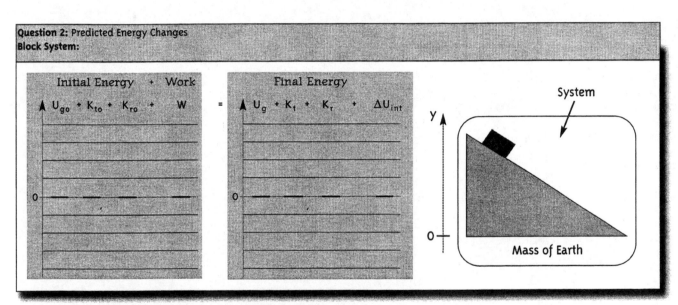

Disk System:

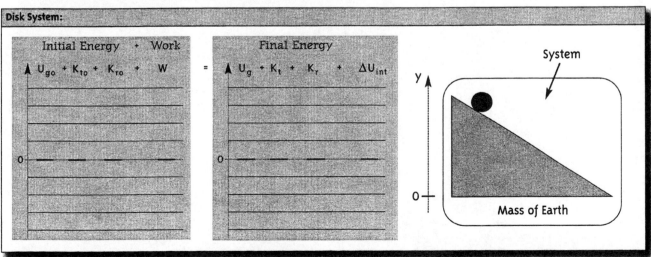

A 60-kg student hangs on a trapeze held by a rope wrapped around a 1.0-m-radius flywheel with a rotational inertia of 180 kg·m². The student starts at rest. Determine her speed after falling 5.0 m towards the ground. Assume that the gravitational constant is 10 N/kg. U_g is the gravitational potential energy, K_s is the student's kinetic energy, K_f is the flywheel's kinetic energy, and U_i is the internal energy due to friction (zero in this problem).

Question 1 — Work-Energy Bar Chart:

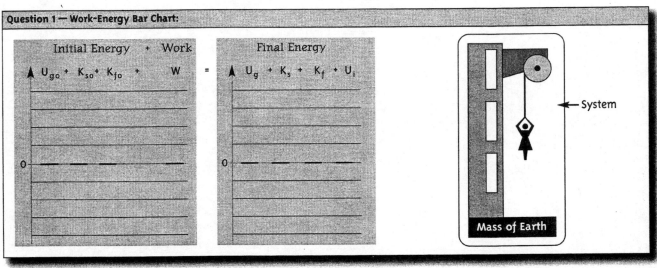

Initial Energy + Work

$U_{go} + K_{so} + K_{fo} + \quad W$

Final Energy

$U_g + K_s + K_f + U_i$

System

Mass of Earth

Question 2 — Apply the energy conservation principle and the generalized work-energy equation.

Question 3 — Relate the translational speed of the student and the angular (rotational) speed of the flywheel.

Question 4 — Solution.

A rotoride has a uniform rod with 80-kg child-occupied pods on each end at 1.0 m from the center of the rod. A parent's continuous 67-N push on one pod causes the pods and rod to rotate at increasing angular speed. The rotational inertia of the rod-and-two-pod system is 168.1 kg•m². Use an energy approach to determine the time interval needed for the first complete turn of the rod, starting from rest. (Ignore friction.)

Question 1 — Work-Energy Bar Chart:

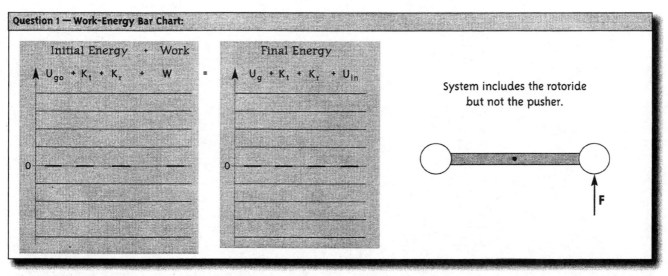

Initial Energy + Work

$U_{go} + K_t + K_r + W$ = Final Energy $U_g + K_t + K_r + U_{in}$

System includes the rotoride but not the pusher.

F

Question 2 — Apply the energy conservation principle and the generalized work-energy equation.

Question 3 — Determine the work done by the person pushing.

Question 4 — Find the final angular velocity.

Question 5 — Determine the time interval for one rotation.

Observe the behavior of the ball and bat in Question 1. Then complete the following information.

Question 2 — Angular Momentum of the Ball: Based on your observations, determine an expression for the angular momentum of the ball.

Question 3 — Angular Momentum of Extended Body: Based on your observations, determine an expression for the angular momentum of the bat.

Question 4 — Angular Momentum Conservation: Based on your observations, write a rule that describes the angular momentum of the ball-bat system during their collisions.

For each of the following situations, determine the missing quantity (or quantities) for the collision. The ball's mass is 0.50 kg, and the bat's rotational inertia is 3.0 kg·m².

Question Number:	5	6	7	Workspace:
Elasticity	1	1	0	
Initial x-velocity (m/s) ball	−4.0	−4.0	−4.0	
Initial y-position (m) ball	−3.0	−0.5	−2.0	
Initial angular speed (rad/s) bat	2.0	2.0	2.0	
Final x-velocity (m/s) ball	_____	_____	_____	
Final y-position (m) ball	−3.0	−0.5	−2.0	
Final angular speed (rad/s) bat	−2.0	1.2	_____	

SUMMARY

- Angular Momentum of Point Particle: $L_z = x\,p_y - y\,p_x = x\,(m\,v_y) - y\,(m\,v_x)$.
- Angular Momentum of Extended Body: $L_z = I\,\omega$.
- Conservation of Momentum Principle: ΣL_z (before collision) $= \Sigma L_z$ (after collision)

  For the ball-bat system:

  L_{zo}(bat) $+ L_{zo}$(ball) $= L_z$(bat) $+ L_z$(ball)

Observe the behavior of the negatively charged ball for Question 1. Then complete the following information.

Question 2: With v_{xo} = +2.00 m/s and y_o = +1.50 m, determine the initial angular momentum of the 1.0-kg ball.

Question 3: Run the simulation with v_{xo} = +1.50 m/s and y_o = +2.00 m. Stop the motion in two quadrants and use the x, y, v_x, and v_y meter readings to calculate the angular momentum of the 1.0-kg ball when it is at these positions. Compare these values to the initial angular momentum calculated in Question 2.

Questions 4-5: Why is angular momentum conserved?

Newton's Second Law can be written in the following form that applies to rotational motion:

Net torque = Change in angular momentum

$$\Sigma \tau = dL / dt$$

Note that if the net torque on an object is zero, its angular momentum is constant. Show that the net torque on the moving particle in this simulation is zero.

Show forces on moving particle: Determine torque caused by these forces:

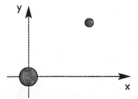

SUMMARY

- Angular Momentum of Point Particle: $L_z = x\,p_y - y\,p_x = x\,(m\,v_y) - y\,(m\,v_x)$.
- Angular Momentum of Extended Body: $L_z = I\,\omega$.
- Conservation of Momentum Principle: If the net torque on a system is zero, the system's angular momentum is constant.

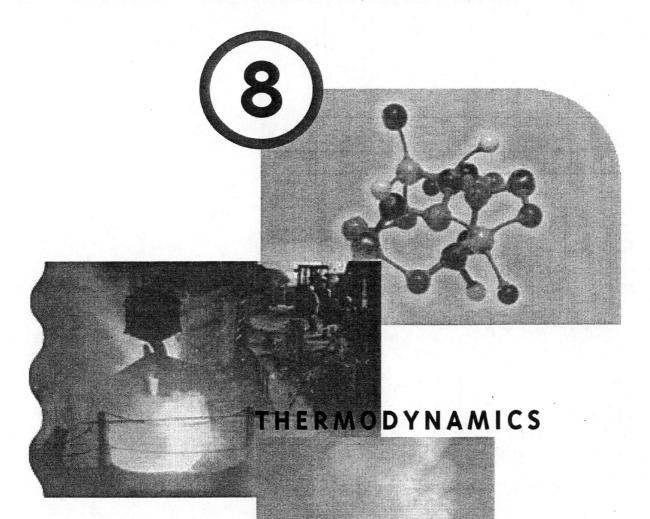

8

THERMODYNAMICS

Thermodynamics Review Notes:

• Ideal gas law: . . . . $PV = NkT = nRT$.

. . . .

• W is the work done *by* the gas on the environment: . . . . $W = \int_{v_0}^{v} P\, dV$.

. . . .

• First Law of Thermodynamics: . . . . $Q = W + U_{in}$.

• Internal energy of an ideal gas: . . . . $U_{in} = (3/2)NkT = (3/2)nRT$.

Units

1.0 dm = 0.10 m

$1.0\ (dm)^3 = 1.0 \times 10^{-3}\ m^3$

$1\ kPa = 1.0 \times 10^3\ Pa = 1.0 \times 10^3\ N/m^2$

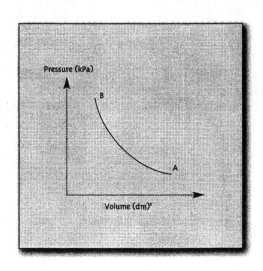

Question 1 — Atom's Speed: Does the colored atom in the simulation always move at the same speed, or does the speed change irregularly?

Question 2 — Reason: What causes the speed of an atom to change irregularly?

Question 3 — Type of Collision with Wall: In this simulation, is an atom's collision with the wall more like an elastic collision or an inelastic collision? Explain.

Question 4 — Instantaneous Kinetic Energy: At one instant of time, do all of the atoms move with the same speed and hence the same average kinetic energy?

Question 5 — Average Speed and Temperature: Set the temperature of the gas to 100 K and make a rough estimate of the average speed of the atom during a one-minute interval. Then predict its average speed at 400 K. After your prediction, set the thermometer to 400 K and estimate the average speed of the colored atom during a one-minute interval. Does the temperature seem to be proportional to the average speed or to the average kinetic energy of the atom?

Question 1 — Number of Atoms with Speed v at Temperature T: How does the number of atoms with speeds between v = 700 and 900 m/s change as the temperature of the gas is increased from 120 K to 960 K?

Question 2: Number of Atoms with Speed v at Temperature T: How does the number of atoms with speeds between v = 2900 and 3100 m/s change as the temperature of the gas is increased from 120 K to 960 K?

A Rule: Based on your observations recorded in Questions 1 and 2, devise a rule that indicates how the distribution of atom speeds changes as the temperature of the gas increases.

Question 3 — Temperature, Root-Mean-Square Speed, and Root-Mean-Square Speed Squared: Record the root-mean-square speed and root-mean-square speed squared for the temperatures listed below.

T (K)	$(v^2_{av})^{1/2}$ (m/s)	v^2_{av} (m/s)^2
120		
200		
400		
600		
800		
960		

Question 4 — Equation Relating Temperature and Speed or Speed Squared: Plot the data in Question 3 on the graphs below and devise an equation that relates the root-mean-square speed or root-mean-square speed squared and the temperature.

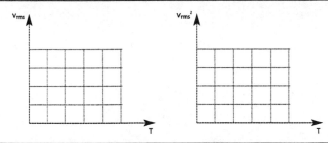

Question 5 — Atom's Mass: Determine the mass of an atom in the simulation. Note that k = 1.38 x 10^{-23} J/K.

Question 6 — v_{rms} at Room Temperature: Determine the root-mean-square speed of a helium atom when it is at room temperature (300 K), m_{He} = 6.65 x 10^{-27} kg.

Question 1: — **Root-Mean-Square Speed of a Helium Atom:** Determine the root-mean-square speed of a helium atom in a gas at temperature 300 K and 600 K. The mass of a helium atom is 6.65×10^{-27} kg, and the Boltzmann constant k is 1.38×10^{-23} J/K.

Question 2 — **Most Probable Speed of a Helium Atom:** Determine the most probable speed of a helium atom in a gas at temperature 300 K and at 600 K. The mass of a helium atom is 6.65×10^{-27} kg, and the Boltzmann constant k is 1.38×10^{-23} J/K.

Question 3 — **Average Random Kinetic Energy of Atom in Gas:** Determine the average random kinetic energy of an atom in a gas that is at temperature 300 K (approximately room temperature). Convert the energy to electron volts (1 eV = 1.6×10^{-19} J).

Question 4 — **Can an Atom Break a Bond?** Compare the average random kinetic energy of an atom in a gas at room temperature to the energy needed to break a bond in a DNA molecule or knock a hydrogen atom off of a protein. Is the average kinetic energy important, or is some other property of the gas important? If so, describe that property.

Question 5 — **Speed to Break a Bond in DNA:** Determine the speed at which a helium atom would have to move in order to have enough energy to break a bond in a DNA molecule.

Questions 1-3: Draw a graph that has the general shape of each process below. The graph must be consistent with the ideal gas law (PV = nRT).

Isobaric Process

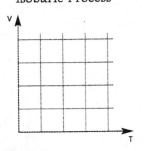

Isochoric Process

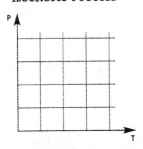

Isothermal Process

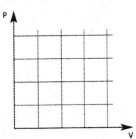

Questions 4-6: For each process below, determine the value of the unknown state variable. The gas has 1.0 mole of atoms.

Isobaric Process	Isochoric Process	Isothermal Process
T = 301.8 K, P = 100 kPa, V = ?	V = 20 (dm)^3, T = 300 K P = ?	T = 300 K, V = 20 (dm)^3 P = ?

Question 7: Determine the temperature of the ideal gas at each corner of the cyclic process shown below. The gas has 1.0 mole of atoms.

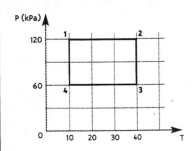

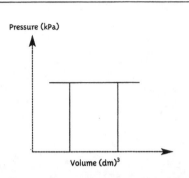

Pressure (kPa)

Volume (dm)³

Question 1: On the simulation for Question 1, pull the top of the left vertical bar on the graph and adjust it to 20 (dm)³ and 100 kPa. Set the top of the right bar to 40 (dm)³ and 100 k Pa. Then calculate the work done by the gas in moving from the first set of values to the second.

Question 2: Adjust the top of the right bar to volume 40 (dm)³ and pressure 200 kPa. (The left bar remains as in Question 1.) Predict the work that will be done by the gas as it moves in a straight line from volume 20 (dm)³ and pressure 100 kPa to volume 40 (dm)³ and pressure 200 kPa. Then, run the simulation to check your answer.

Question 3: The simulation for Question 3 shows an isothermal process in which the pressure is related to the volume by the equation P = (2500 N.m)/V. Determine the work done by the gas as it moves from volume 40 (dm)³ to volume 10 (dm)³.

Question 1 — Isochoric Process: Draw a graph line below to describe an isochoric process in which the temperature increases from 100 K to 400 K. Construct a qualitative work-heat-energy bar chart for the final state. Explain your answers.

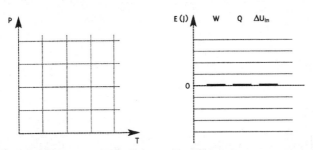

Question 2 — Isothermal Process: Draw a graph line below to describe an isothermal process in which the volume decreases by about one-half. Construct a qualitative work-heat-energy bar chart for the final state. Explain your answers.

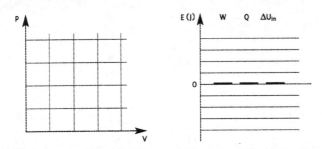

Question 3 — Adiabatic Process: Draw a graph line below to describe an adiabatic process in which the volume decreases by about one-half. Construct a qualitative work-heat-energy bar chart for the final state. Explain your answers.

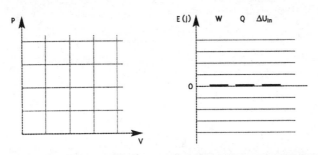

Question 4 — Isobaric Process: Draw a graph line below to describe an isobaric process in which the volume and temperature decrease. Construct a qualitative work-heat-energy bar chart for the final state. Explain your answers.

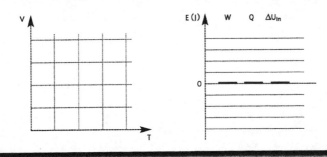

Question 1 — First Law Bar Chart: The bar chart below represents the First Law of Thermodynamics description of heat transfer to a system that remains at constant volume. Why does the bar chart have this shape?

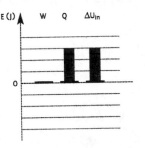

Question 2 — Constant-Volume Heat Capacity (≈): By taking incremental increases in temperature on the simulation, estimate the constant-volume heat capacity. The gas has 1.0 mole of atoms.

$$C_V = \frac{1}{n}\frac{dQ}{dT}$$

at constant volume

Question 3 — Constant-Volume Heat Capacity: Use the simulation numbers as the gas moves at constant volume from temperature 200 K to 800 K to calculate its constant-volume heat capacity. The gas has 1.0 mole of atoms.

$$C_V = \frac{1}{n}\frac{Q}{T-T_0}$$

at constant volume

Question 4 — Expression for Cv: Use the following principles to show that the constant-volume heat capacity of an ideal gas is given by the expression below. Start with the equation in Question 3.

- Use the First Law of Thermodynamics.
- Consider internal energy of a gas in terms of temperature.
- Rearrange to get the expression at the right.
- Calculate the value of C_V using this expression and compare it to the answer in Question 3.

$$C_V = \frac{3}{2}R$$

at constant volume

Question 5 — First Law Bar Chart: The bar chart below represents the First Law of Thermodynamics description of heat transfer to a system that remains at constant pressure. Why does the bar chart have this shape?

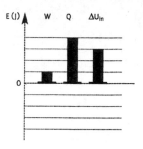

Question 6 — Constant-Pressure Heat Capacity (≈): By taking incremental increases in temperature on the simulation, estimate the constant-pressure heat capacity. The gas has 1.0 mole of atoms.

$$C_p = \frac{1}{n}\frac{dQ}{dT}$$

at constant pressure

Question 7 — Constant-Pressure Heat Capacity: Use the simulation numbers as the gas moves at constant pressure from temperature 200 K to 800 K to calculate its constant-pressure heat capacity. The gas has 1.0 mole of atoms.

$$C_p = \frac{1}{n}\frac{Q}{T-T_0}$$

at constant pressure

Question 8 — Derive Expression for Cp: Use the following principles to show that the constant-pressure heat capacity of an ideal gas is given by the expression below. Start with the equation in Question 7.

• Use the First Law of Thermodynamics.
• Consider internal energy of a gas in terms of temperature.
• Consider work done by the gas at constant pressure.
• Use the ideal gas law.
• Rearrange to get the expression at the right.
• Calculate C_p using this and compare it to the answer in Question 7.

$$C_p = \frac{5}{2}R$$

at constant pressure

The piston encloses the gas so that the cylinder volume is 40.0 (dm)³. Run the simulation and watch the process. The gas starts at 21 kPa and 100 K, moves to 100 kPa and 495 K, and then returns to where it started. Answer the questions below and on the next page.

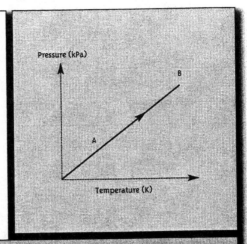

Question 1: What happens to the gas during the first part of the process as the system moves from A to B?

(a) Does the volume increase, remain the same, or decrease?

(b) Does the pressure increase, remain the same, or decrease?

(c) Does the temperature increase, remain the same, or decrease?

Predict the direction of change of bars in the bar chart as the gas moves from A to B:

Q (heat transferred to [+] or from [-] the system), W (work done by the system [+] or on the system [-]), and U (internal energy change of the system).

(d) Q: negative   no change   positive

(e) W: negative   no change   positive

(f) U: negative   no change   positive

After you make your predictions, run the simulation to check them.

Question 2: Use the ideal gas law to determine the number of moles of gas in the system and the number of atoms in the system.

Question 3 — Pressure at B: Determine the pressure in the gas when it is at B. The volume of the gas is 40 (dm)³, and the temperature is 495 K.

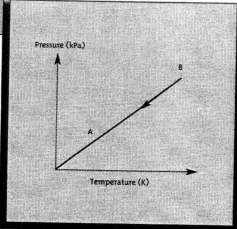

Question 4 — Internal Energy Change: Determine the internal energy change of the gas as it moves from A to B. Use the values of the state variables determined in Questions 2 and 3.

Question 5 — Heat Transfer: Use the First Law of Thermodynamics to determine the heat transfer to the gas as it moves from A to B. Use the results from previous questions.

Question 6: Use a similar procedure to determine the heat transfer to the gas for the following isochoric process.

- The volume remains constant at 20.9 (dm)³.
- The pressure changes from 40 kPa to 197 kPa.
- The temperature starts at 100 K and ends at some unknown temperature.

Watch the piston and graph in the isobaric process simulation. The pressure is set at 200 kPa. The initial volume and temperature at A are 41.6 (dm)³ and 1000 K, respectively. Answer the questions below and on the next page.

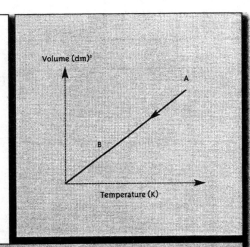

Question 1: What happens to the gas during the first part of the process as the system moves from A to B?

(a) Does the volume increase, remain the same, or decrease?

(b) Does the pressure increase, remain the same, or decrease?

(c) Does the temperature increase, remain the same, or decrease?

Predict the direction of change of bars in the bar chart as the gas moves from A to B:

Q (heat transferred to [+] or from [-] the system), W (work done by the system [+] or on the system [-]), and U (internal energy change of the system).

(d) Q: negative   no change   positive

(e) W: negative   no change   positive

(f) U: negative   no change   positive

After you make your predictions, run the simulation to check them.

Question 2: Use the ideal gas law to determine the volume of the gas when it is at B. The temperature at B is 250 K, and the pressure remains constant at 200 kPa.

Question 3 — Work Done By Gas: Determine the work done by the gas as the gas moves from A to B. The pressure remains constant at 200 kPa. The volume changes from 41.6 (dm)³ to 10.4 (dm)³. The temperature changes from 1000 K to 250 K. (Note that the graph at the right is *not* a pressure-versus-volume graph.)

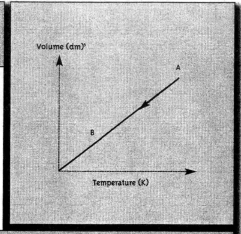

Volume (dm)³ — Temperature (K)

Question 4 — Internal Energy Change: Determine the internal energy change of the gas as it moves from A to B. Use the values of the state variables determined in Question 2.

Question 5 — Heat Transfer: Use the First Law of Thermodynamics to determine the heat transfer to the gas as it moves from A to B. Use the results from previous questions.

Question 6 — Use a similar procedure to determine the heat transfer for the following isobaric process.

- The pressure remains constant at 100 kPa.
- The volume changes from 41.6 (dm)³ to 10.4 (dm)³.
- The temperature starts at 500 K and ends at some unknown temperature.

Watch the piston and graph in the isothermal process simulation. Set the temperature to 300 K. The initial volume and pressure at A are 40 (dm)^3 and 62 kPa, respectively. Answer the questions on this page and the next.

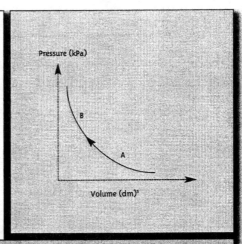

Question 1: What happens to the gas during the first part of the process, as the system moves from A to B?

(a) Does the volume increase, remain the same, or decrease?

(b) Does the pressure increase, remain the same, or decrease?

(c) Does the temperature increase, remain the same, or decrease?

Predict the direction of change of bars in the bar chart as the gas moves from A to B:

Q (heat transferred to [+] or from [-] the system), W (work done by the system [+] or on the system [-]), and U (internal energy change of the system).

(d) Q: negative   no change   positive

(e) W: negative   no change   positive

(f) U: negative   no change   positive

After you make your predictions, run the simulation to check them.

Question 2: Record the values of P and V at several different volumes. Is the product PV constant for the isothermal process?

Question 3 — Work Done By Gas: Determine the work done by the gas as the gas moves from A to B. The temperature remains constant at 300 K. The volume changes from 40 (dm)³ to 10.0 (dm)³. The pressure changes from 62 kPa to 248 kPa. Note: You will have to use the ideal gas law to get the work integral in an integrable form.

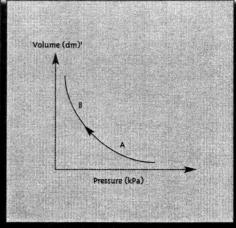

Volume (dm)³

B

A

Pressure (kPa)

Question 4 — Heat Transfer: Use the First Law of Thermodynamics to determine the heat transfer to the gas as it moves from A to B. Use the results from previous questions.

Question 5: What happens to the graph line if the temperature is decreased from 300 K to 250 K?

(a) rises but retains shape
(b) stays the same
(c) drops but retains shape

Explain your answer.

Question 6: Use a similar procedure to determine the heat transfer for the following isothermal process.

- The temperature remains constant at 250 K.
- The volume changes from 40 (dm)³ to 10 (dm)³.
- The pressure starts at 52 kPa and ends at some unknown pressure.

Observe the motion of the atoms in the Adiabatic process simulation. Adjust the initial temperature to 200 K. The initial volume and pressure are 40 (dm)³ and 42 kPa, respectively. Answer the questions below and on the next page.

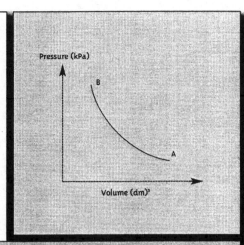

Question 1: What happens to the gas during the first part of the process, as the system moves from A to B?

(a) Does the volume increase, remain the same, or decrease?

(b) Does the pressure increase, remain the same, or decrease?

(c) Does the temperature increase, remain the same, or decrease?

Predict the direction of change of bars in the bar chart as the gas moves from A to B:
Q (heat transferred to [+] or from [-] the system), W (work done by the system [+] or on the system [-]), and U (internal energy change of the system).

(d) Q: negative   no change   positive

(e) W: negative   no change   positive

(f) U: negative   no change   positive

Justify each choice in the space below.

Question 2: Determine the temperature of the gas when it is at B. The volume of the 1.0-mole of gas is 10 (dm)³, and the pressure is 419 kPa.

Question 3 — Internal Energy Change: Determine the change in the internal energy of the gas as it moves from A to B.

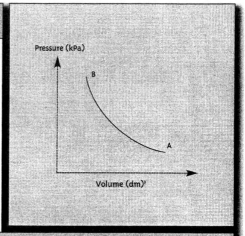

Question 4 — Work Done By Gas: Determine the work done by the gas as it moves from A to B.

Question 5: Repeat this procedure for an adiabatic process that starts at temperature 300 K, volume 40 (dm)³, and pressure 62 kPa and ends at volume 10 (dm)³ and pressure 628 kPa.

Question 1 — Temperature: Use the ideal gas law (PV = nRT) to determine the temperature of the gas at each corner in the process represented by the pressure-versus-volume (PV) graph below.

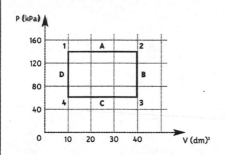

Questions 2–5 — W, ΔU_{in}, Q, and e

• Determine the work done by the gas during each leg (A, B, C and D) of the cycle:

• Use the temperature changes to determine the internal energy change during each leg (A, B, C and D):

• Use the First Law of Thermodynamics to determine the heat transfer during each leg:

• Determine the efficiency of the process: $e = \dfrac{\text{net work done}}{\text{sum of all positive heat transfers to system}}$

Question 1 — Temperature: Use the ideal gas law (PV = nRT) to determine the temperature of the gas at each corner in the process represented by the pressure-versus-volume (PV) graph below.

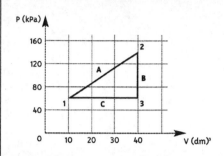

W, ΔU_{in}, Q, and e

- Determine the work done by the gas during each leg (A, B, and C) of the cycle:

- Use the temperature changes to determine the internal energy change during each leg (A, B, and C):

- Use the First Law of Thermodynamics to determine the heat transfer during each leg:

- Determine the efficiency of the process: $e = \dfrac{\text{net work done}}{\text{sum of all positive heat transfers to system}}$

Question 2 — Temperature: Use the ideal gas law (PV = nRT) to determine the temperature of the gas at each corner in the process represented by the pressure-versus-volume (PV) graph below.

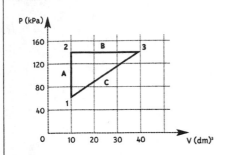

W, ΔU_{in}, Q, and e

- Determine the work done by the gas during each leg (A, B, and C) of the cycle:

- Use the temperature changes to determine the internal energy change during each leg (A, B, and C):

- Use the First Law of Thermodynamics to determine the heat transfer during each leg:

- Determine the efficiency of the process: $e = \dfrac{\text{net work done}}{\text{sum of all positive heat transfers to system}}$

Question 3 — Temperature: Use the ideal gas law (PV = nRT) to determine the temperature of the gas at each corner in the process represented by the pressure-versus-volume (PV) graph below.

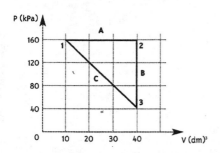

W, ΔU_{in}, Q, and e

- Determine the work done by the gas during each leg (A, B, and C) of the cycle:

- Use the temperature changes to determine the internal energy change during each leg (A, B, and C):

- Use the First Law of Thermodynamics to determine the heat transfer during each leg:

- Determine the efficiency of the process: $e = \dfrac{\text{net work done}}{\text{sum of all positive heat transfers to system}}$

Question 4: Apply the strategies used in the previous cyclic-process problems to determine the efficiencies of the two processes represented on the pressure-versus-volume (PV) graphs below.

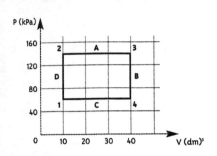

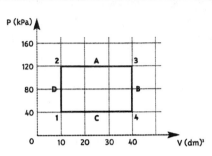

• Why is one process more efficient than the other, even though the same amount of work is done during each process?

Question 1 — U_in, W, and Q Changes: Predict the signs of the changes in the internal energy, work done by the system, and heat transfer to the system for each stage in the Carnot cycle. A and C are isothermal processes, and B and D are adiabatic processes.

ΔU_{in} W   Q

A   + 0 −   + 0 −   + 0 −
B   + 0 −   + 0 −   + 0 −
C   + 0 −   + 0 −   + 0 −
D   + 0 −   + 0 −   + 0 −

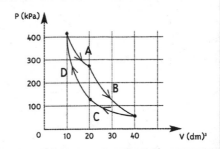

Question 2 — Pressure at Corners: Determine the pressure at each corner. The temperature and volume at the corners are given.

	T (K)	V (dm)^3	P (kPa)
1	500	10	
2	500	19	
3	300	40	
4	300	21	

Question 3 — U_in, W, and Q: Determine the change in the system's internal energy, the work done by the gas, and the heat transfer to the gas for each leg of the process.

	ΔU_{in}	W	Q
A			
B			
C			
D			

Question 4 — Efficiency: Use the numbers above to determine the efficiency e of the process (the ratio of the net work done and the heat input to the system).

Question 5 — Efficiency: Compare the above calculation of efficiency to that obtained using a special equation for efficiency derived from the first and second laws of thermodynamics: $e = 1 - (T_{cool}/T_{hot})$, where T_{hot} is the temperature of the hot reservoir (500 K for this example), and T_{cool} is the temperature of the cool reservoir (300 K for this example).

9

VIBRATIONS

Question 1: Write the amplitude of each block.

Top Block:

Bottom Block:

Question 2: Write the frequency of each block.

Top Block:

Bottom Block:

Question 3: Indicate the initial position, velocity, and phase angle for each block.

Top Block:

Middle Block

Bottom Block:

Question 4: Write an equation that describes the position of the top block as a function of time, and another equation that describes the position of the bottom block.

Top Block:

Bottom Block:

Question 5: Noting that v = dx/dt, write an equation that describes the velocity of the top block as a function of time, and another equation that describes the velocity of the bottom block.

Top Block:

Bottom Block:

Question 6: Noting that a = dv/dt, write an equation that describes the acceleration of the top block as a function of time, and another equation that describes the acceleration of the bottom block.

Top Block:

Bottom Block:

Question 1: Observe the motion of the block and construct a position-versus-time graph (x-vs-t) for the motion. Be sure to include a scale with the correct units.

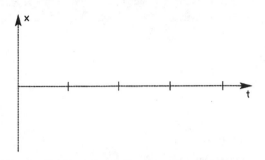

Question 2: Suppose that the equation $x = x_m \cos(2\pi f t)$ describes this type of motion and the above graph. Determine the amplitude x_m, the period T, and the frequency f of this particular motion. Insert any of these values into this equation to get a specific equation that describes this motion. Check to see if the equation gives the correct values of x for different specific times.

Question 3: Use the equation for x in Question 2 and the fact that velocity is the rate of change of position ($v = dx/dt$) to determine an equation for the block's velocity as a function of time. Be sure to include an estimate of the block's maximum speed. Compare the value of v given by your equation to the value of v given in the simulation for the five times listed.

Question 4: Run the simulation that shows both x-vs-t and v-vs-t graphs at the same time. Does the value of v at every time seem to equal qualitatively the slope of the x-vs-t graph at that time?

Question 5: Use the equation developed in Question 3 and the fact that the acceleration is the rate of change of the velocity ($a = dv/dt$) to determine an equation for this block's acceleration as a function of time. Be sure to include an estimate of the block's maximum acceleration a_m. Compare the value of the acceleration given by your equation and from the simulation graph for several specific times.

Question 6: Acceleration is the time derivative of the velocity ($a = dv/dt$). This derivative is also the slope of the velocity-versus-time graph. Move the slider back and forth to compare slopes and accelerations at specific times.

• The slope of the v-vs-t graph and the acceleration at times 1.0 s, 2.0 s, and 3.0 s

• The slope of the v-vs-t graph and the acceleration at times 0.5 s and 2.5 s

• The slope of the v-vs-t graph and the acceleration at times 1.5 s and 3.5 s

Summary: Draw below the x-vs-t, v-vs-t, and a-vs-t graphs described in this activity. Indicate roughly the vertical scale for each graph. Note that the slopes of the graphs are consistent with the definitions of velocity and acceleration.

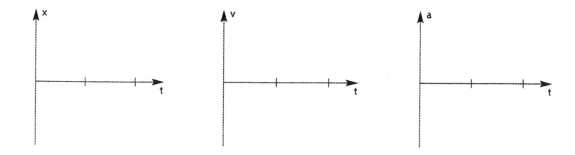

Question 1: Determine two positions where the block's kinetic energy and velocity are greatest.

Question 2: Determine two block positions where the spring's elastic potential energy is greatest.

Question 3: The block's mass in this simulation is 2.0 kg, its maximum speed is 8.0 m/s, and the force constant of the spring is 40 N/m. Determine the amplitude of the vibration.

Question 4: The block's mass in this simulation is 4.0 kg. Note the meter readings and determine the force constant of the spring.

Question 5: The block's mass in this simulation is 2.0 kg, the spring's force constant is 40 N/m, and the vibrational amplitude is 1.8 m. Determine the speed of the block when the spring is displaced 0.90 m from equilibrium.

Tarzan Jr. is on a spring, ready to be weighed. Based on your careful observations of the simulation, use a frequency approach and then an energy approach to independently measure Tarzan Jr.'s mass. The spring force constant is 200 N/m, and the gravitational constant is 10 N/kg.

Question 1 — Frequency Approach:

Question 2 — Energy Approach:

A 20-kg ape holds the 40-kg aging Tarzan as they vibrate up and down at the end of a springlike vine. At the lowest position in the vibration, after vibrating for 1.5 s, the ape accidentally drops Tarzan.

Question 1: How does the ape's maximum acceleration change?

(a) increases   (b) remains the same   (c) decreases

Explain the reason for your choice:

Question 2: How does the ape's maximum velocity change?

(a) increases   (b) remains the same   (c) decreases

Explain the reason for your choice:

A 90-kg skier holds a 30-kg cart that vibrates at the end of a spring. After one vibration, the skier lets go of the cart when it is at its maximum displacement from equilibrium.

Question 1: After the skier's release, how does the cart's new maximum displacement from equilibrium compare to before?

___ 1/4   ___ 1/2   ___ same   ___ 2 times   ___ 4 times

Explain.

Question 2: After the skier's release, how does the cart's new frequency compare to before?

___ 1/4 .   ___ 1/2   ___ same   ___ 2 times   ___ 4 times

Explain.

Question 3: After the skier's release, how does the cart's new maximum speed compare to before?

___ 1/4   ___ 1/2   ___ same   ___ 2 times   ___ 4 times

Explain.

A 60-kg skier holds on to a 20-kg cart that vibrates at the end of a spring. After 1.75 vibrations, the skier lets go of the cart when the cart is passing through its equilibrium position at maximum speed.

Question 1: After the skier's release, how does the cart's new maximum displacement from equilibrium compare to before?

___ 1/4   ___ 1/2   ___ same   ___ 2 times   ___ 4 times

Explain.

Question 2: After the skier's release, how does the cart's new frequency compare to before?

___ 1/4   ___ 1/2   ___ same   ___ 2 times   ___ 4 times

Explain.

Question 3: After the skier's release, how does the cart's new maximum speed compare to before?

___ 1/4   ___ 1/2   ___ same   ___ 2 times   ___ 4 times

Explain.

Question 1 — Force Constant: A 1.0-kg block vibrates at the end of a spring. Based on your observations, determine the force constant of the spring.

Question 1 — Speed: Now, based on your observations and previous calculations, determine the maximum speed of the block.

Question 2: A 1.0-kg block is attached to two 3.0-N/m springs on each side. The springs are initially relaxed, and the block is moving right at speed 8.0 m/s. Determine the time interval needed for one vibration and the frequency of vibration. Note that you will have to determine the effective force constant of the two-spring system. Construct a force diagram for the block and apply Newton's Second Law when it is displaced a distance x from equilibrium. Compare this equation to the equation for a block at the end of a single spring.

(a) Calculate the force constant of the spring attached to the 510-g cart. The incline is 168 cm long and the height of the end of the incline is 65 cm. You may need to use other quantities shown in the video. (b) Then, estimate the coefficient of friction between the cart and incline. (c) Finally, predict the frequency of a similar system with two springs attached in parallel to the cart.

Concept(s) to be used:

Unknown to be determined:

Known or estimated quantities:

Calculations:

A 50-kg skier, after coming down the slope, travels at 12 m/s on a level surface, raises a ski pole, and runs into a 25-kg cart. The ski pole attaches to the vibrating cart. A spring on the other side of the cart compresses and expands, giving the skier a Vibro-Ride at the end of the ski run—what fun! Determine the amplitude of the vibration and the period for one vibration.

Questions 1-3 — Amplitude of Vibration:

• Plan a strategy for determining the amplitude of the vibration.

• Solve the problem parts and determine the vibration amplitude.

Question 4 — Period for One Vibration:

Question 1: How does the frequency of a pendulum depend on the mass of the pendulum bob?

___ Frequency is lower for a larger mass bob.

___ Frequency is higher for a larger mass bob.

___ Frequency is independent of the mass of the bob.

Explain your answer.

Question 2: How does the frequency of a pendulum depend on the amplitude of the vibration?

___ Frequency is lower for a larger amplitude vibration.

___ Frequency is higher for a larger amplitude vibration.

___ Frequency is independent of the amplitude of the vibration.

Explain your answer.

Question 3: How does the frequency of a pendulum depend on the length of the string?

___ Frequency is lower for a longer length pendulum string.

___ Frequency is higher for a longer length pendulum string.

___ Frequency is independent of the length of the pendulum string.

Explain your answer.

Three different length pendula hang from a metal rod. Harold can move the rod back and forth and cause only one pendulum to have large amplitude vibrations. How can he do this?

Explanation:

Question 1: As a visiting scientist on planet Zeus, you are asked to assist in the design of a pendulum timer for use on the planet. The gravitational constant on Zeus is 6.0 N/kg = 6.0 m/s². The pendulum bob you will be using has a mass of 0.10 kg. You are to choose the length of the pendulum string so that the bob completes one vibration in 3.0 s. Complete your calculations. Then adjust the length of the string and run the simulation to check your work.

Question 1: You must decide the constant speed to walk in order to make it under the 4.0-m-long pendulum with its 400-N bob. If you choose the wrong speed, you get a good bump on the head — or somewhere else. The pendulum starts at rest in the position shown. The grid lines in the simulation are separated by 1.0 m. The gravitational constant is 10 N/kg.

Solution:

First construct a free-body diagram for the physical pendulum and then apply the rotational form of Newton's Second Law to its motion. This leads to a differential equation with a standard solution. Finally, examine the solution to determine the frequency of the motion. Then solve for the length of the string of the simple pendulum that has the same frequency.

Free-Body Diagram: Construct a free-body diagram for the hanging uniform rod when it is displaced from its equilibrium position.

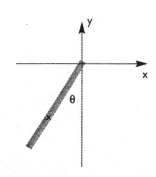

Rotational Form of Newton's Second Law: Apply the rotational form of Newton's Second Law to the free-body diagram for the rod. Note: The rotational inertia of the rod about a pin through its end is $mr^2/3$. Also, use the small angle approximation ($\sin \theta \approx \theta$, if θ is in radians).

$$\Sigma \tau = I \, \alpha$$

Solution of the Equation: Show that $\theta = \theta_{max} \cos (2\pi f \, t)$ is a solution to the above differential equation. What must be the expression for frequency f in order for this equation of motion to be a solution to the rotational form of Newton's Second Law? Finally, show that the frequency of this physical pendulum rod is the same as the frequency of a simple pendulum [$f = (1/2\pi)(mg/mL)^{1/2}$] that is two-thirds as long as the rod.

A ball hits a uniform beam, or bat, at different distances from the handle. Suppose you lightly hold the handle when the ball hits the bat. Your goal is to decide where along the bat to make contact with the ball so that the bat handle makes the smallest impulse with your hands. The best spot for the ball to hit the bat is called the sweet spot.

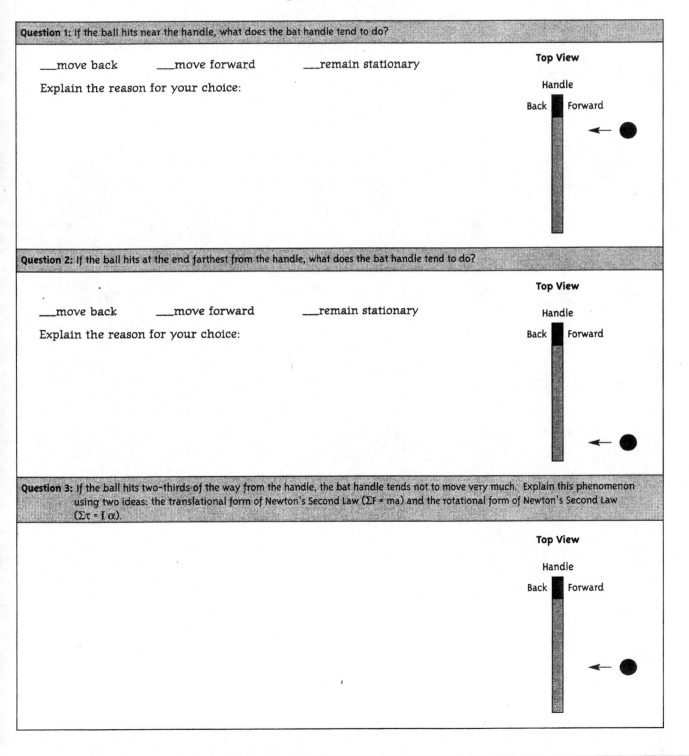

Question 1: If the ball hits near the handle, what does the bat handle tend to do?

___move back   ___move forward   ___remain stationary

Explain the reason for your choice:

Top View

Handle

Back   Forward

Question 2: If the ball hits at the end farthest from the handle, what does the bat handle tend to do?

___move back   ___move forward   ___remain stationary

Explain the reason for your choice:

Top View

Handle

Back   Forward

Question 3: If the ball hits two-thirds of the way from the handle, the bat handle tends not to move very much. Explain this phenomenon using two ideas: the translational form of Newton's Second Law ($\Sigma F = ma$) and the rotational form of Newton's Second Law ($\Sigma \tau = I \alpha$).

Top View

Handle

Back   Forward

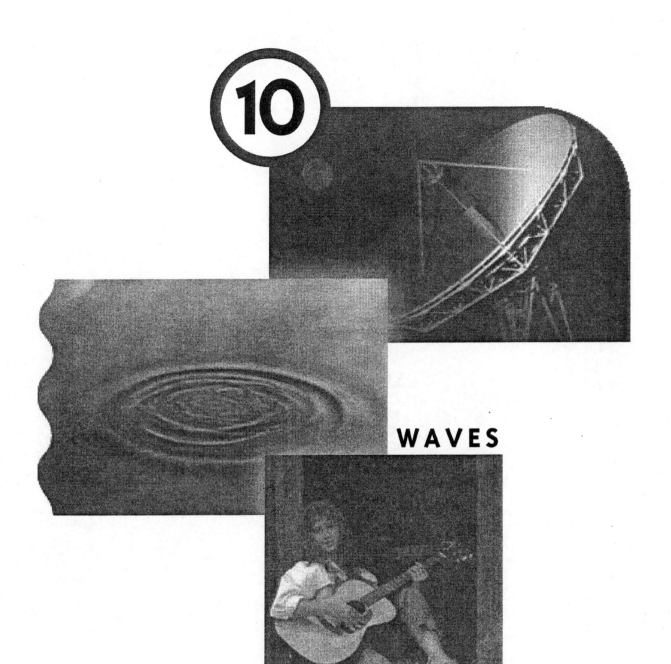

10

WAVES

Question 1 — Transverse or Longitudinal: Describe in the space below the difference between transverse waves and longitudinal waves.

Question 2 — Amplitude and Wave Speed: Does the wave amplitude affect the wave speed? Support your answer with measurements.

Question 3 — Frequency and Wave Speed: Does the wave frequency affect the wave speed? Support your answer with measurements.

Question 4 — $v = f\lambda$: Measure on the screen the wave speed and wavelength and show that $v = f\lambda$.

Question 1 — Units of $[T/\mu]^{1/2}$: Show that the units of $[T/\mu]^{1/2}$ are m/s, the same as the units of speed.

Question 2: Write an equation that describes the graph line:

Question 3: Calculate the speed of a wave on a horizontal string of 0.08 kg/m linear density that is pulled by a 2.0-N force.

Question 4: Determine the tension and the linear mass density that produce the slowest wave speed on the string.

Question 5: Determine the tension and the linear mass density that produce the fastest wave speed on the string.

Question 1 — Units of $[B/\rho]^{1/2}$: Show that the units of $[B/\rho]^{1/2}$ are m/s, the same as the units of speed.

Question 2: Write an equation that describes the graph line.

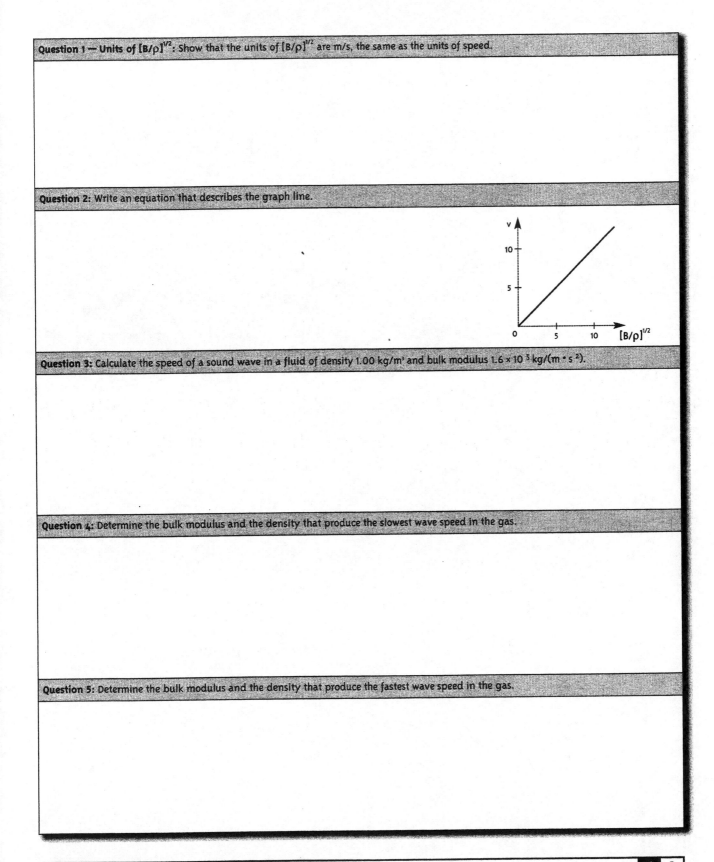

Question 3: Calculate the speed of a sound wave in a fluid of density 1.00 kg/m³ and bulk modulus 1.6×10^5 kg/(m·s²).

Question 4: Determine the bulk modulus and the density that produce the slowest wave speed in the gas.

Question 5: Determine the bulk modulus and the density that produce the fastest wave speed in the gas.

Questions 5 - 7: Set the sliders on the simulation to the following values: mass/length = 30 g/m, tension = 3.0 N. Calculate the wave speed on the simulation and predict the frequencies of the first harmonic (fundamental) vibration and the second harmonic. After completing your work, adjust the sliders to evaluate your prediction.

First harmonic (fundamental)

Second harmonic

Follow-Up Question: Set the mass/length slider to 100 g/m and the tension to 3.6 N. Calculate the wave speed and the frequencies of the lowest two harmonic vibrations. After completing your predictions, adjust the frequency slider to check your work.

To answer the questions, you will use the following standing-wave-on-a-string concepts:

- The speed v of a wave on a string is $v = (T / \mu)^{1/2}$.
- The allowed standing-wave wavelengths are $\lambda_n = 2L / n$ for n = 1, 2, 3, ...
- Since frequency $f = v / \lambda$, the allowed standing-wave frequencies are $f_n = (v / 2L) n$, for n = 1, 2, 3, ...

Question 1: Set the mass per unit length on the simulation to 100 g/m and the frequency to 4.0 Hz. Determine the string tension that will cause the 1.0-m-long string to vibrate at its second harmonic frequency. Check your answer by running the simulation with the predicted tension.

Question 2: After you have selected the correct tension (your answer to Question 1), the string will be vibrating in the second harmonic frequency. List below three other harmonic frequencies at which the string will vibrate. Check your predictions by adjusting the frequency slider to these frequencies.

Question 3: With the tension at 1.6 N, the mass per unit length at 100 g/m, and the frequency at 2.0 Hz, the string will vibrate in its fundamental mode (n =1). Now, double the tension to 3.2 N. How would you have to change the frequency to see a fundamental-frequency vibration again? After your prediction, adjust the simulation to your predicted frequency to check your result.

To answer the questions, you will use the following standing-wave-on-a-string concepts:

- The speed v of a wave on a string is $v = (T / \mu)^{1/2}$.
- The allowed standing-wave wavelengths are $\lambda_n = 2L / n$ for $n = 1, 2, 3, \ldots$.
- Since frequency $f = v / \lambda$, the allowed standing-wave frequencies are $f_n = (v / 2L) n$, for $n = 1, 2, 3, \ldots$.

Question 1: Set the mass per unit length on the simulation to 98 g/m, the tension to 1.0 N, and the frequency to 11.2 Hz. Predict the frequencies of the other six standing-wave vibrations. Check each answer by adjusting the frequency on the running simulation.

Question 2: Set the tension to 2.5 N, the mass per unit length to 40 g/m, and the frequency to the 4.0-Hz fundamental frequency. Suppose that you want another string of the same length and pulled by the same tension to vibrate at 8.0 Hz. Determine the mass per unit length needed for that string. Check your prediction by adjusting the slider in the simulation so that its fundamental vibration frequency is 8.0 Hz..

Question 1 — Beat Patterns: Study the graph below, which shows how pressure of sound produced at one point in space varies with time. This disturbance is caused by the combination of two sound waves of different frequencies. The resultant wave fluctuates in amplitude. Each fluctuation is called a beat, and two beats are shown. You will shortly learn how this beat pattern is formed.

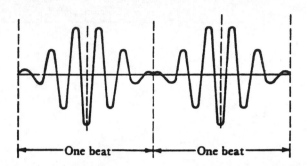

|← One beat →|← One beat →|

Question 2: Try several frequency combinations and record the frequencies and the beat frequency.

f_1 (kHz)	f_2 (kHz)	f_{beat} (kHz)		f_1 (kHz)	f_2 (kHz)	f_{beat} (kHz)

Question 3: Compare the beat frequencies for the following two combinations:

(a) 3.4 kHz and 4.0 kHz

(b) 4.6 kHz and 4.0 kHz

Question 4: Is the beat frequency higher for frequencies of 2.0 kHz and 2.4 kHz or for frequencies of 4.0 kHz and 4.4 kHz? In short, is the beat frequency higher for higher frequency waves?

Question 5 — Beat Frequency: Based on your observations, invent a rule in the form of an equation for how the beat frequency f_{beat} is related to the frequencies f_1 and f_2 of the two waves that are producing the beats. Be sure that your rule applies to all possible combinations of the frequencies: $f_2 > f_1$, $f_2 = f_1$, and $f_2 < f_1$.

Question 8 — Does wave interference produce the beat pattern? Set both amplitudes to +30 and one frequency to 3.4 kHz and the other to 4.0 kHz. Observe that the red and green waves add together to produce large amplitude waves in the beat pattern when the red and green waves are in phase and small amplitude waves when they are not in phase. It may be easier to do this addition with the waves shown below. Add the disturbances caused by each wave at the times represented by the vertical lines. See if the resultant disturbance in the beat pattern is just the sum of the individual disturbances. When you are finished, you should be convinced that the formation of beats is just another example of wave interference.

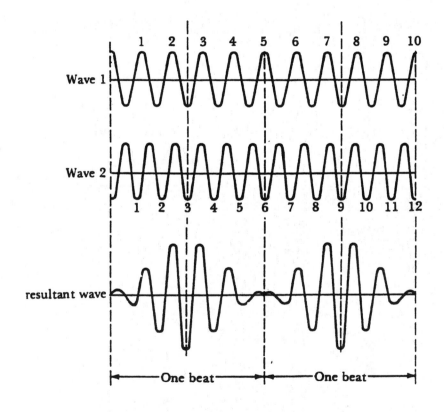

Question 9 — Complex Waves, Another Example of Wave Interference: Shown below are three wave patterns. Each pattern is the variation in pressure at different positions in space at one instant of time. The resultant wave at the bottom is simply the sum of the pressure variations caused by the two top waves if present at the same time. You can produce the same pattern with the simulation by adding two waves each of amplitude +30 with the first at frequency f_1 = 2.0 kHz and the second at twice the frequency, or f_2 = 4.0 kHz. In the music business, the first wave is called the fundamental, and the second is the second harmonic, or the first overtone. The resultant complex wave produced by adding the two is the pattern seen in the simulation and reproduced below. Show that the bottom wave is just the sum of the two waves at each position of space.

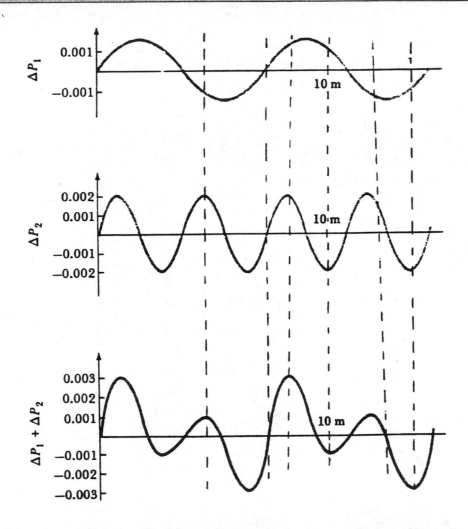

SUMMARY

- Beats are produced by adding two waves of slightly different frequencies.
- The beat frequency is the absolute value of the difference in frequency of the two waves:

$$f_{beat} = | f_2 - f_1 |$$

- Complex waves are formed by adding a fundamental-frequency wave with higher-frequency harmonics that are integral multiples of the frequency of the fundamental wave.

A source (the bell in the simulation) emits a sound at the source frequency f_S. A listener or observer (the person in the simulation) detects the sound at what may be a different frequency f_L. Under what conditions are these frequencies the same? Under what conditions are they different? Which frequency is greater? Is there any useful application for this frequency difference? These questions are the subject of this Doppler-effect activity.

Note: The signs for the velocities in the simulation indicate the velocity of the source or listener relative to an axis that points toward the right.

Questions 1 - 2 — Doppler Frequency, Qualitative: For each situation described below, decide if the listener (observer) frequency is greater than, equal to, or less than the source frequency.

(a) The listener moves toward the stationary source: $f_S > f_L$ $f_S = f_L$ $f_S < f_L$

(b) The source moves toward the stationary listener: $f_S > f_L$ $f_S = f_L$ $f_S < f_L$

(c) The listener moves away from the stationary source: $f_S > f_L$ $f_S = f_L$ $f_S < f_L$

(d) The source moves away from the stationary listener: $f_S > f_L$ $f_S = f_L$ $f_S < f_L$

(e) The listener and source move in the same direction at the same speed: $f_S > f_L$ $f_S = f_L$ $f_S < f_L$

Invent a qualitative rule (without an equation) that indicates under what conditions the listener frequency is greater than the source frequency, less than the source frequency, and equal to the source frequency. Write the rule in the space below.

Question 3: Have you ever experienced the Doppler effect? Describe the experience(s).

Questions 4 - 5 — What causes the moving-source Doppler effect? In the simulation, set $v_{listener}$ = 0.0 m/s, v_{source} = −10.0 m/s, and the source frequency f_s = 10,000 Hz. Run the simulation. You should see a pattern such as shown below but with many more wave crests. Look at the pattern below and pretend that you are looking down from above on a very large swimming pool. Each crest is a wave that was created by a large beach ball that is bobbing up and down in the water as it moves from the right to the left. The larger radius crest was created when the ball was at position 1, and the smaller radius crest when it was at position 2. The wavelength of waves leaving the source is the distance between crests. Explain in the space below why the listener frequency is greater than the source frequency when the source moves toward the listener and less when the source moves away. Think about the wavelength, and how wavelength is related to wave speed and frequency.

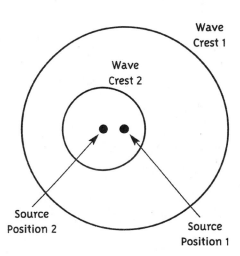

©1997 Addison Wesley Interactive & Alan Van Heuvelen

Question 6 — What causes the moving-listener Doppler effect? In the simulation, set $v_{listener}$ = +4.0 m/s, v_{source} = 0.0 m/s, and the source frequency f_s = 10,000 Hz. Run the simulation. Note in particular the rate at which the listener moves past wave crests. Now, change the listener velocity to $v_{listener}$ = -4.0 m/s. Run the simulation again and note again the rate at which the listener moves past wave crests.

(a) If the listener was moving left at the same speed as the waves, what frequency would the listener observe? Explain.

(b) Explain in the space below why the listener frequency is greater than the source frequency when the listener moves toward the source and why the listener frequency is less than the source frequency when the listener moves away from the source.

SUMMARY

- $f_{listener} < f_{source}$ when the listener and the source are moving farther apart.
- $f_{listener} > f_{source}$ when the listener and the source are moving closer to each other.
- $f_{listener} = f_{source}$ when the listener-source separation is constant.

DOPPLER EQUATION

- $f_{listener} = f_{source} \left(\dfrac{v \pm v_{listener}}{v \pm v_{source}} \right)$ where

  v = the speed of sound in the medium (about 340 m/s for sound in air);

  $v_{listener}$ = listener speed (use + in equation if moving toward source and − if moving away); and

  v_{source} = source speed (use − in equation if moving toward listener and + if moving away).

SUMMARY

- $f_{listener} < f_{source}$ when the listener and the source are moving farther apart.
- $f_{listener} > f_{source}$ when the listener and the source are moving closer to each other.
- $f_{listener} = f_{source}$ when the listener-source separation is constant.

DOPPLER EQUATION

- $f_{listener} = f_{source} \left(\dfrac{v \pm v_{listener}}{v \pm v_{source}} \right)$ where

  v = the speed of sound in the medium (about 340 m/s for sound in air);

  $v_{listener}$ = listener speed (use + in equation if moving toward source and − if moving away); and

  v_{source} = source speed (use − in equation if moving toward listener and + if moving away).

For each of the following situations, predict the listener (observer) frequency. After your prediction, adjust the sliders to see how you did.

Question Number:	1	2	3	4
Listener velocity (m/s)	0	0	+4.0 (right)	−4.0 (left)
Source velocity (m/s)	−10 (left)	+10 (right)	0	0
Source frequency (Hz)	10,000	10,000	10,000	10,000
Predicted frequency (Hz)				

Question 7: You and a friend decide to test the Doppler effect by walking along a street as you blow identical 1000-Hz whistles. Your friend is ahead and moves right at speed 2.0 m/s. You (initially on the left) move right at 4.0 m/s. (a) What beat frequency do you hear when playing your whistle and while still behind your friend? (b) What beat frequency do you hear after passing your friend? Make your predictions. Then check your predictions by running the simulation.

Why does a violin playing concert A at 440 Hz sound different from a flute or a clarinet playing the same frequency sound equally loud? The answer is in part due to what we call the harmonic content of the complex waves produced by these musical instruments. A complex wave consists of one wave at a fundamental frequency — such as the 440 Hz frequency of concert A played by a violin. The wave also consists of other waves at integral multiples of the fundamental. All of these waves are added together to form the complex wave. In this activity, you can construct some very special complex waves by adding the fundamental and the right combination of higher harmonics.

in Construct a Sawtooth Wave:

 • Open the simulation, which displays the wave pattern that looks like the teeth of a saw (upper right box).

 • Leave INITIAL SIGNAL checked.

 • Click on SYNTHESIZED SIGNAL to remove the check mark.

 • Move the slider for n in the floating window to 1. (You may have to scroll down the simulation window to see this slider.)

 • Now check SYNTHESIZED SIGNAL. You will see a sine wave at the same frequency as the sawtooth wave.

Finish the Sawtooth Wave:

 • Change the slider to n = 2. You see a combination of the fundamental (n = 1) and the second harmonic (n = 2) superimposed on the sawtooth wave.

 • Click the slider again to add the n = 3 wave to the other two waves.

 • Keep adding more harmonics to produce a wave that looks very much like a sawtooth wave.

A sawtooth wave can be produced by combining a fundamental-frequency wave with a carefully selected combination of higher frequency harmonics.

Other Complex Waves: You can repeat this activity with other types of wave patterns. They are formed by different amplitude combinations of the fundamental and its higher harmonics.

PART IV

ActivPhysics User Guide

Acknowledgments

Author: Alan Van Heuvelen
The Ohio State University

Addison Wesley Interactive

Director:	Chip Price
Project Manager:	Arati M. Nagaraj
Production Manager:	Lee Stayton
Production:	Beverly Brissette
	Syed Ali
	Erik Klemetti
	Gabe Weiss
	Erich Burton
Art Director:	Erik Johnson
Web Engineer:	Mark Moline
Package Designer:	Dusan Koljensic
Marketing:	Elizabeth O'Neil
	William Danon
Accuracy Checking:	Professor Maria Falbo-Kenkel
	Northern Kentucky University
Software Engineering:	Doug Stein
	Paul Tu
	Glenn Howes
HTML Production:	Brenda Baugh
	Ellen Berrigan
	Kristy Shriver
Copy Editing:	Barbara Mindell

Partners and Consultants

Simulations:	OpenTeach Software, Inc.
ActivPad:	Sophist Solutions, Inc.

Trademark Notices

Macintosh, the MacOS logo, QuickTime, the QuickTime VR logo are trademarks of Apple Computer, Inc., used under license. Windows is a trademark of Microsoft Corporation. **Netscape Navigator**™ is a trademark of **Netscape Communications**™**, Inc.** **ActivPhysics**™ and **ActivPad**™ are trademarks of Addison Wesley Longman. All other trademarks are property of their respective owners.

Copyright © 1997, 1999 by Addison Wesley Longman

Contents ·

Special Acknowledgments

Our special thanks and appreciation to the many individuals who tested and reviewed *ActivPhysics 1*.

Student Reviewers

John Andrews - Tufts University; Marc Von Deylen - The Ohio State University; Mike Dishong - The Ohio State University; Mathew Eckstein - Tufts University; Mark Fisher - Arizona State University; Dave Grillo - The Ohio State University; Izydor Gryo - Arizona State University; Kristin Hamilton - Tufts University; Jason Henry - Arizona State University; Lisa Izzie - The Ohio State University; Anthomny Johansson - Arizona State University; Emily Jutkiewicz - Tufts University; Brandon Kahle - Arizona State University; Aaron Lynott - The Ohio State University; Jon Mann - Tufts University; Joel Melamed - Tufts University; Ed Murphy - The Ohio State University; Lucia Nurman - Arizona State University; Newton - Arizona State University; Terresa Pietro - Tufts University; Christian Price - Arizona State University; Ricardo Da Ros - The Ohio State University; Jessica Rosenthal - Tufts University; Josh Schulz - Arizona State University; Donald Thomas Sechler - Arizona State University; Raphael See - Arizona State University; Abbas Syed Shabbar - The Ohio State University; Geoffrey Shaver - The Ohio State University; Stephen Siler - Arizona State University; Mark Smertneck - The Ohio State University; Jeffrey Staw - Tufts University; Anthony Strattos - Arizona State University; James Suh - Arizona State University; Sandra Szela - Tufts University; Lohi Tevel - Arizona State University; Brian Thurow - The Ohio State University; Branimir Toyaganov - Arizona State University; Jeremy Wolford - The Ohio State University

Faculty Reviewers

Special thanks to Paul D'Alessandris (Monroe Community College), George Zimmerman (Boston University), Teodoro Halpern (Ramapo College), Gordon Aubrecht (Ohio State University), M Rajlakshmi (Ohio State University), Thomas Keil (Worcester Polytechnic University), Michael Ziegler (Ohio State University), Meg Hickey (Mass College of Art).

Donald Bowen - SFA Station; Mark Bunge - San Jose City College; Juan Burciaga - Colorado College; Bradley Carroll - Weber State University; S. Raj Chaudhury - Norfolk State University; Victor Cook - University of Washington; P.J. Conney - Millersville University; Roger Freedman - University of California-Santa Barbara; John Gastineau - North Carolina State University; Dennis Harp - Purdue University; Sadri Hassani - Illinois State University; Curt Hieggelke - Joliet Junior Community College; James Huddle - U.S. Naval Academy; Richard Jacob - Arizona State University; Randy Knight - California Polytechnic-San Luis Obispo; Harvey Leff - California Polytechnic University; David maloney - IPFW; Kandiah Manivannan - Southeastern Louisiana University; Riachard Martin - Illinois State University; David Meltzer - Southeastern Louisiana University; Daniel Mioduszewski - Lawrence Technological University; David Peak - Utah State; Gordon Ramsey - Loyola University-Chicago; Vladimir Visnijc - Temple University; David Weaver - Chandler Gilbert Community College.

Class Testers

Rick Lewis - Spokane Community College; Thomas Keil - Worcester Polytechnic Institute; Briane Desilets - Marist College; John Foley - Mississippi State University; Paul Sokol - Pennsylvania State University; Donald Bowen - Stephen F. Austin State University; Ina Brownridge - SUNY-Binghamton; Jack Brennan - University of Central Florida; Robert Lind - University of Wisconsin-Platteville; Doyle Davis - New Hampshire Technical College-Berlin; Ntungwa Maasha - Coastal Georgia Community College; S. Deonarine - Bronx Community College; Jerry Meisner - UNC-Greensboro; Mani Manivannan - Southern Louisiana University; William Skocpol - Boston university; Ron Gautreau - New jersey Institute of Technology; Roderich Engelmann - SUNY-Stony Brook; Mike Politano - Arizona State University; Richard Vawter - Westrern Washington University; Bob Peterson - College of Marin; Todd Leif - Cloud County Community College

About *ActivPhysics*

ActivPhysics 1 is a collection of 122 guided, interactive activities that present mechanics, thermodynamics, and waves at an introductory level. All the activities are simulation based and emphasize a qualitative perspective.

Designed by a leading professor in physics education, Alan Van Heuvelen, *ActivPhysics* contains many features that convey concepts and information in a visual, interactive way, unlike most traditional methods.

The *ActivPhysics* Author

Dr. Alan Van Heuvelen, of The Ohio State University, is a respected physics professor, author, and pioneer of active learning methods. Since 1992, Professor Van Heuvelen has given 76 invited talks and workshops in five continents. His Active Learning Problem Sheets (the ALPS Kits) encourage student participation and learning in large and small classes and while working alone and in small groups. Now these same interactive techniques are easily extended and better visualized with the *ActivPhysics* simulations and activities.

Navigating *Activ*Physics

Menu Bar Buttons

Main
Brings you back to the main menu of the unit you are in.

AWI Site
Brings you to the Addison Wesley Interactive Web site. Here you can get technical support, ask questions, leave comments; and get updates on tools and simulations.

ActivPad
Launches *Activ*Pad, an interactive notebook you can use to keep notes and create customized links to any place in *Activ*Physics or the World Wide Web.

Help
Outlines navigation features and provides tips on how to integrate the product into your course.

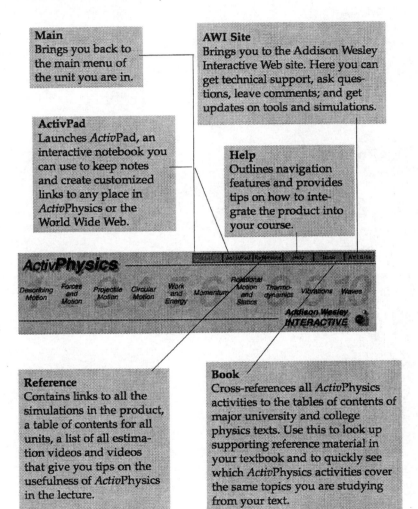

Reference
Contains links to all the simulations in the product, a table of contents for all units, a list of all estimation videos and videos that give you tips on the usefulness of *Activ*Physics in the lecture.

Book
Cross-references all *Activ*Physics activities to the tables of contents of major university and college physics texts. Use this to look up supporting reference material in your textbook and to quickly see which *Activ*Physics activities cover the same topics you are studying from your text.

Units and Activities

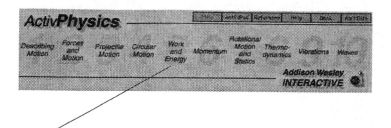

You can move to a unit by selecting one of the unit names or numbers along the middle of the menu. Once you have made your selection, the titles of the activities for that unit will appear in the frame on the right (see below). Simply click on an activity to launch it. The activity will appear in the frame on the right, and all simulations, videos, and animations will appear on the left.

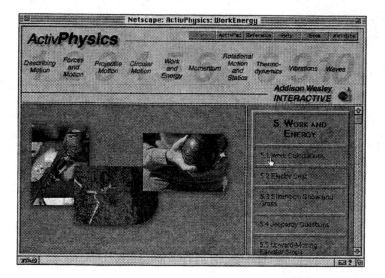

Navigating an *ActivPhysics* Activity

The Help button in the main menu brings you to a sample interactive activity that illustrates what each button and link in an *Activ*Physics activity does. This interactive Help activity is a great way to learn how to use the *Activ*Physics interface. It is recommended that you review this section before working with an *Activ*Physics activity.

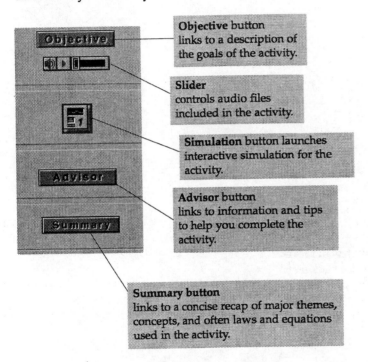

Objective button
links to a description of the goals of the activity.

Slider
controls audio files included in the activity.

Simulation button launches interactive simulation for the activity.

Advisor button
links to information and tips to help you complete the activity.

Summary button
links to a concise recap of major themes, concepts, and often laws and equations used in the activity.

Some *Activ*Physics activities contain computer tools to help you solve problems and make predictions:

- **Force Diagram Tool:**
  Allows you to create force diagrams on the screen. See an example in Activity 2.8.

- **Bar Chart Predictor:**
  Allows you to qualitatively predict the shape of work-energy bar charts See an example in Activity 5.3.

For more information on using these tools, see the on-line help section in *Activ*Physics.

Some *Activ*Physics activities also include video or animation with a problem relating to the activity, which can be launched by clicking on this icon.

Left-pointing broken arrow Rewinds video.

Solid arrow Begins video.

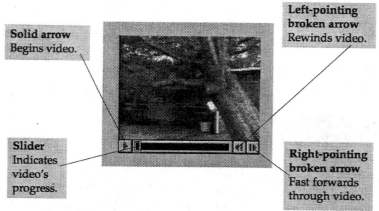

Slider Indicates video's progress.

Right-pointing broken arrow Fast forwards through video.

 To enjoy smooth video playback, please allow a few moments for the video to completely load. (In Windows, the black bar in the middle of the slider will indicate the loading progress.)

Using the Simulations

Simulations are launched by clicking on this icon:

The simulations contain sliders and controls that allow you to alter the conditions of the physical system represented by the simulation. Simulations can be accessed through the on-screen activity or through the Reference section.

As you roll the cursor over the simulation screen, information about the simulation, including descriptions of what the various controls do, appears at the bottom of the interface screen:

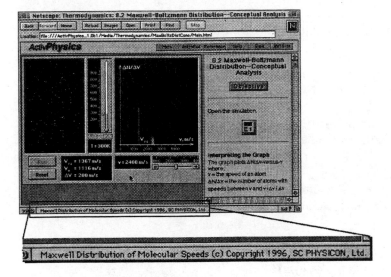

To get simulation help, click anywhere on the simulation. (In Windows, right mouse click).

More Navigation Hints
All of Netscape Navigator's navigation features can also be used with *Activ*Physics. To learn about these features, be sure to see the Netscape Navigator Help section in the Netscape menu bar.

Appendix 1: Using *ActivPad*

*Activ*Pad is an on-line, interactive notepad you can use to keep notes and "bookmark" places in *Activ*Physics. You can also use *Activ*Pad to create hyperlinks to sites on the World Wide Web. *Activ*Pad is ideal for creating lecture notes or custom homework problems, because you can have instant hyperlinks to *Activ*Physics tools or other Web sites.

Students: Use *Activ*Pad to
- keep your notes about the various activities, questions you want to ask an instructor or TA later, etc. ;
- post your answers to *Activ*Physics questions and paste in material from *Activ*Physics, or graphs and charts from other programs;
- "bookmark" places in *Activ*Physics and, if you have a live Web connection, to add links to physics sites or other related material on the Web. You can also link to your course home page if your instructor has posted one.

Instructors: Use *Activ*Pad to
- organize your lecture notes and class demonstrations. Type your notes into *Activ*Pad and/or use the active linking feature to create links to the simulations or other portions of *Activ*Physics that you want to show in class.
- create new questions or problems to accompany the existing *Activ*Physics simulations. You can then save your *Activ*Pad assignment to a server where your students can access it.
- save links to physics resources out on the Web, including your course home page.

To Set Up *Activ*Pad on Windows

1. With *Activ*Physics open, from the **Options** menu select **General Preferences**. A Preferences window opens.

2. Select the **Helpers** tab and click **Create New Type...**

3. In the dialog box enter:
   - MIME type: **application**
   - MIME SubType: **led**

4. Click **OK** to close the dialog box and return to the Preferences window, then enter:
   - File Extensions: **led,Led**
   - Click the **Launch the Application** radio button.
   - Click the **Browse** button and locate *Activ*Pad 1.0 by browsing your hard drive for the application.

5. Select the *Activ*Pad application icon and click the **Open** button.

6. Close the dialog box by clicking **OK**.

To Set Up *Activ*Pad on Macintosh

1. With *Activ*Physics open, from the **Options** menu select **General Preferences**. A Preferences window opens.

2. Select the **Helpers** tab and click the **[New]** button.

3. In the dialog box type:
   - Description: **ActivPad**
   - MIME Type: **application/led**
   - Suffixes: **Led**

4. Select *Activ*Pad as the application by clicking the **Browse** button to locate the *Activ*Pad application on your hard drive and then clicking **Open**.

5. Click the **File Type** pop-down menu and select **LDDC**.

6. Click **OK** to close the Helpers dialog box.

7. Click **OK** to close the Preferences window.

Managing Your *Activ*Pad Documents

*Activ*Pad documents are like any other documents that you save on your computer. You can save them all in one folder, or in various locations. You decide where an *Activ*Pad document will be stored when you name and save it.

 If you work with *Activ*Physics and *Activ*Pad on more than one computer, be sure to see "Sharing *Activ*Pad Documents".

Taking Notes in *Activ*Pad

Note taking using *Activ*Pad is straightforward. The program behaves much like a regular word processor.

1. In the **Main** menu bar, launch *Activ*Pad by clicking on the **ActivPad** button.

 *Activ*Pad *does* not launch from within Internet Explorer. If *Activ*Pad is not launched from the Main Menu, locate the ActivPad application on your hard drive and launch it from there.

Cutting and Pasting in *Activ*Pad

You can cut and paste material from other documents into *Activ*Pad. This includes material from *Activ*Physics, word processing documents, clip art, graphics, charts and tables from spreadsheets, etc. Simply open the document you want to paste from, copy the material, then open your *Activ*Pad document and paste the material in.

 *Activ*Pad is not a full math processor, so check the pasted material for accuracy when cutting and pasting formulas or other math text.

 Depending on your computer's memory allocations, you may not be able to have many documents open at once. You may have to open and close documents while copying and pasting.

 Windows users using Netscape cannot paste images into *Activ*Pad directly from *Activ*Physics; those using Internet Explorer can do so.

Creating a Link in *Activ*Pad

Make sure that both *Activ*Pad and *Activ*Physics (or the Web document you want to link to) are open. It is easiest to create the link if you can see the *Activ*Pad document you are working with and the document you want to link to at the same time. To do this you can reduce the size of the windows of each application in such a way that they are side by side or one on top of the other. An example of how to do this is shown below:

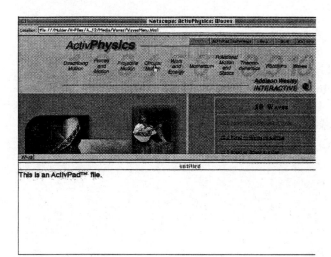

Grab Current

Grab Current is a method to "bookmark" useful resources in *Activ*Physics or the Web.

1. With *Activ*Pad open, go to the spot in *Activ*Physics or the Web to which you want to create an *Activ*Pad link.

2. From the ActivLinks pull-down menu, choose **Grab Current URL**. The link will appear in your *Activ*Pad document.

Drag and Drop

Drag and Drop is helpful when you want to grab many links from one page and put them into a single *Activ*Pad document.

1. With *Activ*Pad open, select the place in *Activ*Physics or on the Web that CONTAINS the link you want to add to *Activ*Pad. *Do not activate the link.*

2. Select the link and DRAG it over to the open *Activ*Pad document and release the mouse. The link will appear in your *Activ*Pad document.

3. Double-click on the new link to activate it.

 You need to have either *Activ*Physics or a Web connection open in order for your links to work (depending on where they point to.)

 You can delete any links that you have created in *Activ*Pad by simply selecting them and hitting the delete key.

 *Activ*Pad links will open any framed links full screen instead of in their original framed window.

Customizing Your *ActivPad* Links

When you bring a link into *Activ*Pad from *Activ*Physics or the Web, it will look like this:

4.1 Determining Acceleration Direction Graphic
$ActivPhysics$Media/CircularMotion/DetAccDirGraph/Main

The link label shows the title of the link, information about the link's point of origin, etc.

 The symbols contained in the label are slightly different between Macintosh and Windows machines.

You can rename the label or customize it so that the link is represented by an image. You may want to do this to make the link easier to remember, to connect an image to a link for study purposes (e.g., an image of a graph linking to material about the physical phenomena it represents), or to make your *Activ*Pad document visually interesting if you are using it for demonstration purposes.

Creating a Link Represented by an Image

1. Paste the image you want to use to represent a link into the *Activ*Pad document (See "Cutting and Pasting in *Activ*Pad" for help with this.)

2. Select the place in *Activ*Physics or on the Web that CONTAINS the link you want to connect to the image. **Do *not* activate the link.**

3. Select the link (Right click for Windows; click and hold for Mac) until the pop-up link menu appears. From the menu, select **Copy this Link Location.**

4. Return to the image you pasted in the *Activ*Pad document. Select the image.

5. From the **ActivLinks** menu, select **Edit ActivLink.** A new window will open.

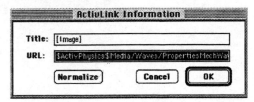

6. Highlight any text in the URL line of this window, and then select **Paste.** This replaces the old link information with the new information you copied from your desired link. If there is no text in this line simply select **Paste.**

7. You have now created an image link in *Activ*Pad, which works like every other *Activ*Pad link. Remember that the document you are linking to must be open, whether it is *Activ*Physics or a web browser.

Changing a Link's Label

1. Select the link in *Activ*Pad.

2. Go to the menu bar at the top of the screen and open the **ActivLinks** menu. From that menu, select **Edit ActivLink.** A new window will open.

3. Replace any text in the TITLE line of this window with whatever text you want to change it to.

4. Your link still goes to the same location it originally did, but now has the title of your choice. Remember that the document you are linking to must be open, whether it is *Activ*Physics or a web browser.

Sharing *Activ*Pad Documents

Standardizing *Activ*Pad Links

If you intend to use *Activ*Pad documents on a different computer or to share *Activ*Pad documents with other *Activ*Physics users, you should use *Activ*Pad's standardizing feature.

When an ActivLink is created, *Activ*Pad records a URL, or digital address, so that the program will later be able to retrieve that same location on the CD-ROM or Web. Because different computers are configured differently, this address varies from computer to computer. While one computer may have the CD-ROM drive designated as drive D, another may call it drive G, and yet another (a Macintosh, for example) does not use a letter to denote its CD-ROM drive. Thus, the same *Activ*Physics home page may have several different addresses, depending on the computer it is being viewed on:

Your computer:	file:///D I/ActivPhysics1.html
PC 2:file:	///E I /ActivPhysics1.html
Web server:	http://www.phys.university.edu/ActivPhysics1.html
Macintosh:	file://ActivPhysics_1_CD/ActivPhysics1.html

*Activ*Pad's standardizing feature will automatically replace the first part of these URL's with a variable name like "$ActivPhysics1$". Thus, the URL's from above will be recorded in *Activ*Pad as follows:

Your computer:	$ActivPhysics1$ActivPhysics1.html
PC 2:	$ActivPhysics1$ActivPhysics1.html
Web server:	$ActivPhysics1$ActivPhysics1.html
Macintosh:	$ActivPhysics1$ActivPhysics1.html

Now all standardized links will work properly when shared among the above users.

 Make sure that everyone is using the same variable name.

 You do not need to standardize links to the World Wide Web.

Standardizing *Activ*Pad Hyperlinks

You should standardize *Activ*Pad hyperlinks if you intend to do any of the following:

- Share *Activ*Pad documents with other users.

- Distribute *Activ*Pad documents as class notes or custom homework sets.

- Use *Activ*Pad documents on multiple computers.

You must perform the following steps with the *Activ*Physics home page open.

To Standardize *Activ*Pad Documents

1. Launch *Activ*Pad by clicking the **ActivPad** button on the Main Screen of *Activ*Physics.

2. From the **ActivLinks** menu, choose **ActivLink Preferences.** A window appears listing *Activ*Physics in a **Variable** box.

3. Click on the **Grab** button to the right of the *Activ*Physics **Variable** box.

4. Click the check box under the **Standardize New URL's** heading, if a check is not already there.

5. *To test:* From the **ActivLinks** menu, select **Grab Current Location.** The following hyperlink should be inserted into the current *Activ*Pad document:

   URL: $ActivPhysics1$ActivPhysics1.html

If the link is not inserted properly, check your **ActivLink Preferences** to make sure that the **Standardize new URL's with this prefix** checkbox is checked.

Appendix 2: Getting Help with *Activ*Physics

If you find that you need help or technical support:

Try reading the section of this User Guide that covers the part of *Activ*Physics about which you have a question. There is also a README file and a Help file on the *Activ*Physics CD-ROM. You may find an answer to your question in one of these.

Addison Wesley's physics web site (http://www.awl.com/physics) is also a good source for updates on new products, technical information, frequently asked questions, and user comments.

If your problem is related to installation or defective media, please contact Addison Wesley's Technical Support Division via e-mail at mailto:techsprt@awl.com, or by phone at 800-677-6337. The hotline is staffed from 9 A.M. to 4 P.M., Monday through Friday (Eastern time). If you do not get through immediately, please leave them a message describing your problem. A software technician will return your call. Please note that Technical Support provides installation guidance and defective media replacement only. Questions on program usage should be directed to Addison Wesley Longman Physics via our web site. If you are a student, you can also direct questions on program usage to your professor or lab coordinator.

*Activ*Physics 1 Installation

Installation for Windows 95 or NT 4.0

1. Place the CD-ROM in the CD-ROM drive. A launcher window will open.

   NOTE: If the launcher window does not automatically open when you insert the *Activ*Physics CD-ROM, you should open the *Activ*Physics CD-ROM via Windows Explorer, then double-click the "Launcher" or "Launcher.exe" application.

2. Install Netscape Navigator 3.0, QuickTime 2.5, and *Activ*Physics Plug-ins onto your hard drive.

   NOTE: If you use Microsoft Internet Explorer (version 3.0 or higher), or if Netscape Navigator (version 3.0 or higher) is already installed on your machine, you do not need to install Netscape from this CD-ROM.

3. After this installation, click "RUN" from the Launcher window to launch *Activ*Physics 1.

   See the on-line Help to get more information on how to use *Activ*Physics.

Installation for Macintosh

1. Insert the *Activ*Physics CD-ROM into your CD-ROM drive. A window will open.

2. Install QuickTime 2.5- this is the standard installer from Apple Computer, which is also available at **http://quicktime.apple.com**

   NOTE: If you have QuickTime 2.5 already installed, you can omit this step.

3. Install Netscape Navigator 3.01- this is the standard installer from Netscape Communications, which is also available at **http://www.netscape.com**

   NOTE: If you have Netscape 3.0 or higher or Internet Explorer 3.0 or higher installed, you can omit this step.

4. Install *Activ*Physics 1— this will install the required plug-ins and *Activ*Pad on your hard drive.

5. Launch *Activ*Physics by double-clicking the **ActivPhysics1.html** icon.

   See the on-line Help to get more information on how to use *Activ*Physics.